THE FORGOTTEN INDIAN PRISONERS OF WORLD WAR II

THE FORGOTTEN INDIAN PRISONERS OF WORLD WAR II

SURRENDER, LOYALTY, BETRAYAL AND HELL

GAUTAM HAZARIKA

Pen & Sword
MILITARY

AN IMPRINT OF PEN & SWORD BOOKS LTD.
YORKSHIRE – PHILADELPHIA

First published in Great Britain in 2025 by
PEN AND SWORD MILITARY
An imprint of
Pen & Sword Books Limited
Yorkshire – Philadelphia

ISBN 978 1 03612 438 0

Typeset in Times New Roman 10/13 by
SJmagic DESIGN SERVICES, India.
Printed and bound in the UK by CPI Group (UK) Ltd.

The Publisher's authorised representative in the EU for product safety is
Authorised Rep Compliance Ltd., Ground Floor, 71 Lower Baggot Street,
Dublin D02 P593, Ireland.
www.arccompliance.com

For a complete list of Pen & Sword titles please contact
PEN & SWORD BOOKS LIMITED
George House, Units 12 & 13, Beevor Street, Off Pontefract Road,
Barnsley, South Yorkshire, S71 1HN, England
E-mail: enquiries@pen-and-sword.co.uk
Website: www.pen-and-sword.co.uk

or

PEN AND SWORD BOOKS
1950 Lawrence Rd, Havertown, PA 19083, USA
E-mail: uspen-and-sword@casematepublishers.com
Website: www.penandswordbooks.com

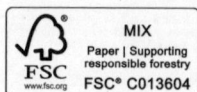

MIX
Paper | Supporting
responsible forestry
FSC
www.fsc.org   FSC® C013604

ADVANCE PRAISE

for THE FORGOTTEN INDIAN PRISONERS OF WWII
by GAUTAM HAZARIKA

'[Gautam Hazarika] weaves in nuanced positions on history that sometimes challenge popular conceptions. Informative, exciting and at times provocative, this book makes an interesting read indeed'.—**Vijay Balan, author of** *The Swaraj Spy*

'A page turner… fills a gap on a subject that has been neglected by historians and film makers reflecting their Euro and American centric biases'.—**Mihir Bose, award-winning broadcaster, journalist and author**

'Hazarika's research shows a human side and story to the lives of these Prisoners of War caught up in this often-forgotten part of a global conflict whose legacy continues to inform and shape the Indian diasporic experience in this region and beyond.'—**Romen Bose, Author of** *Singapore At War: Secrets from the Fall, Liberation and Aftermath of WWII*

This book is different and it is this difference that makes it so important. Gautam Hazarika through his detailed research, has revealed the details of a sordid story unknown to most…. a 'must read' for every citizen of India, and of the world, not only because it gives us a story of the INA (Indian National Army) never known in such detail, but also because it exposes the brutality of war and the sordid side of human nature.—**Major General Ian Cardozo (retd), Gurkha officer, military historian and author of** *Cartoos Saab, 1971 Stories of Grit & Glory* **and many other books on the Indian Army**

'[An] entirely fresh and original account of a tale that is little told and little understood in India itself, and barely even mentioned in Britain – the saga of the Indian troops who fell into the hands of the Japanese in the early months of 1942 … a beautifully crafted and constructed book.'— **Phil Craig, author of** *1945 The Reckoning: War, Empire and a Struggle for a New World*

'This book sheds new light on certain lesser-known aspects of India's involvement in the war, with a particular focus on the war in East Asia, and the saga of suffering, loyalty and sacrifice of the forgotten Indian FEPOWs (Far East Prisoners of War), whose story was overshadowed by that of the Indian National Army and the tumult and chaos of independence and partition.'—**Squadron Leader Rana Tej Pratap Singh Chhina (retd), MBE (retd), author, military historian and director, Centre for Military History and Conflict Studies, United Service Institution of India**

'History is always the combination of individual stories, whether we look at it that way or not. For the prisoner of war experience this vantage point must surely be privileged. The many stories brought to light here are often vivid and compelling as well as shocking. This is a valuable addition to our literature on that sad wartime chapter. '**Professor Brian P. Farrell, Department of History, National University of Singapore**

'A powerful and deeply human account of Indian soldiers held by the Japanese in WWII. Gautam Hazarika brings long-forgotten voices to life with care and clarity. I'm glad I could assist in a small way with this important work that finally gives these men the recognition they deserve.'—**Major General Syed Ali Hamid (retd), author of** *Sahibzada Yaqub Khan* **and** *At the Forward Edge of Battle*

'This truly is a history of the Unknown Indian POW, who suffered extensively at the hands of the Japanese … a remarkable story, told well and which the author brings up to date with personal interactions with survivors.'—**Sanjoy Hazarika, award-winning journalist, author and International Director of the Commonwealth Human Rights Initiative**

'[A] largely forgotten story of Indian prisoners of war in Southeast Asia during the Second World in an accessible narrative style. He also charts lesser-known stories about the Indian National Army (INA) such as that of Captain Mohan Singh the commander of the first incarnation of the INA.'—**Dr Alan Jeffreys, FRHistS, military historian and Head of Collections and Research, National Army Museum**

'Lucid account of the dilemma of Indian soldiers taken prisoner by Japan, the book clears away clouds of wishful thinking and nationalist mythology, and allows light to fall on many lost scenes of courage, survival and humanity.'—**Raghu Karnad, author of** *Farthest Field: An Indian Story of the Second World War*

'A calm, detailed and revealing account of the lost Indian POWs of 1942. A brilliant debut.'—**Dr Robert Lyman, MBE, FRHistS, author of** *A War of Empires* **and** *Bill Slim*

'A long-forgotten story that needed to be told. Sacrifice, loyalty, heroism and tragedy abound. Huge congratulations to the author for bringing this vital WWII history to light.'—**Damien Lewis, author of** *The Ministry of Ungentlemanly Warfare*

'This timely, very well researched book tells the story of the Indian officers and rank and file of the British Indian Army …..Singapore historian Gautam Hazarika tells the complex story of Japanese duplicity and intrigue within the Indian leadership. It is the story of those who joined the Indian National Army; those who chose captivity and those who joined the INA but very soon had second thoughts and ended up as POWs…... This book is a 'must read' to those interested in that story and the events of WW2 in South East Asia. It will certainly add to our knowledge of POW captivity.'—**Jonathan Moffat, co-author of** *Moon Over Malaya A Tale of Argyll's and Marines*

'[A] remarkable work. It is the Indian point of view, yet as far as possible unemotional, one-volume retelling that this episode of India's history demands … Highly recommended.'—**K.S. Nair, author of *December in Dacca* and *The Forgotten Few***

'An important book that highlights the suffering and fortitude of the forgotten Indian prisoners of the Japanese. This is a vital contribution on a neglected subject, and it deserves a wide readership.'—**Kevin Noles, author of *Indian Prisoners of War in Japanese Captivity during World War Two***

'[Hazarika's] breezy and well-researched narrative never falters, gripping you with every clever twist.'—**Mukund Padmanabhan, distinguished professor of philosophy, Krea University, former editor of *The Hindu* and author of *The Great Flap of 1942***

'Richly detailed and remarkably researched . . . a fascinating account of a lost chapter in India's freedom struggle.'—**Manu S. Pillai, historian and author of *Gods, Guns and Missionaries***

A signal merit of Gautam Hazarika's book is the story that it tells of how Mohan Singh—soon elevated to the rank of General—worked with the Japanese to establish the first Indian National Army after the fall of Singapore….. Hazarika paints a vivid portrait of this remarkable, if rag-tag, military outfit that was forged in the heat of the war, including several dramatis personae who seldom feature in standard histories of the INA. …Hazarika rightly holds that the INA's postwar political importance outstripped its military contribution… The fluent, yet often dramatic, narrative presented in this book is undergirded by in-depth research in archives across countries.—**Srinath Raghvan, Professor and author of *India's War, The Making of Modern South Asia 1939-1945***

'[A] powerful and moving account …Through painstaking research and compassionate storytelling, this book resurrects the tortured voices of those silenced by captivity, torn from home and erased from memory.'—**Rajesh Rai, Associate Professor and Head, South Asian Studies Programme, National University of Singapore, and author of *Indians in Singapore***

'The history of Indian soldiers in WW2 is rarely told except perhaps in the context of Netaji Subhas Bose and the Azad Hind Fauj. There are, however, other stories that can be told …In his very first book, Gautam Hazarika explores these side streets to bring alive an important but chaotic period in world history.'—**Sanjeev Sanyal, economist and bestselling author**

'Newcomer Gautam Hazarika connects two aspects of WWII history: the familiar – the Indian National Army – and the unknown Indian PoWs of the Japanese. He tells these stories vividly, skillfully weaving a tale of loyalists and renegades, and heroes and villains, all caught up in the great conflict that changed all Asia 80 years ago.'—**Prof. Peter Stanley, Historian of the Indian Army and Professor at University of New South Wales Canberra**

EAST ASIA IN WORLD WAR II

SOVIET UNION

MONGOLIA

Peking

KOREA

Sea

CHINA

Shanghai

Yellow Sea

NEPAL

BHUTAN

Okinawa

INDIA

BURMA

Hong Kong

Formosa

Rangoon

Hainan

THAILAND

Bangkok

Manila

Philippine Sea

FRENCH
INDOCHINA

South China Sea

Saigon

PHILIPPINES

PALA

MALAYA

MALAYA

Singapore

Equator

DUTCH EAST INDIES

Batavia

Soerabaya

Indian Ocean

4 June 1942 Extent of Japanese Occupation

AUS

(SJmagic DESIGN SERVICES, India)

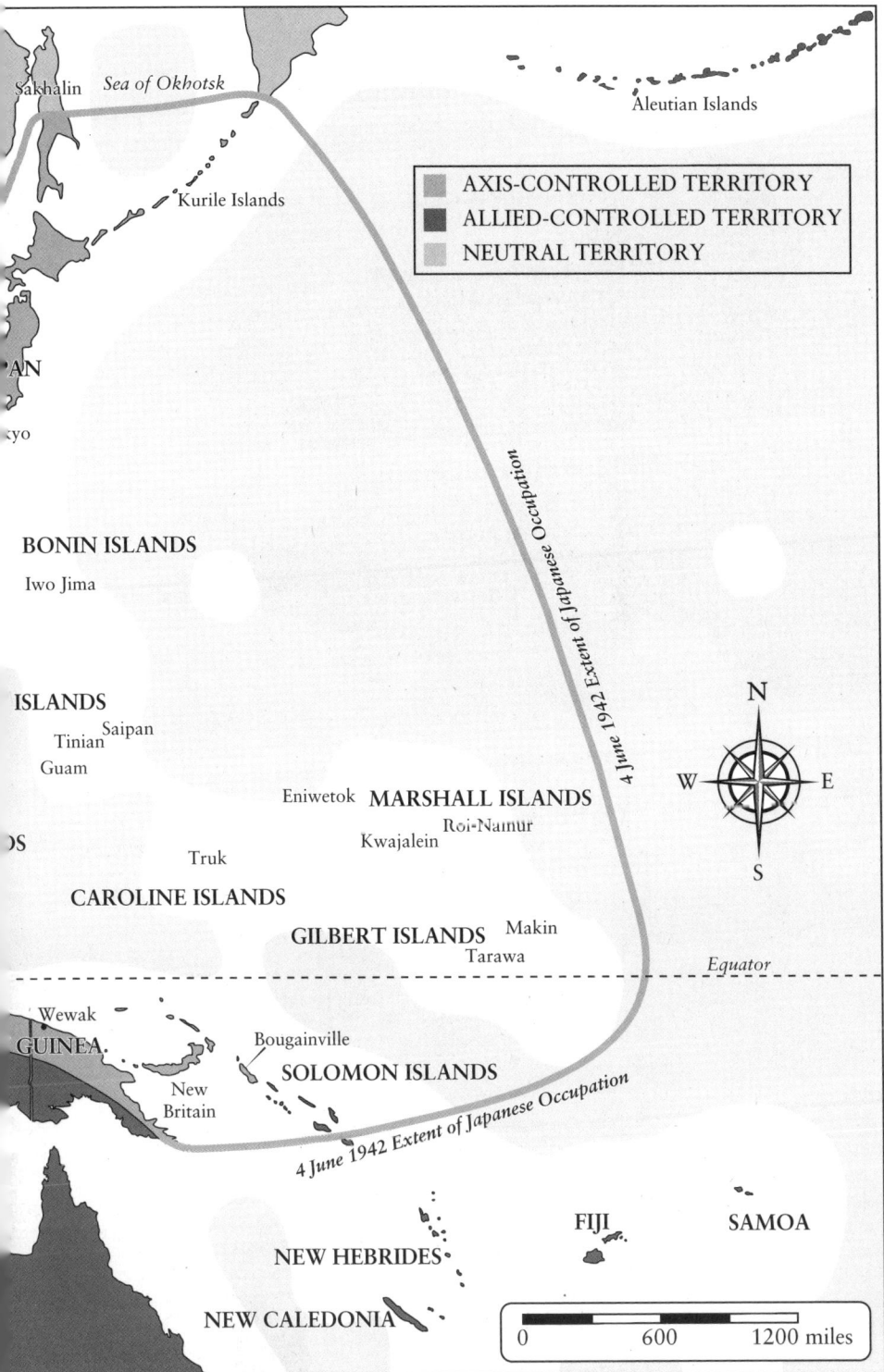

Sakhalin *Sea of Okhotsk*

Aleutian Islands

Kurile Islands

'AN

:yo

BONIN ISLANDS

Iwo Jima

4 June 1942 Extent of Japanese Occupation

N

W   E

ISLANDS

Saipan
Tinian
Guam

Eniwetok **MARSHALL ISLANDS**

Roi-Namur

Kwajalein

S

)S   Truk

CAROLINE ISLANDS

GILBERT ISLANDS   Makin

Tarawa

Equator

Wewak

GUINEA   Bougainville

New
Britain   **SOLOMON ISLANDS**

4 June 1942 Extent of Japanese Occupation

FIJI   SAMOA

NEW HEBRIDES

NEW CALEDONIA

| 0 | 600 | 1200 miles |

CONTENTS

FOREWORD

1942 was a cataclysm for the British empire as it came under sustained challenge in Asia by the armed forces of Japan. Japan had been fighting in China since 1931 and was now focused resolutely on expanding its empire in East Asia and the Pacific, at the cost of the possessions of Britain, the Netherlands and the USA.

It was also a personal cataclysm for the millions of people caught up in the tsunami of blood that swept through Asia in 1942 for, despite the assertions from Tokyo that it wanted to create an 'Asia for the Asiatics', this piece of egregious propaganda was not what was practiced in reality. As time would demonstrate, this actually meant an 'Asia for the Japanese in the lead, and all others as their slaves.'

For the men of the Indian Army caught up in the surrender of Malaya and Singapore in February 1942, and for the scores of thousands of domestic Indians living across British Asia who saw the ignominious departure of the British and the sudden arrival of new masters, a profound challenge was now faced. In this remarkable book, Gautam Hazarika calmly steps through the choices these men faced, and the consequences of these decisions on each personally as the war went through its various phases. He powerfully includes the different decisions of different men and some women, explaining what happened in each of a number of scenarios. What was a sepoy of an Indian regiment to do at the surrender to the Japanese, when all around him he could see the end of something he'd taken for granted from birth: the mighty British Empire humbled in the face of an Asian enemy? What is more, these men – or many of them – were encouraged by their departing British officers to obey their new masters. This cataclysm represented what appeared to be the end of an old world, and the start of a new. It's hard not to be sympathetic with honourable men in this utterly unforeseen predicament, finding themselves seemingly at an inflection point in history, and having to make a decision as to whether they accepted this new reality, or stick with the old.

The first challenge was to accept that the defeat they had experienced in truth represented the end of the British in Asia and that it was time to take up arms to push the tottering edifice of the Raj aside, alongside the Imperial Japanese Army. Many officers and men in the Indian Army had nationalistic views, and looked forward to the time when India might achieve its independence. Was that time now? Was it right therefore to accept Japanese urging to join the new Indian National Army (INA)? Hazarika describes this challenge, explaining the decision made by those who accepted and those who did not. The nature of the INA, as a reflection of Indian nationalistic as well as Japanese military imperatives, is a fascinating part of the study, exposing the fault lines that led to the demise of the first INA, and the birth of the second.

But what stands out for me is Hazarika's description of those Indian POWs who fell outside the INA, for one of several reasons, and who as a result have tended to be forgotten, especially in the modern retelling of the INA story in India. Modern India knows all about Subhas Chandra Bose, or thinks it does. It likewise knows all about the INA, or thinks it does. But as this book demonstrates, there was more than one INA and there were many scores of POWs who have not been remembered because their experience sat outwith that of Mohan Singh or SCB. This deficiency in our memory of the lost POWs of the Second World War is powerfully rectified by Hazarika: he unflinchingly describes the impact of an 'Asia for the Asiatics' on India POWs who became not much more than slaves at the hands of a rapacious empire that ended up leaving perhaps 20-million dead in its wake. These men deserve our remembrance and our understanding. In this fine study Hazarika is to be congratulated for doing precisely this.

Dr Robert Lyman MBE FRHistS

TABLE OF RANKS OF THE INDIAN ARMY IN WORLD WAR II

INDIAN ARMY Infantry	Equivalent in BRITISH ARMY
Sepoy*	Private
Lance-Naik	Lance-Corporal
Naik	Corporal
Havildar	Sergeant
Havildar-Major	Sergeant-Major

Between Havildar-Major and commissioned officers were Viceroy Commissioned Officers (VCO) equivalent to Warrant Officers in the British Army. There were three grades of VCOs:

Jemadar
Subedar
Subedar-Major

Officers had the same nomenclature in both armies.

---

* Sepoys are called Rifleman in the Gurkhas and Sowars in the Cavalry.

PROLOGUE

War comes to Singapore – Suddenly

At 4.30am on December 8, 1941, the 28-year-old Shiraz Mohammedali of slight build and with a smart moustache, was asleep in 14 Malacca Street in the central business district of Singapore. Suddenly awoken by a loud noise, followed by a tremendous shaking of the building, he rushed outside clad just in his singlet and sarong. There he heard the groans of men in pain and the voices of others running about in a panic. The previous evening Shiraz had watched an Indian war movie "Watan"* or homeland, and realized this was not an earthquake, but a bombing. War had suddenly come to Singapore and caught the people unawares. It had also surprised the British, Australian, Indian, Malay and Chinese troops present.

Indian soldiers in Singapore

The British were defending their empire, the local Malays, Chinese and Indians their city, but there were also Indian troops from India there. The Indian people had no interest in Malaya nor any fight with Japan. At that time, India was a British colony, and though there were many who came from families with a long tradition of serving in the army and loyal to the empire, to others it was just a profession, so they were in effect mercenaries[1] and did what they were ordered to do by their paymasters, the British. In this case it was to defend a part of its global empire, Malaya, from an attack expected from Japan. Indians had been used by the British in this manner for two centuries – it began with Indians helping the British defeat other Indians, and once India had been conquered in this way, to extend and hold their empire across the world. This was how 67,000 Indian troops[2] ended up defending Malaya and Singapore, half of the Allied army there.

---

* Family archive of Shiraz Mohammedali with his son Asad Shiraz, Singapore.

The (not) Sudden Attack by the Japanese

Japan had deliberately kept itself isolated from the rest of the world for centuries, when the American Commodore Perry arrived in Tokyo in 1853 and forced her to restart relations with the west. Trade followed, but Japan also embarked on an expansionist policy enabled by them modelling their armed forces on the German army and the Royal Navy. In the first case in recent history of an Asian power defeating a European one, Japan won its war with Russia hands down in 1905. She then made Korea a colony and in 1931 invaded Manchuria. In 1937 she attacked more of China and that's where her troubles began. After the collapse of the Qing dynasty in 1911 China was split between powerful warlords, the communists under Chairman Mao, and Chiang Kai Shek supported by the Allied powers. Divided this way, China was open to attack but was also too vast to conquer, so the Japanese got bogged down. Besides this, lacking her own oil, steel and other natural resources, Japan depended on US and British supplies. When they further extended their reach into Vietnam in 1940 and 1941, the US imposed an embargo on oil and Japan's financial assets to stop them.

It was then that Japan decided to invade Southeast Asia, rich in the resources she lacked. Maintaining a fig leaf of negotiating for peace, at the same time they prepared for war. As the Americans and the British did not expect them to attack, they ignored all the signs. So, when on December 8, 1941, Japan simultaneously attacked Hong Kong, Singapore, Malaya, the Philippines, and the US naval base in Pearl Harbor (December 7 local time), it came as a big shock.[3]

The Defence of Singapore

Besides the Americans, the main adversary of the Japanese in Asia was Britain with a vast empire including much of southeast Asia, as well as Hong Kong. Weakened by World War I, Britain could not maintain a large naval fleet both in the Atlantic and the Pacific. Prioritizing the Atlantic for any attacks by a possibly resurgent Germany, she decided to send capital warships (battleships and aircraft carriers) to Asia when the need arose. After a long study, many delays, fits and starts, a naval base to house them was inaugurated in Singapore on 14 Feb1938. To ensure they had a free hand in the region, the Japanese had to capture the island city and this base. The triple irony of the British defence of Singapore, was that at the time when they were needed there were just two capital warships there as Churchill could not spare more from his war with Hitler. But this was far in the future when in the 1930s, to defend the naval base a large (but ill-equipped) army was deployed and to defend them, air bases built that had just a handful of outdated planes. To top this, more troops were sent to defend these airbases. So, to defend a naval base with no ships, an army was sent with no tanks, and to defend the army, air bases were built that had few modern planes.[4]

The failure of Operation Matador

The British correctly anticipated that if the Japanese invaded Malaya and Singapore, they would first land in south Thailand and then move down Malaya to the island city. They also guessed where exactly the Japanese would land in Thailand – Singora and Patani on the eastern coast. The best way for an army to stop such an invasion was to destroy it on the beaches of Thailand where they would be most exposed. Plans were drawn up, named Operation Matador, to do so, but the timing of when this would happen was key. If it started late, it would fail and that is what happened.

To stop the Japanese, the British had to be at the beaches before they landed. And this involved invading Thailand before any actual Japanese assault had occurred. The British quandary was that they wanted to respect Thai sovereignty and not hand the Japanese the fig leaf of an excuse by invading first. In early December 1941, Japanese ships were sighted heading towards Thailand, but the British waited for them to land to trigger Matador. By then it was too late.

The Collapse of the Allied Defence

Lieutenant-Colonel Leslie Vernon Fitzpatrick was the commanding officer (C/O) of the 1/14 Punjab Regiment based in north Malaya, one of the battalions assigned to Matador. In a post-war report he said "On 8 December 1941 at Tanjong Pau 0315 hours, orders were received for scheme Matador to operate. By 0630 hours the battalion had arrived at Anak Bugit Railway Station where the Leicesters* were already entrained. Battalion was dispersed in slit trenches pending the arrival of its train".[†] After waiting almost all day "at about 1600 hours orders were received to return to Tanjong Pau". Once the battalion marched back, Fitzpatrick "was informed that scheme Matador was off and the Jitra position was to be held".

This is how the war began for the 1/14 Punjab, as for many other units. Decisions were taken too late, valuable time wasted and orders kept changing. And this is how it largely continued for the rest of the campaign. As Matador could not stop the Japanese, the back-up plan to stop their advance in Malaya went into motion.

---

*   1st Leicester's, a British battalion fighting alongside.

†   Fitzpatrick quotes from India MOD 601/639/H.

However, once the Japanese had established themselves, it was difficult to stop them. For the Allies, there was also a feeling of inevitable defeat embedded – from the start, the orders invariably said hold on as long as you can and then fall back. This continued all the way down the Malayan peninsula and later in Singapore.

The Retreat

With a well-planned Japanese advance and an equally well-planned Allied retreat, the battle slipped rapidly from the hands of the Allies. The Japanese were well-trained, equipped and informed. They moved fast, famously on bicycles, with each soldier carrying all the food he needed for a week. They were audacious, attacking at times and places least expected. They had almost total control of the air from the start with more modern planes than the British. Flying from bases close by in Saigon, they destroyed many of the British planes on the ground, then their troops captured those airfields which were in turn used to intensify their bombing. They air base-hopped down the Malayan peninsula, capturing all the well built but ill-equipped RAF bases.

Churchill had finally sent two large warships – HMS *Prince of Wales* and *Repulse* that arrived in Singapore on December 2, 1941. On December 10, both were sunk off the eastern coast of Malaya by Japanese planes. Now the land, the air and sea were controlled by Japan.

Strange Happenings – The Bridge over the River Muar[*]

Given the overwhelming Japanese superiority on all fronts, the strange events that happened to some Indian units did not impact the battle but were a precursor of things to come. Men disappeared, then some came back mysteriously with stories of good Japanese and a Sikh General who was leading Indian POWs.

The 5/2 Punjab Regiment had been in Malaya since 1939 and was in Singapore when war broke out. On December 13, 1941, they were moved to Sungei Patani in northern Malaya to bolster its defence. When they arrived, the battalion was faced with news of fifth columnists[†] working against the British and shaken by reports of false orders being relayed to deliberately create chaos.

---

[*] This section including quotations from Captain I.J. Kiani from CSDIC S Section Report 1110 in INA383 henceforth I.J. Kiani, Lt Col Deakin NAM 6509-15, Havildar Shiv Singh CSDIC (I) No. 2 Section Report 612/INA 499 part 3.

[†] A term used for people who undermine from within.

With these fears clouding over them, on the 16th, they took control of the Pakaka bridge on the Muar river. The overall retreat strategy had already taken hold, and they were ordered to blow it up to slow down the Japanese advance. C Company of the battalion commanded by the 30-year-old 5-foot 10-inch Captain Inayatullah Jan Kiani was in charge at the bridge when at 2.00pm he was told that a British officer was waving a white flag from the other bank. He went to investigate and saw him along with forty to fifty men in non-descript clothing. Kiani could not make out who they were, though he did think at least one was Japanese. This officer then shouted in Hindustani, "*Ham dost hain, dushman nahin, fire mat karo*" (we are friends, not enemies, don't fire). Kiani thought he recognized him and shouted back "Ward you fool what are you doing down there?" He received a reply in guttural English "I am not Ward".[*] Kiani told him that he alone should cross the bridge to the other side for his story to be verified.

The bridge had not been destroyed properly, and this mysterious European started walking across it towards Kiani on the other bank. While he did this, he was covered by one of Kiani's men, Havildar Gurbachan Singh, armed with a Tommy gun. When the European reached the other side, he suddenly swept Singh's gun aside, grappled with him and they both fell into the water. From across the river, someone shouted out to him "you fool, they'll fire now". Exactly on cue, another of Kiani's men, Havildar Pritam Singh shot the European in the head with his pistol, killing him. Then the men on the other bank started firing at Kiani's Indians who were able to hold their ground. After the skirmish ended, the mysterious European's body lay there all day, but at night it was missing, preventing the Indians from finding out who he really was. Besides his dead body, Kiani and his second in command were also missing, so Havildar Pritam Singh officiated until they reappeared the next afternoon.

"Salooni" and the Sikh General

After this incident, the 5/2 Punjab withdrew down Malaya with more men disappearing and some returning, as did the slight 25-year-old Sepoy Ghulam Mohammad, nicknamed Salooni. On January 2, 1942, when encamped on the Slim river, Salooni was sitting with Sepoy Fazal Din driving a water truck, when they apparently inadvertently crossed over into Japanese territory. Din was not heard of again, but Salooni returned the next day wearing a spotlessly clean pair of canvas shoes bearing no mark of being lost in the jungle for a day. There was no news

---

[*] I.J. Kiani.

of Din or the water truck. To the battalion C/O Lieutenant-Colonel C C Deakin he said nothing about his disappearance but soon whispered to the men the story of his experiences. Soon the whole battalion was aware that the Japanese treated Indians very well, allowed him to return and there was a Sikh General fighting with them. These events became even more mysterious. Salooni had obviously met the Japanese and probably Indians already working with them and returned to spread the news that he did.

This was later called the strategy of "quick release", to be sent back soon so he would not be suspected of having become indoctrinated with anti-British emotion, while he could spread exactly this feeling. It did not work in his case as he was removed from the front line. But before he left, word of the friendly Japanese and the Sikh General had spread. The aim was to get more men to desert, and it worked, for a few days later some did.[5] However, this seems to have affected only a few men during the campaign, as despite these ominous events, the battalion fought well, as recorded by the Official History.[6]

On Singapore Island

After further defeats, the Allies evacuated Malaya on January 31, 1942, blew up the causeway linking it to Singapore and gathered there to make their last stand. Then followed a week of incessant shelling and bombing by the Japanese for which the British had no response. They had no planes to shoot down the bombers and the big guns on the island intended to attack ships did not have the right ammunition to fire at targets on land. On the night of February 7/8, 1942, the Japanese began their invasion focusing on the north-west of Singapore, exactly where the British commander General Percival did not expect them, so had concentrated his forces elsewhere. The men did what they could and then the familiar pattern of retreats began.

The last days in Singapore

Warrant Officer Abdul Hayat Khan of the 3 Mixed Reinforcement Centre, a slightly built 38-year-old from Badaun in the United Provinces of India, gives us a graphic account of the confusion of those days. Once the battle was almost over, many soldiers including Khan were in the city centre. On February 13, he was headed to the Robinsons department store (at that time in Raffles Place) where two anti-British fifth columnists in military uniform were found, so Gurkhas were appointed to guard the building. That night when everyone was asleep, they returned, threw brickbats and shouted "Fire fire". In the confused melee, dozens died. The next day, Khan went to Bidadari camp to collect rations and found "Klings" (the colloquial term for South Indians) hoisting Indian National Congress* flags. That day Robinsons was bombed and this continued incessantly until the sudden ceasefire on the evening of the 15th.

At 9.00am the next morning, Japanese tanks rode triumphantly through the city and soon their officers came with trucks to collect arms and ammunition from the Allied soldiers. At noon, all British and Chinese shops were forcibly shut down. That night Khan slept at a building near the main Post Office (now the Fullerton Hotel). Unknown to him, the next day he was to see Salooni's mysterious Sikh General.

---

* The INC is a leading Indian political party that fought for her independence.

Chapter 1

THE SPECTACLE AT FARRER PARK

"The whole crowd erupted in cheers, throwing their turbans and caps in the air."[*]

On Tuesday, February 17, 1942, in Singapore at the old racecourse in Farrer Park adjacent to today's Little India, the mysterious Sikh General, who was in fact Captain Mohan Singh of the 14th Punjab regiment, was enthusiastically greeted when he took the microphone and spoke to the thousands of Indian soldiers gathered.

Two days earlier, in the biggest military defeat in their history,[1] Britain had surrendered Singapore to Japan. Addressing them as friends in Hindustani (a mix of Hindi and Urdu), Singh asked what had brought them together that day? It was the British, who always used them for their own purposes, as there was no reason for Indians fighting in Malaya. However, now the British had been defeated, making Indians their own masters, and this was met by more cheers. A new Indian National Army would be formed with the help of the Japanese to expel Britain from India, and together with his fellow soldiers Captains Akram[2] and Allah Ditta,[3] he had agreed to join the Japanese in doing so. When Singh ended by asking the soldiers to swear an oath to fight for India's freedom, the whole crowd erupted in cheers, throwing their turbans and caps in the air.[4]

These were extraordinary words from Singh and an even more extraordinary response from the soldiers. The Indian Army had sworn an oath to the British king, and this cheering broke that oath. For the soldiers on that day however, it may have seemed obvious to do so. They had been totally demoralized by a campaign of continuous retreats and a chaotic defence with some units not fighting at all.

---

[*] Major Toye's CSDIC (I) S Section Report 1007 para 67 on Singh's interrogation INA File 386 National Archives India henceforth MS-Toye, This has been described in similar terms by many including Captain Balbir Singh 4/19 Hyderabad who said of the crowd "They cheered MOHAN SINGH at the end of his speech most enthusiastically", IWO Abdul Hayat Khan said he was greeted by "loud shouts" (CSDIC (I) No. 2 Section Report 16 and 80, INA499, henceforth Balbir Singh and Khan).

The mighty British had surrendered two days ago and on the next day the Indian Army was left leaderless when their British commanding officers were segregated. Then on that day they heard Singh urging them to join the Japanese to throw out defeated Britain from India, an India Japan had promised to leave free. If they did, the soldiers would be treated as allies and not suffer ill-treatment as prisoners of war, so it's no surprise that most cheered.

In an interview with the British after the war, Singh said he noticed many officers with downcast eyes, and thought to himself, if he could convince these naysayers, they would certainly succeed. But there was no doubt that Captain Mohan Singh had struck a chord with the soldiers, and many officers. Though Singh had a slight build, his proud and erect bearing, piercing eyes[5] and a very clearly evident belief in what he said, had its effect. The British Major Hugh Toye, who interviewed many of those present after the war, said Singh "made an intensely nationalist speech that roused the hearts and raised the hopes of his audience".*[6]

Captain Mohan Singh

One of the lesser known figures in the history of modern India, Captain Mohan Singh's role as the first leader of the INA is overshadowed by his illustrious successor, the prominent nationalist politician Subhas Chandra Bose.† It is remarkable that Singh, a relatively junior officer quite unknown outside his unit, was chosen by the Japanese and accepted by thousands of soldiers and dozens of officers senior to him, as their leader.

His journey to Farrer Park began with a tough childhood, his father dying two months before he was born 1909 in Sialkot now part of Pakistan. His mother moved them to her maternal home, but she too died when he was just six. He joined the army as a sepoy or private in 1927, and soon being recognized as having higher potential, was included in the first batch of Indians groomed as officers at the Indian Military Academy Dehradun in 1932.[7] He served with the 14th Punjab Regiment and was with the 1/14 Punjab when they reached Malaya in March 1941. Singh was one of several Indian officers who felt discriminated against by the British, and away from the cantonments of India when they mingled with European civilians in Malaya, faced racism.[8] At this time desire for Indian independence was also at

---

* MS-Toye.
† Bose started off as a mainstream Indian nationalist, becoming the President of the Indian National Congress in 1938–1939. Wanted to follow a more aggressive stance to achieve Indian independence he broke away and that path eventually led him to the INA in mid-1943.

a peak,* so all that was needed was a spark to ignite the flames – one big enough to bridge the gap between discontentment and rebellion. It would however need to be a big spark, as there is a difference between feeling discriminated against, and acting on that by rebelling against the British.[9]

Giani Pritam Singh

That big spark was about to come. Shortly after Singh's arrival in Malaya, Japan's Army HQ started actively to seek the help of locals in the Southeast Asian countries they were planning to invade. They wanted them to join Japan in expelling their Western colonial rulers and reclaim "Asia for the Asiatics". Bangkok was chosen as their intelligence base, Thailand being the only independent Asian country in a sea of colonies so a hotbed of espionage,[10] as well as bordering the soon to be invaded Malaya. Japan had no interest in India but knew there were two million Indians in Southeast Asia including prominent traders, priests and lawyers. Not only that, there were organizations to protect interests of the Indians, and one right there in Bangkok, was headed by ardent nationalists who kept the flame of independence alive overseas.[11] And so no one needed convincing when in June 1941 they met a prominent Sikh preacher, Giani Pritam Singh, who wanted their help. His goal was to galvanise Indian civilians in Southeast Asia to fight for India, raise funds and an army not only from them, but also the thousands of Indian soldiers in Malaya, Singapore and Burma who had been sent there to protect the British Empire.[12]

Major Fujiwara

To cement this alliance, Major Fujiwara Iwaichi, a Japanese intelligence officer, arrived in Bangkok on October 1, 1941.[13] Other authors have used parentage metaphors to describe the roles played by these three men – Fujiwara, Giani and Singh on the birth of the INA. To put them all together, Singh was the mother, Fujiwara the father and the Giani the mid-wife of the INA.[14] They were coincidentally the same age (32), committed and very good at what they had decided to do. Tasked to get Asian civilians and Indian soldiers in Malaya to collaborate with the Japanese Army, Fujiwara had visited Southeast Asia in disguise in May

---

* After supporting Britain in World War I, India expected Dominion status as in Australia. There was some devolution of power in the 1930s but it was far from being a Dominion. When the British declared war on behalf of India in 1939 without consulting any Indians, there was an outcry that raised the pitch for the demand for independence.

to assess the possibilities, and after his arrival in Bangkok soon met the Giani. Expecting a burly Sikh, he was surprised to find a slight man but with a fire burning in his eyes, and his nationalist zeal impressed him a great deal.[15]

Despite being a relatively junior officer given the scope of his role, he was allowed much leeway. Added to that he believed that his focus should be more on what his Indian partner wanted, to enable the help desired. An agreement was signed in early December once Japan's invasion of Malaya was imminent, that said that in return for help by Indians in Malaya, Japan would support forming a volunteer army from Indian soldiers and civilians to achieve Indian independence and protect Indians in occupied areas. Fujiwara had gone beyond the scope of his orders which were to get their help, and not to promise anything in return.[16]

The Giani's Leaflets to Indian soldiers

Fujiwara and the Giani were aligned, but what of the Indian Army? The Giani had met them[17] and it is probably because they were willing to join him in seeking Japanese help to oust the British. that he proposed the formation of a volunteer army from the soldiers. There were two Indian divisions in north Malaya to whom the Giani's men distributed anti-British leaflets in Indian languages to rile up the men with content such as this:

> English Dogs bark before the innocent Indians to show they that they are
> saving India from Germany, Japan. But it is wrong. No country has done
> any wrong to India except these English pirates and thieves in of disguise.*

Having known of links between the Japanese and Indian nationalists, when war clouds were in the air the British sent the most senior Indian officer in Malaya, Major Narandar Singh Gill, 4/19 Hyderabad Regiment on a secret mission to Bangkok to investigate how bad things were. His report was that besides the Giani, most Indians were not political.[18] It is possible that after investigating, he decided to join them as he became the most senior INA officer after Mohan Singh, who was rumoured to have accompanied him. Singh went on leave at the same time, his battalion was in the Thailand/Malaya border and he could have slipped across. At a farewell party hosted for him in Malaya on November 30, 1941 at the end of his leave, Singh announced to the guests that he did not plan to die for the British and they should not be surprised to see him rise up against them. Was this him, excited with his mission to achieve a new destiny for India inadvertently letting the cat out of the bag? Or, as he tried to explain it after the war, something inexplicable, as he flatly denied any pre-war contact?[19]

---

* INA 295, pg13–14.

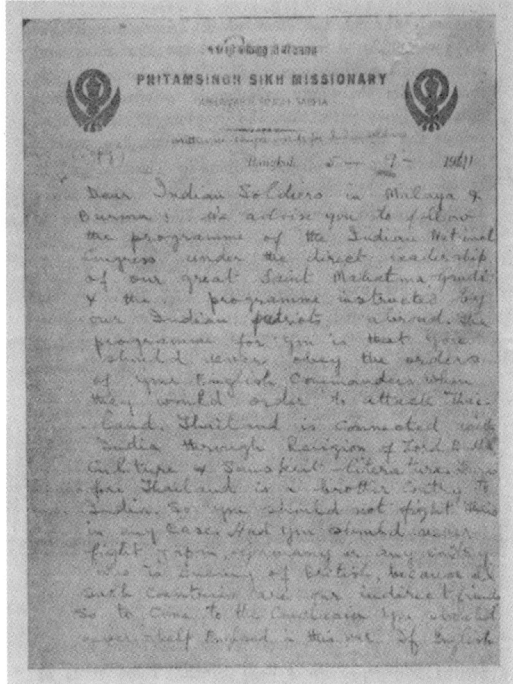

Giani Pritam Singhs handwritten text for poster addressed to Indian soldiers in Malaya in September 1941. (National Archives India)

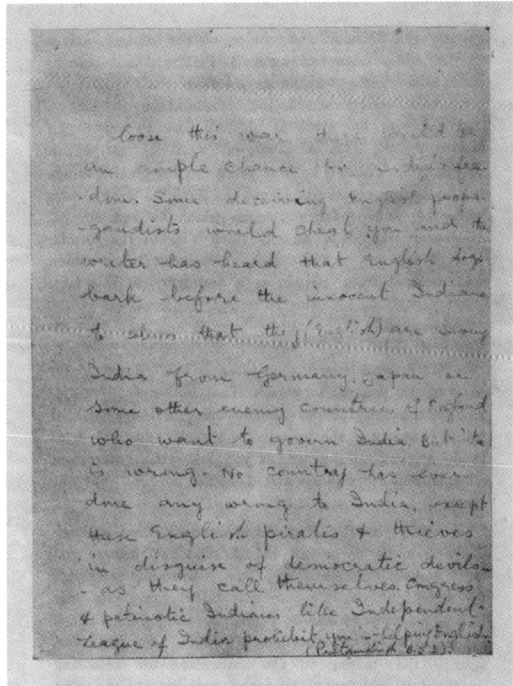

The Fujiwara Kikan at the start of the war

Whether there was active Indian Army involvement at this stage or not, Fujiwara and the Giani went to work. In anticipation of the invasion and the agreement, spies had been sent to Malaya in November to incite the local Indians against the British.[20] The Japanese invasion began in the early hours of December 8, 1941. New leaflets were printed in Bangkok to be dropped by Japanese planes urging Indians to join Japan in their effort to reclaim "Asia for the Asiatics", urging them to "Kick out the white devils from the East". The Japanese added that "We have come to liberate Asia from the deadly clutches of the Anglo-Saxons" and "No Asiatic is our Enemy" and so on. A unit was created with Fujiwara's small staff and with a few Indians selected by the Giani. They were assigned to each of the three Japanese Army groups leading the invasion who were instructed to handover all captured Indian soldiers to them. As the Japanese tend to name teams after their commander, this was called the Fujiwara Kikan (liaison team).

Loudspeakers on the Front Lines

On December 10, 1941, Fujiwara and the Giani arrived at the border between Thailand and Malaya where the Giani's men began reaching out to Indian soldiers, shouting out to them using loudspeakers to stop fighting for the manipulative British and join Japan who wanted to free India. Some of those who surrendered were fed well and sent back, to spread the word about how good the Japanese were, a precursor to Saloon's actions in the prologue. From the very first days of the invasion, Indian Army men started deserting the British.[21]

Fujiwara and the Giani meet Mohan Singh[22]

Meanwhile, Mohan Singh's battalion had been tasked with defending the border and then withdrawing to the main defensive line at Jitra in northern Malaya. They did what they could, but crumbled and dispersed when the Japanese attacked with tanks on December 11. In the melee Mohan Singh came across his wounded battalion commander Lieutenant-Colonel Leslie Vernon Fitzpatrick.[23] By now he had decided to join the Japanese, and took a calculated risk. He could have sent Fitzpatrick to safety towards Jitra where the main defence line was. That would have kept him away from Singh's men whose resolve could have been weakened by the commanders presence. Instead Mohan Singh decided to keep him close as a fig leaf – with Fitzpatrick there, his eventual surrender to the Japanese would look honourable, in case things did not work out as hoped. He took this risk as he knew his men were more loyal to him.

Once decided, he headed east, away from the Indian Army positions at Jitra. On the way he rendezvoused with Captain Akram who had disappeared on the day before the tank attack. Together, they made their way to Kuala Nerang, 10 miles east of Jitra. When they reached on December 14, the latest news was that the Japanese had not only captured Jitra, but were now further south at Alor Star. Mohan Singh sent a message to them saying they were ready to surrender. The next morning Fujiwara and the Giani arrived.

The meeting of these three men in the middle of the Malayan jungle was not a coincidence at all, for in the last few days while heading to Kuala Nerang, Mohan Singh had met Colonel Sugita, the head of intelligence of the invading Japanese troops and Fujiwara's superior in the field. After negotiations, Mohan Singh arranged for his surrender and joined the Japanese on December 15.

Captain Mohan Singh joins the Japanese

At the start of the jungle meeting, Fitzpatrick was segregated from the Indians and Singh never saw him again. He was handed over to the Japanese Army who were in charge of all non-Indian POWs. When they reached Alor Star, Singh and his men became "part and parcel"* of Fujiwara's team that day and started wearing the soon to be infamous F armband, white with the letter F in red so they could be recognised. Fujiwara said the F stood for "Fujiwara, Freedom, Friendship".[24]

Fujiwara asked him to restore order to the town where looting had broken out after the sudden departure of the British. Singh tasked Akram with a group of twenty of their men to do this, which they did armed just with batons and handcuffs.[25] The long talks that began that night were a sight to be imagined. There would have been at least five people present, Fujiwara nursing his bottle of whisky, Lieutenant Otaguru of the Fujiwara Kikan translating for him since he spoke no English, an inquisitive Singh and Akram, his constant partner in those crucial first weeks. The fifth person would have been a quiet Giani, for despite his enthusiasm in the field, he did not speak during these political meetings. This is perhaps why Singh thought he was not up to those aspects of his role. These talks continued late into the night, with the sound of the cock crowing telling them dawn had broken. Singh said in the beginning he did not help Fujiwara finish the whisky as he needed to be sober

---

* Singh reminiscences in Fujiwara.

when discussing such major events. Despite not speaking English, in a few weeks in Bangkok Fujiwara had clicked with Giani Pritam Singh, and in a few days in Alor Star with Mohan Singh.[26]

Though he had hardly met any Indian soldiers or officers so early in the campaign, Fujiwara did not hesitate and offered Singh the role of leading the INA, and to further demonstrate Japan's support, the next day took him to meet General Yamashita, the Japanese commander, who reiterated their commitment.[27] Singh took on the mantle immediately and decided to form a core set of volunteers, starting with, as advised by Captain Akram, the "pukka" or "cent per cent"* early adherents from Alor Star. This group of eventually 250 soldiers became the new members of the Fujiwara Kikan, the earlier set of the Giani's followers from Bangkok being sent back as he had managed to recruit many civilian followers in Malaya in just a few days. These new Fujiwara volunteers were notorious as they preached what was considered treason and many Indian soldiers recalled them vividly years later, wearing the infamous armband. They started collecting and controlling hundreds of surrendering Indian POWs, and by preaching the fight for independence, encouraging deserters. As there were thousands of Indians living in Malaya, it would have been possible for Indian soldiers to melt into the local population, as some of them did, and create trouble for the Japanese. This had been worrying Fujiwara, so he was pleased that Singh's men were corralling the Indians.[28]

The Birth of the INA

While Singh and Akram rounded-up the POWs, Fujiwara and the Giani focused on getting Indian civilians to join them, both sides achieving remarkable success. The four met on December 30 and 31 to finalize plans, and in a written proposal, Fujiwara outlined the strategic partnership and asked Singh for his men to fight the Allied army, including Indian soldiers there and then in Malaya. Singh was agreeable, but his men were not, refusing to fight their own unit and other Indian soldiers.

In a letter to Fujiwara dated January 1, 1942 which had the first use of the term Indian National Army, Singh and Akram said they would join the Japanese as proposed, with conditions. They asked that Subhas Chandra Bose be invited from Germany to lead the movement and clarify the political aspects, that Indian soldiers not be asked to fight their compatriots in Malaya as they were not ready yet, and finally that the INA be treated equally as an allied army. The later conflict

---

* MS-Toye para 51.

between the INA and Japan were clear here – did the Japanese have any territorial aims on India and how the Indian troops who joined them were to be used and treated?[29]

However, at that time, the partnership progressed smoothly. Both Fujiwara and Singh decided to skate over the unresolved ally status of the INA hoping that things would get resolved later. Singh was also aware that without Japan succeeding in Malaya, there was no hope for the INA, so he had to support them now as best he could. He also decided that if later the Japanese would not live up to their promises, he would withdraw his support. Fujiwara knew ally status was a problem. Both kept things from each other to enable the moment to happen, and that it did.[30] New leaflets were printed in early January using hand held presses, with simple and short messages in Indian languages explaining why Indians should not fight for the British and how many had already joined Singh, who signed off as GOC (General-Officer-commanding) INA. These were scattered by Japanese planes over Indian soldiers.[31] Singh joined the Fujiwara volunteers in all night missions to shout out to Indian soldiers to join them that netted hundreds of men as they moved down Malaya.[32] To protect themselves from air attacks Singh instructed his men to spread out a Japanese flag on the ground if Japanese planes were flying overhead and a British flag otherwise. This ingenious air defence to make attacking planes think his men were friendly worked, as they were not bombed.[33]

As Malaya was rapidly captured, almost 8,000 Indian POWs were collected by late January.[34] The largest group was in Kuala Lumpur where Singh created a microcosm of the future INA. He promoted a Viceroy Commissioned Officer (VCO)* over Indian officers present as the Camp Commandant and started propaganda lectures. When delivering these, Mohan Singh said "One had to be an orator of hatred and rouser of discontent",† to arouse anti-British emotions. Besides this, in a novel measure, he created common kitchens that cut across caste and religion.[35]

---

* The VCO was a device created by the British in the nineteenth century. In a vast Indian Army with only British officers, they needed to have senior Indians in positions of authority. Not wanting Indian officers until the 1920s, they created the VCO who was between the Indian soldiers and the British officers. Indians had to salute them, but even British privates (the lowest rank in the army) did not. Becoming regular officers in the INA instead of "in-betweens" in the Indian Army attracted many VCOs. The VCOs had decades of service and had great influence over the soldiers, perhaps more than the Indian officers who were still comparatively junior. The VCO ranks in descending order were Subedar-Major, Subedar and Jemadar, all equivalent to Warrant Officers in the British Army.

† Singh's oratory, see his book pg99.

The new Fujiwara Kikan in the Battle for Singapore

The Fujiwara volunteers were prepared for the upcoming invasion of Singapore with training in boats for the seaborne attack. A farewell party was held for them attended by Major Fujiwara, Mohan Singh and others. Wine flowed and in speeches the volunteers were exhorted not to let the movement down.

In early February 1942, they were split into groups, one of which helped to supply Japanese gunners in Johore pounding the island, resulting in legends that they were directing the shelling, and in fact fired the guns. Though this was untrue, their leader in the field, Subedar Allah Ditta, 7/22 Mountain Regiment said he did not deny it then as he wanted to build up the reputation of his force. Most Fujiwara volunteers accompanied the Japanese Army invading Pulau Ubin, an island between Johore and the eastern end of Singapore. When it was taken, three of the Fujiwara's from Singh's battalion raised the Japanese flag at its eastern tip. After this, most of them moved to Singapore via the quickly resurrected causeway linking it to the mainland at Johore.[36] There the battle had been raging and they were very active, informing the Indians about Japan's offer of help and the formation of the INA under Singh. Feelers were sent to some Indian officers, who were alleged to have surrendered prematurely.[37] In the last few days before Britain capitulated on February 15, captured Indian POWs were collected at Kranji police barracks. There, Captain Tehl Singh of the 1/8 Punjab Regiment recalled meeting the by now captain in the INA, Allah Ditta, wearing a British uniform with a captain's three pips on the shoulder, a Sam Browne belt worn by officers and a Turkish Fez symbolizing his Islamic heritage, who then went on to tell him about Singh's INA.[38]

Preparations for the Announcement of the INA

Meanwhile, Captain Mohan Singh had reached Singapore on the night of February 14, where he met Fujiwara and the Giani. Singh learnt that surrender was expected that day (i.e. February 15) with about 35,000 Indian POWs. The date was correct, but the number was much higher. On surrender night, Fujiwara was busy celebrating, but on the next day, February 16, lots happened. After a discussion at the Japanese HQ, Captain Singh was informed by Fujiwara that all the Indian POWs would be handed over to him, and he was required to arrange to look after them. Singh was then established in a bungalow near his own on Mount Pleasant Road, near today's Polo Club.[39]

For a handover of so many POWs to an unknown 33-year-old Captain when there were many officers senior to him, it had to be a mass, public spectacle and was carefully planned. The British were told that all Indian POWs must be segregated from their British officers and sent to the old polo grounds at Farrer Park the next morning, February 17th, at 8.30am. More importantly, Singh had to assert his authority with his fellow officers, the most senior being the same Lieutenant-Colonel Gill* who had been in Bangkok in November 1941. A power sharing was agreed, with Gill running the Indian POW camps and Singh the political aspects at INA HQ. This happened on that hectic day, February 16th, as Gill played a major role at Farrer Park the next morning. This was a critical negotiation as not having Gill on his side would have "wrecked the whole movement"[†] according to Lieutenant-Colonel Deakin of the 5/2 Punjab Regiment who spent his captivity in Singapore.[40]

Besides this, a careful sequence of speeches was planned, translators strategically selected and loudspeakers put up so everyone could hear. As the ceremony would last a long time, arrangements were made for food and medical support, and to drum up morale, a band was present. Lastly, some Fujiwara's were tasked with spreading INA propaganda amongst their fellow soldiers during the ceremony.[41]

Farrer Park and IWO Abdul Hayat Khan

As February 17th dawned, the segregation of the British officers from their Indian men began. Poignantly recorded by Lieutenant-Colonel George Clough who commanded the 4/19 Hyderabad Regiment, he said

> On 17 Feb at 0700 hrs the Indian ranks including all officers of Indian nationality fell in. The British officers said Goodbye. It was a very sad moment. Many were unable to speak, some had tears in their eyes, others were crying. Leaving their arms behind they marched off to their prison camp. Approximately 350 went. Many had fought extremely well, others could not stand the pace. Still they had tried.[‡]

At the same time, Warrant Officer Abdul Hayat Khan was told by his Commanding Officer, Lieutenant-Colonel Edward Claude Pine-Coffin, 14 Punjab Regiment, to head to Farrer Park.[42] In a long account of this very interesting and historic event, Khan says he drove the few kilometres to the park in a truck loaded with food for his unit and when he arrived, it was already packed and extremely noisy. A Japanese film of this gathering made at that time and now in the archives shows

---

*   Gill had got a battlefield promotion to temporary Lt-Col.
†   Deakin pg22 (INA History/ INA 403).
‡   Manuscript in Clough family, courtesy of his daughter-in-law, Joan Clough.

several seconds of footage panning the packed masses. Imagine over 40,000 young Indian soldiers gathered here and you can picture the squeeze and almost hear the racket.[43]

After the shock of the surrender just two days ago, and then the separation from their British commanding officers leaving them leaderless, what must have been going through the minds of the Indian soldiers? Relief for surviving, uncertainly, or perhaps many just didn't care. The same film shows a group of soldiers sitting on the ground happily playing cards, glad to be alive and just enjoying some peace after weeks of chaos, bombardment and confusion.

Lieutenant-Colonel Hunt's Handover to Fujiwara

In the park, Khan saw a pavilion in front. On the upper floor was a verandah with a few Japanese and Indians. Behind and on either side were crowds of civilians, many holding flags of India's Congress Party, very similar to the Indian flag today. It took a long time to organize the crowd on the field, as the officers were asked to come to the front, and the soldiers to group together in their Muslim, Gurkha, Sikh and other classes. When the ceremony finally started, Khan missed out one significant event in the confusion, probably as it lasted just a few minutes. Before the speeches, Lieutenant-Colonel William Shapter Hunt of Hodson's Horse, one of the oldest cavalry regiments of the Indian Army, brought the massing crowds to order. Representing the British, he addressed the Indian POWs in Hindustani and told them that the British had surrendered and were handing the Indians over to the Japanese. Henceforth, as they had earlier obeyed British orders, the Indians must now obey the Japanese. Hunt then saluted and left, spending the rest of his captivity in Singapore. This handover was not required as per the rules of war and not done for British and Australian soldiers who were also POWs of the Japanese. It had been deliberately arranged to be a public humiliation of the British, by making them acknowledge their surrender before the assembled Indian soldiers. After the war, Hunt said he had been told by his British superiors to do what the Japanese asked even if it crossed boundaries, so that the Indian POWs would not be mistreated in retaliation. In fact any retaliation would have been on Hunt and the British officers. He did this as his only choice was compliance or ill-treatment.[44]

Fujiwara's handover to Mohan Singh[45]

This was the first part of the carefully planned event – the British who commanded the Indians, telling them they were now under Japan. Then Fujiwara, representing Japan, stepped up to the microphone. The speeches are taken from Khan, a soldier and not an officer, but as they comprised over 99% of the army, what they remembered is critical, even if these were not the actual words and the sequence of subjects may have been different. Fujiwara's speech was translated sentence by sentence, first into English by Lieutenant Kunizuka from his team, and received with nods from the officers in the front. And then when it was translated into Hindustani by Lieutenant-Colonel Gill, it was received by nods from the thousands of soldiers behind.[46] At the very beginning Khan mistook Fujiwara for the Japanese Prime Minister Tojo, possibly as the latter started by reading out a statement from Tojo that said Japan was going to free Asia for the Asiatics and would support in any way possible India's freedom. In his own speech Fujiwara said a tyrannical British government that had deceived Indians and brought them here to fight the Japanese, had been extirpated. Japan had no desire to fight Indians as the two countries shared a common heritage in their respect for Buddha. Continuing, Fujiwara said he had tried to prevent them from getting killed by dropping leaflets from planes that in many Indian languages asked them not to fight. On them being bombed by Japanese planes, he explained that this was unfortunate as from the air, Indian and British soldiers could not be distinguished.

Fujuwara went on to congratulate the Indians for being able to now bask in the sunshine of liberty for which they had been agitating for so long. This was greeted with loud cheers. He said all civilians in Malaya and Singapore would be free and that Indian soldiers who had fought the Japanese were forgiven and would be treated as allies. He went on to berate their lack of discipline, commenting on their disorganized arrival at Farrer Park as if they were sheep and goats, and that in future strict discipline must be maintained. Continuing, he said the present battle had not been fought by Japan to conquer Malaya but to free India from British Imperialism, and that now the Indian POWs should get ready to fight the British with Japan's help. On the matter of food, he asked the POWs to excuse him as atta, milk, ghee, dal and sugar were in short supply, but hoped the situation would improve. He announced that an Indian Independence League (IIL) would be formed in Singapore as a step to the liberation of India. He ended by thanking the Indians who had helped Japan win this war and invited them to speak, and finally, announced that henceforth Captain Mohan Singh would be their commander.

Cheering for Captain Mohan Singh[47]

Until now, the thousands of Indian POWs there may have heard a bit, understood little and followed nothing of what was going on. But when Captain Mohan Singh stepped up and spoke, they listened with rapt attention. Singh started by stressing on the need for discipline and warned that under Japanese law the punishment for defying it was death. He went on to say that the replacement of British officers by Indians had been the first step to Home Rule granted by the Japanese. The Indian regiments were no longer to be called by their existing titles, but renamed as units of the INA, and would be asked to fight only for the freedom of India and not help Japan in their other battles. Moving on to the IIL, he said besides working for independence, they would help protect the civic rights of Indian civilians in Malaya, a concession that had been granted by Japan immediately after the surrender of Singapore.

Describing his own interactions with the Japanese, he said when he first met representatives of their government near Alor Star he was convinced of their sincerity in fighting for India's independence, and had been further comforted on this by Giani Pritam Singh when the three of them (including Fujiwara) had met under a tree near the battle front line. He said that unlike the British, all the Japanese saluted him, and that Fujiwara treated him like a friend, consulted him on all matters and even ate dal and mutton with him like a glutton, a comment that was greeted with great laughter. Comparing Japanese and British soldiers, he said the former cared less about their appearance but had a keen fighting spirit whereas the latter cared more about the beauty of their clothing and person. He urged the Indians to follow the Japanese lead in this matter.

Besides this, Singh vehemently condemned Churchill who had accused Indian soldiers of cowardice, saying that the Indians had lacked the right equipment, air support and that British units had withdrawn without being ordered to, leaving Indians exposed.

Singh asked the soldiers – would they fight the British? In response, the crowd went wild. That Khan remembered so much detail of what Singh said shows how strong an impact his speech had on him. Singh was remembered by many for being able to reach out to the common soldier. Lakshmi Swaminathan, who later commanded the INA's Rani Jhansi Regiment, the first unit of women soldiers in an army in modern times, was not at Farrer Park, but heard him speak later. Mirroring the view of many, she said "He had an emotional way of speaking. He seemed convinced he had taken the right step, he didn't have any doubts of any kind".*

Giani Pritam Singh

After Singh, the Giani was cheered when he came on stage. He said he had prepared with the Japanese before the war for this movement and had himself thrown leaflets from Japanese aeroplanes over British and Indian troops all the way down the

---

* MS belief coming across in his speeches, see Fay pg108.

Malayan peninsula from Alor Star to Singapore. He was disappointed it took two months for the Allies to surrender as he had promised the Japanese that Indian soldiers would not fight them. However, he thanked those Indian soldiers who had deserted due to his efforts and ended by congratulating the Japanese on this splendid victory.

The spectacle ended with shouts of Inquilab Zind bad (long live rebellion) and the band of Havildar-Major Ram Singh Thakur of the 2/1 Gurkha's leading the singing of songs like *chal chal re naujavan* (let's march on young men).[48]

Drinks for the Officers

After the ceremony, all officers above the rank of Lieutenant (there were about 100) were invited to the pavilion and this allowed them to ask about the shocking plan of fighting the British they had just heard about. Preparations had been made in advance and while the officers mingled, they were served alcohol. Fujiwara, told them Rangoon would fall in a month (it did) and this considerably affected their morale.[49]

While the soldiers digest what has happened

Meanwhile, Khan reported, the soldiers were discussing this extraordinary event. They were happy that the Japanese would treat them better as allies instead of prisoners, but were worried about breaking an oath, as once one did, all credibility was lost. In fact, despite cheering in the heat of the moment, many soldiers were then thinking exactly this. As the two main Indian speakers, Singh and the Giani, had confessed their dealings with the Japanese before and after the war started, it seemed to them that treachery had resulted in British defeat. They feared that these men would deceive them, as they had done the British. This was the rumour mill. It is true that 250 Fujiwara Indians had joined the Japanese before surrender, however they were too few to have had any impact on the battle.[50]

The soldiers were faced with an unprecedented predicament – break their oath to the British king and join the Japanese in a fight to free India, or face the wrath of the Japanese? What were they to do?

Chapter 2

THE RISE AND FALL OF CAPTAIN MOHAN SINGH'S FIRST INA

After the post-speech gossip, some of the Indian POWs stayed at Farrer Park overnight, and the rest moved to camps across Singapore. The Japanese, overwhelmed by having to manage almost 100,000 Allied POWs, left the half of them who were Indian to run their own camps. The next day, the Indian POW administration under Lieutenant-Colonel Gill was created and approved by Singh. They got to work on their biggest challenges, food and medical care for the thousands of wounded in hospitals. With 50,000 Indian POWs in Singapore (there were about 10,000 more in Malaya), crowded into camps built for half that number, poor sanitation resulted in outbreaks of dysentery and cholera that took many lives. Food was insufficient and of poor quality. Even orthodox Hindus were having fish-based food to make up for the lack of protein. In fact, fish, not the standard food for most Indians, became the protein source for everyone. Very soon, the rosy picture of amity presented at Farrer Park broke down. There was little food or medicine. Even the food that was scrounged was not palatable to many of the Indian soldiers used to atta and milk. Japan was then unfamiliar with milk and in a famous incident proudly presented bulls to the Indians, not knowing that they don't generate milk.[1]

Changi Guards – Indians over the British

In the days after surrender, all Allied POWs were made to clear the rubble of the battle and make Singapore tidy again.[2] With the Indians, Japan went even steps further and made them perform military duties which was forbidden as per the Geneva Convention. It started by them being asked to guard British POWs who were all at Changi in the east of the island. This created controversy as the 100 former Fujiwara volunteers appointed to do so under Subedar Santa Singh of 1/14 Punjab were now lording over British officers and men, who until a few days ago were their superiors in the military hierarchy. In a matter of days the Subedar was replaced by Lieutenant Gurbaksh Singh Dhillon, also of 1/14 Punjab, who took over on March 11. According to him, Lieutenant-Colonel Gill specially requested him to take this on as all the other officers declined to take on this distasteful job, and someone else had to be appointed as Subedar Singh did not speak English.

When he started, Dhillon found that the Japanese would slap British POWs who would not salute them or the Indians. He protested, but they persisted. Some Britishers asked him, "Why do you do this?" referring to his role as a camp guard commander, to which he replied he had been ordered to. More awkward situations arose when others questioned his authority. Dhillon also saw that some of his men enjoyed their new found power, status and seeing their former commanders having to salute them. According to him, while he was in charge, twelve British soldiers had attacked two Indian guards and in the resulting melee, the guards shot one dead and injured another. After an investigation by the Japanese, they probably decided that the Indian guards were trigger happy, and ordered that they should keep their rifles unloaded and carry only five bullets each.[3]

In June 1942 Dhillon fell ill and was replaced by Lieutenant Mohammad Azim Khan Rana of the 1st Kapurthala Infantry, who soon was asked to go a step further. In July, two British and two Australian POWs who had escaped from another camp, were sentenced to death by the Japanese, and Rana was asked to provide the firing squad. The two Britons were in their twenties, as was one of the Australians, the other being in his forties. In the presence of some British and Japanese officials, they were taken to the seashore and made to kneel before graves that had been dug for them about five feet apart. A British priest read them the last rites and gave each of them some water and a cigarette before the firing squad took over. Rana admitted that providing just one Indian soldier for each POW to be shot was a mistake. Normally more are assigned, so that if one missed, the other completed the job. In the first volley, three of the POWs were killed but the fourth screamed as he was shot in the shoulder and did not die. The Indian soldier in the firing squad assigned to him, nick-named "Pineapple", fired again but that too hit his elbow and once again he survived. According to Rana, this POW managed to get up and as he knew him slightly said "this man cannot shoot straight, you shoot me". Rana shot him with his revolver, killing him. This event became infamous, both for the fact that Japanese shot escaping prisoners, and that Indian soldiers had been used as a firing squad.[4]

The Gunners

Besides guard duty, the Japanese demanded that the Indian POWs who had manned the now captured Allied anti-aircraft guns defend the Japanese Army against Allied air attacks in Burma and the Philippines, where their invasion was ongoing, as well as Singapore. Pressured by Singh himself, groups of gunners were sent to these places in March 1942 and effectively became part of the Japanese Army. In addition, in an ingenious use of Indian POWs, some were sent as the advance party of an invasion of the Andaman Islands, arriving on March 23, 1942. When they beached, they shouted to the handful of defenders "We are Indians – don't fire on us".[*] It worked and the main Japanese contingent landed unopposed.[5]

Recruitment Starts

Meanwhile, the entire POW population experienced the full gamut of the ambitious program Singh launched immediately to seek INA volunteers.[6] He made regular speeches, as did most of his key officers,[7] and they spoke to smaller groups with soldiers of the same class together. Officers were addressed separately, probably in English. To the soldiers, the messaging was blunt, based on re-education and slogans, and the same theme was repeated again and again – the British were bad, it was time the soldiers fought for India's independence and in doing so cooperate with the Japanese who were trying to reclaim Asia for the Asiatics. Those who joined got promotions, plum jobs, better food, medical care and passes to go into the city to entertain themselves.[8]

To cut off news from the outside world, the Japanese started confiscating radio sets. The only information people got was from tightly controlled radio broadcasts, the Japanese run English newspaper, *The Syonan Times*, and the Azad Hind (Free India) newspaper, all of which only gave anti-British and pro-Japanese news. This newspaper was distributed free and published in Indian languages so had a very wide reach. The only films shown were of Allied defeat, such as the surrender of General Percival, and of the victorious Japanese armies.

Slogans in daily life

Indian pride was built through the introduction early on of national days commemorating the infamous Jalianwala Bagh, the popular Indian revolutionary Bhagat Singh,[†] and Gandhi's birthday. Later on, an annual calendar with a similar

---

[*] CSDIC (I) Report 16, pg8 (INA 379 Part 7).
[†] On April 13, 1919, scores of Indian civilians were massacred by Indian soldiers on the order of their British commander at Jalianwala Bagh (garden) in Amritsar, Punjab. They had gathered to protest against a new draconian law, the Rowlatt Act. Though the assembly was declared illegal, the killing of so many, including women and children shocked India. This became a seminal event in India's independence movement. Bhagat Singh was hanged on March 23, 1932 for shooting dead a British police officer serving in India, mistaking him for another police officer, the actual target.

number of national, Hindu, Sikh, Muslim and Christian holidays was announced, very much like the Singapore calendar today. From June 1942, evening roll call was accompanied by shouting the slogans *Inquilab Zindabad*, *Hindustan Azad* and General Mohan Singh *Zindabad* (long live rebellion, India should be free, and long live Mohan Singh). The army language, that is the words of command used, was also changed from English to Hindustani, and Romanized Hindustani began to be used in communications.[9]

One of the most popular entertainments was nationalist plays staged by drama groups. Their names indicate the subject – Dukhia Bharat (*Wretched India*), Inquilabd (*Revolution*), Milap (*Unity*), Ek Hi Rasta (*There Is Only One Way*) and Balidan (*Sacrifice*). After the war, Subedar Dharam Chand Bhandari described the plots and how they shared resources like instruments and clothes, and so kept the soldiers entertained and the nationalist momentum going.[10] However, behind all this, there was a veiled threat of ill-treatment if men did not volunteer or interfered, a veil that was soon to be cast aside.

Fujiwara unites Indian civilians with the INA

Besides getting the army in line, a clear understanding between Indian civilian and military leaders of their joint political objective and structure was needed. Fujiwara and the Giani had already convinced Indian civilians in Malaya during the campaign to join Japan and wasted no time in doing the same in Singapore. On February18, Fujiwara met Sirish Chandra Goho, a successful lawyer and the most prominent Indian in Singapore. At a dinner in his bungalow on February 21, Fujiwara introduced the Indian civilian and military leaders, Goho and Singh respectively. Another prominent Indian lawyer, K.P. Keshava Menon (known as KPK) was also present, and a couple of others. The Gurkha Ram Singh who led the singing at Farrer Park provided music, alcohol flowed as did informal anti-British speeches by Fujiwara and Singh. Goho was to run the soon to be formed Indian Independence League in Singapore, with KPK as his deputy.[11]

Goodwill Mission to Tokyo

The next step in this delicate process, was an invitation from the Japanese Army HQ for the leading Indians to come to Tokyo for talks.[12] This missive mentioned a Rash Behari Bose (no relation of Subhas Chandra Bose). Rash Behari was an Indian nationalist who had fled India after a British crackdown following the attempted assassination of the Viceroy Lord Hardinge, in which he was implicated. He found refuge in Japan in 1915 and came under the protection of the Black Dragons, a powerful underground society, who were able to prevent the British from extraditing him. Rash Behari married a Japanese woman with whom he had a daughter and a son, who later died in the war serving in the Japanese Army. He became a Japanese citizen and also started the local branch of the Indian Independence League and maintained close links with the Japanese government over the years. He was trusted by them and considered a "Japanese amongst Indians*".[13]

In Singapore, the Indian leaders decided that they would send a Goodwill Mission, the name carefully chosen so there is no implied allegiance to Japan. The attendees too were carefully selected. There were six civilians, with Goho/KPK Menon representing Singapore, Nedyam Raghavan (a prominent Penang lawyer) and Neelkanth Iyer for Malaya. Thailand was represented by the Giani, as well as Swami Satyanand Puri who was outspokenly anti-Japanese. The three army men chosen were Captains Mohan Singh and Mohammad Akram and Lieutenant-Colonel Gill.[14]

The Air crash of March 24, 1942

On the travel arrangements, at short notice Fujiwara told Singh four seats had suddenly become available on the scarce flights and picked the Giani, the Swami, Akram and Iyer to be on this flight that left Singapore on March 13, including Lieutenant Otaguru, the translator Fujiwara had been using from the beginning during his talks with the Giani in Bangkok and Singh after his surrender.[15] The second flight with the rest of the Indians and Fujiwara left Singapore on March 15 and arrived in Tokyo on the 19th. They were surprised that the first flight that had left earlier had not reached and waited for its arrival every day. Finally, after six days, on March 25 they were told that the flight had crashed on the previous day during its last leg to Tokyo due to bad weather, with no survivors. It was an astounding event. Though the Japanese aircrew and Otaguru were also reported dead, conspiracy theories abounded – mainly around the Giani, who knew of the pre-war agreement with Japan. Now, so the theory went, having already got enough of the Indian Army on their side, they did not need to live up to this commitment, and Fujiwara was rumoured to have gone to the Giani's house after his death to retrieve these documents. After the war, Singh said he did not think the crash was deliberate, but if it was, the Japanese waited for bad weather, that did indeed occur on the 24th, before telling them on the 25th about the incident. He also added that it was unlikely that Akram was a target and was chosen to disguise the main targets, the Giani and the Swami to whom the Japanese had made wild promises.[16]

---

* Colonel Kadomatsu (Hikari Kikan INA 974 pg6) and Fujiwara in INA254 pg7.

After this ominous event, the conference began. The visitors were not impressed by Rash Behari, believing him to be more on the Japanese side[17] and though many resolutions were made, the main decision was that a larger group of Indian would meet soon in a suitable location in Southeast Asia to work out the details of the movement.[18] More importantly, on April 8, the delegation spent forty minutes with Japanese Premier Tojo, who said Japan was on India's side, but, in a veiled reference to the recent April 6 raids by planes from Japanese aircraft carriers on Ceylon and Madras, that if India did not decide soon about joining Japan, its people would suffer. After an inexplicable and long sightseeing tour of Japan, Singh and the others returned to Singapore on April 22, 1942.[19]

Bidadari Resolutions

Almost immediately, he convened a meeting on April 25 with senior Indian officers where the Bidadari Resolutions were framed, named after the POW camp where they met. They had four points, one of which was "We are prepared to take any action for India on demand by the people of India, in India".* Singh seemed to be looking for legitimacy for the creation of the INA in stating that they would act if asked to do so by India. Despite there being no way to know what India wanted them to do, 25,000 Indian POWs volunteered within a month.[20]

"An Impossible Dilemma" or "A great attraction"?†

What was going through the minds of these 25,000, and of the other 20,000 who had not volunteered? They faced a loyalty challenge that soldiers were rarely confronted with – whether to remain loyal to their oath (to the foreign King of England), or break it and fight the British to free their own country, India? One view was that the soldiers did not like the political atmosphere and wanted to be left alone to live out the rest of the war as POWs. They liked the idea of independence, but not of invading their own country and fighting their own men, amongst whom were many relatives. Also reluctant to break their oath, they were being confronted with an impossible dilemma. An alternative view was that the INA held a great attraction for the rank and file in the army. Most of the current batch of soldiers were from the millions who had earlier been inarticulate, but now politically

---

* INA-History pg112 (INA 403) and Report 953/INA 499.
† Dilemma – Captain Balbir Singh 4/19 Hyderabad, Report 16, Attraction – Captain Pritam Singh 2/16 Punjab Report 19 in INA 499.

conscious due to the efforts of the Congress Party. They were also from families without a long army tradition, so did not have relatives serving elsewhere. It just needed a real or imaginary grouse to stoke the embers for them to join the INA and pit it against the Indian Army.

The Indian POWs were given a choice the British and Australians were not, better treatment in the INA or remain as POWs with the terrors that entailed. Their dilemma was complicated by the vital role of Japan in this fight as without their support there would be no INA. Their behaviour left much to be desired to say the least. Captain Pritam Singh, 2/16 Punjab Regiment, was in a hospital adjacent to the famous Raffles Hotel taken over by the Japanese at the time of surrender and said:

> It seems that the Japanese did not like modern furniture. Beautiful sofas...were thrown onto the street...They struck me as complete barbarians...They were extremely fond of beating and slapping people. Car loads of Chinese girls were seen being brought to the hotel every evening and taken away the next morning. All these created a revulsion in my heart.[*]

The Massacre of the Chinese

The Chinese community had been badly hit, as besides the ill-treatment of women, young men were rounded up and thousands massacred in the first few weeks.[21] A great process of Japanization had also begun in Singapore. No one dared speak English in public, signboards were changed to Japanese, teaching the language in schools became compulsory, and by the end of May 1942 it seemed the British never ruled Malaya.[22] This did not bode well for when, or if, the Japanese reached India.

Besides this, even though the Japanese were trying to get Indian POWs to join them, that did not stop them from ill-treating them. Captain Pritam Singh reported that one day, Captain Bishan Singh 3/16 Punjab and he were walking towards the city from their camp, when they were stopped by a well-known Japanese officer. When he found they did not have a pass to leave the camp, he "boiled up like a volcano"[†] and tried to slap Captain Bishan Singh but was unable to as he was too tall for him. Then he caught hold of a stick and hit each of them, threatening to have them shot for disobedience. This was just one of many instances.

---

[*] Pritam Singh Report 19 and similar Pillai debrief AWM 54-779-10-4 pg33, henceforth Pillai.
[†] Pritam Singh Report 19.

Half the Indian POWs join the INA

Given these examples of what Japan was really about, why did 25,000 soldiers volunteer? Before the war began, like most armies Indian soldiers were not political and followed their colonial masters' orders to fight the Japanese, even if they were not enemies of India. During the battle they had seen the defeat of the British empire by an Asian power, and witnessed the brutality of the Japanese against POWs and civilians. With the disastrous retreats, the cocoon of unit cohesion was crumbled 'like a clump of earth thrown into a flowing river' as eloquently described by Srinath Raghavan. Finally, with Fujiwara enthusing and empowering a core set of Indians like Singh who guided the propaganda, and the elevation of the influential VCOs, it was quite inevitable that many volunteered. For some, patriotism was indeed the main factor, and with propaganda this feeling grew (becoming a "great attraction"), but for many it was a way of rationalizing this impossible dilemma.[23]

The Bangkok Conference in June 1942

With the strength of 25,000 volunteers behind him, Singh reached Bangkok on June 11 where 90 prominent Indian civilians from Southeast Asia and 25 Indian Army officers met. In talks, decisions were made about how the IIL leading the movement was to be organized, and how as the Congress Party was the only political organization that truly represented India, they would be guided by it. Regarding Japan, the Bangkok Resolution asked that they treat the INA equal to its own army as an ally, use Indian soldiers only to achieve India independence, and declare that they would respect the territorial integrity of India.[24]

Mohan Singh's long and emotional speech lasted over a day and deeply affected the audience. Fujiwara noticed his transformation before his eyes and Radio Berlin announced his role.[25] The Bangkok Times quoted his speech: "The responsibility of deciding the fate of 400 million brothers has now finally been put on our shoulders. Indians inside India are like a bird in cage and decreed not to sing. The world has great hopes on us and our countrymen are staring in askance".*

Concentration Camps – The "Nimbu Parade"

When Singh returned to Singapore on July 12, 1942, he was fired up with enthusiasm as the undisputed commander of the INA and one of five members of the newly formed

---

*   Quote from Kevin Noles, *Divided Loyalties in The People's War*, ed, Wilson and Fennell published by McGill University Press 2022, pg261.

Council of Action of the IIL, akin to a war cabinet. Emboldened, he did two things. First, in late July 1942 an unconditional oath to the INA and to Singh himself was drawn up. Normally oaths are to a country, in a rare instance this one was to Singh. After the war Singh said he did this to keep the INA out of the control of Rash Behari and the Japanese.[26] Second, he warned all those spreading anti-INA propaganda to stop. He told them to stay out if that is what they wanted, but they must not try to convince others. Everyone must decide on their own. Many refused to listen, and it was these men who were taken to a concentration camp and harshly treated until they agreed to stop.

This camp was on Braddell Road in Bidadari. It had been originally made by the British to house Japanese POWs, but as the defence failed and few Japanese surrendered, it was not used for that purpose. After surrender, it housed the Indian POWs who had infringed rules as there was rampant indiscipline. It was reused as a concentration camp, with a separate area marked out as a detention camp for the discipline cases. Singh knew how influential the VCOs were so sent the recalcitrant ones there.[27] At first the most senior VCO would be contacted, and if he did not cooperate, was sent to the camp. Then the INA worked down the chain to other VCOs, and finally the NCOs under them, until finally only INA friendly seniors remained who convinced the soldiers to volunteer.[28]

Jemadar Mohammed Nawaz of the 5/2 Punjab Regiment was one of the hundreds who were sent there. He was beaten with lathis (thick wooden rods), spent hours collecting dung and then mixing it with ash and earth. Nawaz added that if anyone said they were too sick to work and the INA doctor didn't agree, they would be given twelve lathi strokes. The most infamous person meting out these beatings was the tall (5 feet 11 inches) dark, bald, clean-shaven and well-built sweeper Nibua (or Nimbu as he was known), who had been specially chosen having been an experienced flogger in Lahore, Aligarh and Multan civil jails in India. For those who were caste conscious,[*] being beaten by a sweeper in the "Nimbu parade" was specially humiliating.[†]

The "Kranji *ke bahadur*"[‡] (brave men of Kranji)

Perhaps the most famous inhabitants of this camp were the "Kranji *ke bahadur*" or the brave men of Kranji. It could also mean the foolhardy if said sarcastically,

---

[*] The caste system in India is an ancient practice that continues until today amongst some. It was a strict hierarchy that one is born into and could not move out of during life. Sweepers were considered the lowest of the low, in fact outside the system as "outcasts". Hence, for caste conscious Indians, being beaten by a sweeper was considered the worse possible treatment.

[†] Nawaz see Red Fort Trial INA File 495 part 4 pg113, Nimbu trial INA File 493.

[‡] Shingara Singh trials INA File 492 parts 1 and 2.

as may have been intended when Subedar Shingara Singh of the 5/14 Punjab Regiment called them that. In the new era of coercion and concentration camps, INA men were fanning out to arrest NCO and VCOs who worked against it. One such group was in the 22 Mountain Regiment based at the POW camp in Kranji, in the north of Singapore near the Woodlands checkpoint to Johore. On August 23, 1942, Shingara Singh's subordinate and battalion-mate Jemadar Fateh Khan came to the camp with orders to take twelve men of the regiment to INA HQ. That very day fellow soldiers of the 22nd had visited Kranji and told them how they had been inveigled into the concentration camp and badly beaten. The twelve refused to go unless the whole unit was taken, so Khan left saying he would be back.

The account that follows comes from transcripts of the court martial of Shingara Singh and Fateh Khan in Delhi in 1946 where they gave a different version of events and denied any wrongdoing, but were found guilty. The day after Fateh Khan's visit, August 24, 1942, was remembered by many for the "mutiny" at Kranji and the bloodbath that followed. According to the prosecution witnesses, at around 2.00pm Khan came in a truck with over a dozen armed guards, and Shingara Singh on his motorcycle dressed in civilian attire, with a white shirt, khaki trousers and a green turban. Singh and Khan, accompanied by four guards with rifles, went to the barracks, asked the men to come out, unholstered their pistols and harangued them to join the INA. When they all refused, Singh fired his pistol in the air and blew on his whistle, the signal for the guards with them and others spread out around to camp, to open fire with their rifles. Lance Naik Mohammad Alam of the 7/22 Mountain Regiment was shot in the head, probably by Khan with his pistol. Gunner Allah Ditta was shot in the chest by a rifle, and Sepoy Said Zaman RIASC (aka Bumbu) also had a rifle wound in the head and had his brains blown out. Besides these three POWs dying, fourteen were wounded, many losing limbs.

At first the POWs tried to avoid the bullets, but soon turned on the INA men and started fighting back. One of the INA guards, Sardara Singh of the Kapurthala Infantry, was hit on the head with a spade cracking open his skull and killing him. Running out of ammunition after firing at least 250 rounds, the guards dragged Sardara Singh (probably now dead) by his hair and got back onto their truck and left. Sometime later, Japanese and INA officers with guards came to the camp. Major Aziz of the Kapurthala Infantry translated – the Japanese supposedly said "if you kill one INA man, we will kill one hundred of you". This sounds fanciful, but similar threats were reportedly made on other occasions. That evening, fourteen men of the 22nd Mountain Regiment, the "Kranji *ke bahdur*" were taken to the concentration camp where eleven of them were kept in a small cage with a diameter of just 6 feet. The same guards were present, meting out beatings that hospitalized many for weeks.

The Officers' Separation Camp

There was also the infamous Separation Camp in the gardens of Alsagoff Mansion, the former home of one of the prominent families of Singapore. This was started on August 18, 1942, for the most anti-INA officers and when Captain Krishan Purshotam Dhargalkar of the 3rd Cavalry was sent there, he joined the over forty already imprisoned. So far in the camps, officers still had their batmen who looked after them, who of course were not allowed here. Dhargalkar was with fifteen others in a 10-foot-square room, they slept on the floor with no electricity, were made to clean the garden for hours every day, sweep their rooms, clean their own utensils, and dig their own latrines outdoors. The officers were being made to live a basic life without any comforts. They were not beaten and even had better food than at the concentration camp (where Dhargalkar had been briefly), and the purpose was to separate them from their men and unleash a reign of terror on the latter. Mohan Singh, in his regular visits to these camps, said he wanted the officers to know what the life of the average Indian was like. After a while the camp had outlived its purpose as the hardcore non-volunteers refused to change their mind, and it was closed on October 2, 1942, Gandhi's birthday.[29]

Almost everyone volunteered

Eventually, 40,000 volunteered in 1942, 90% of the 45,000 Indian POWs in Singapore.[30] We have examined the possible motives of the initial 25,000 volunteers. Once coercion and torture was ramped up, it's likely the additional 15,000 who joined later did so mainly to avoid ill-treatment. The impact of the camps cannot be exaggerated. Of this phase, Subedar SC Pandya said the biggest driver of recruitment was fear of the camps, about which they received daily news of ill-treatment and death. The hundreds of POWs at Bidadari overlooked the concentration camp and would have seen what was going on. News spread to other camps, as was the intention.[31]

In an overall assessment from one who was there, Lieutenant-Colonel Gill said some volunteered to re-join the British when they moved close to India, most to avoid hardships and some for patriotism (though this feeling spread). Subedar Pandya added that the main methods of recruitment were threats, shootings, beatings, bribery and promises of high posts. He said no one admitted to having joined willingly, giving their reasons as wanting to re-join the British and avoid hardships as Gill said, and protect Indian women from what happened to those in Singapore.[32]

The Soldiers did NOT follow their Officers

There is a belief that most soldiers did what their commanding officer told them to do. The senior officer indeed had a big influence in many units – he was the "*Mai Baap*" (the mother-father figure) and in some cases they did what he directed such as the 1st Kapurthala Infantry led by Major Aziz Ahmed Khan – ten out of eleven officers and all but twenty to thirty soldiers joined. The most well-known case of no volunteers was the Jind Infantry led by Lieutenant-Colonel Gurbaksh Singh. For those like him, it was clear an oath could not be broken and his men followed his lead, and no one joined. The most important values in an army were and remain today "*naam, nishaan* and *namak*", or the name of the regiment, the colours of the regiment and most of all, loyalty (symbolised by namak or salt*). The oath was taken in a solemn ceremony, swearing upon one's sacred religious book in the presence of many men and all the officers of the unit. Once an oath was broken, trust also was broken. When Gurbaksh Singh was courted later personally by Subhas Chandra Bose, as quoted in his post-war CBE recommendation he said "if I could betray one master, I could betray another". Mohan Singh said the toughest obstacle was convincing men that the oath they had taken was not honourable and instead swearing to fight for one's own country was indeed the right thing.[33]

However, most soldiers did not follow their officers lead, as almost all of them joined while less than half the officers did. Similarly, of the few soldiers who did not volunteer many chose a different path from their officers, such as the Gurkhas, Baluchis and junior medical officers.[34] Looking at the officers, many had the same motivation as the soldiers. A few admitted to joining as opportunists, just enjoying promotions and perks while they lasted. According to Aziz of the Kapurthala Infantry, a senior INA member, 10% of the officers joined for patriotic reasons, 45% were opportunists and 45% did so to avoid ill-treatment.[35] Others said they joined so that by being inside the INA they could take better care of their men, or sabotage the whole scheme, or ensure they could protect civilians in India once the Japanese reached.

What motivated the men?

Some or all of this could have been true, and the actual motives of the men are difficult to determine. Interrogated when they eventually reached India, in what would have been a very awkward meeting, explaining to the winning side

---

* Salt is considered an ancient symbol of loyalty, as the most additive to food to make it palatable and used in ancient times as a form of payment.

(British India) why they had joined the INA, many motives were mentioned. Some remained defiantly nationalistic, others said they were coerced or wanted to avoid ill-treatment. What they actually thought is unknown, but the interrogations tell us what they said.[36] Of 653 INA soldiers grilled after the war in Singapore, 94 said they joined for patriotic reasons, 113 from peer pressure, 228 to avoid ill-treatment, 201 due to threats and propaganda, 2 as they wanted to escape when they got a chance and 15 did not say. Sometimes peer pressure was such that some, like one soldier from Madras who could not understand the Hindustani propaganda, joined as did the rest of his unit. One confessed he was an opium addict and hoped to feed his habit by joining.*

British officers in Singapore thought that given the conditions it was surprising that more had not volunteered. Some had even smuggled out messages to their Indian officers and men telling them to join.[37]

The INA is Formed

Finally, on 1 September 1942, the INA was launched with Special Order No. 1 by Captain Mohan Singh, general officer commanding (GOC), Indian National Army, equivalent to the gazette used by the British to make major announcements. In this Order, Singh announces the appointment of dozens of Indian Army officers to the INA. On this day, for some strange reason, though Singh is GOC, his rank is still Captain, so all the officers were appointed as Second Lieutenants, two ranks lower than his captaincy. This is perhaps a unique document in military history – it's an order by a Captain (Singh) directing a higher ranked Major (who issued the document) informing officers senior to him (such as Lieutenant-Colonel Gill) that they were being promoted, but to Second Lieutenant, a rank junior to that which they held then. On September 9, 1942, just eight days later, the now General Mohan Singh announced many promotions up to the rank of Lieutenant-Colonel, most of whom finally returned to the ranks they had held in the Indian Army until eight days ago.[38]

In addition, in a revolutionary move, Mohan Singh abolished the VCO ranks and made them all Second Lieutenants.[39] Becoming officers in the INA instead of "in-betweens" in the Indian Army attracted VCOs, but some regular officers were not pleased. Major K.P. Thimaya who remained defiant about joining the INA and whose younger brother Captain K.S. Thimaya had been in Singapore before the war and later became Chief of Staff of the Indian Army, said this was aimed at

---

* The idea of studying a sample came from Kevin Noles and this survey was done by Roshini Dadlani.

making officers join the INA so they wouldn't have to salute the newly promoted VCOs. Overall, however, only one-third of them joined, the lowest proportion, compared to half the officers and 90% of the men.[40]

Gandhi, Nehru and Azad Regiments

Besides the promotions, the INA's structure was formally announced. One division was to be formed of 16,700 men, with 9,000 in the main fighting units named Gandhi, Nehru and Azad regiments after leaders of the Congress Party, with the remaining in command, support and propaganda units. The unit names were carefully chosen. Mohan Singh knew how well respected they were in India, amongst his soldiers and by him personally. In Bangkok, Singh had said – "Congress alone was the voice of India. Congress was the people of India".[*] Barracks were also re-christened with these names. As many units had volunteered en masse, to retain their camaraderie they were incorporated as a whole into INA units. For example, the 2nd Battalion of the Gandhi Regiment consisted of soldiers from the 1/13 Frontier Rifles and the Kapurthala Infantry. They were equipped by the Japanese from captured British supplies, though enough was provided for only 6,000 fighting men.[41]

Communal Harmony

This was a major focus for Mohan Singh and he worked very closely with Captain Akram and his other early adherents to stress this at every opportunity. Subedar Shingara Singh, who we encountered in the concentration camp, was once hesitating to share the dining table with the Muslim Akram (common then with every creed and class eating separately), when Mohan Singh told him to "come and show that you are bigger than you look". Shingara Singh was over 6 feet tall and said this "puny man (referring to Mohan Singh) made me realise my limitations, the small circle I had been perambulating so far. He gave me courage, he gave me hope and he made me think and be a better man henceforth".[†] This is from his statement at his post-war trial and though his denial of any ill treatment at all seems fanciful and he was found guilty, these words seem true.

Reflecting the dining table conflict in Shingara Singh's mind, the most important day-to-day aspect was food – managing kitchens for the Indian Army had always

---

* MS-Toye para 102.
† Shingara Singh on Mohan Singh, see trial INA File 492 part 1.

been complex, with different religions and castes wanting separate arrangements. For caste conscious Hindus, even who made and touched their food was vital. The slaughter of cows (considered sacred by Hindus) and pigs (considered unclean by Muslims) was forbidden. By far, the biggest issue was how meat was prepared. Hindus and Sikhs wanted it made the Jhatka way, Muslims the Halal way, both akin to Kosher requirements. The British in the past had been scrupulous in having different kitchens to ensure this. To promote communal harmony and make arrangements easier, Singh wanted to scrap different kitchens and dining halls. He first said everyone will eat fish. That did not go down well as most Indians were not familiar or comfortable with fish. The khatka-halal issue eventually prevailed, though soon how to cook meat became less of a problem, as there was not much available.[42]

Though Singh tried, communal tension simmered below the surface. Though proportionately more Muslim officers (52%) joined the INA than Hindu/Sikh (45%), some Muslims considered Akram and other INA officers of their faith as Quislings. Also, with Mohan Singh, a Sikh, at the head, many Sikhs brandished their new-found power and a Sikh Raj seemed to be in the air.[43] Despite these undercurrents, undoubtedly September and October 1942 were heady months for Mohan Singh's INA. The force was organized, equipped and the administrative structure built.

Trouble Brewing with the Japanese

Soon though, the unequal relationship with Japan holding all the cards began to rear its head. At the core of it, each had different objectives. For Japan, India was peripheral and they thought enough had been said by their Prime Minister, and done on the ground by their officers. For the Indians, the only objective was their independence, and to ensure that Japan must only use the INA to fight for it and that they had no ambitions on India. These were encapsulated in the Bangkok resolutions that by now they had been waiting five months for Japan to confirm. So far they had not done so, and only supported the forming of one INA division of 16,700 men, that too with insufficient arms. Any successful invasion of India would in fact need many, many more soldiers and the Japanese had said they would support a force of 250,000 including civilians. Even if that number was far away, Singh already had 25,000 more volunteers ready to be equipped, but the Japanese had not agreed to arm them. If they were only interested in one division he feared they probably only wanted to use the INA as support troops or propaganda, and not as a real army. This would also leave the Indians in a poor bargaining position if India was conquered. Due to this, Singh refused to send the entire INA division to Burma as requested, but only a small "advance party" in mid-November. This upset the Japanese, but they accepted it, for now. Both sides were losing patience.[44]

The new war reality – Japan stalled

There were many discussions amongst the Indian leaders in Singapore in November 1942. Besides unhappiness with no response from Japan on the Bangkok resolutions, the strategic war situation had changed dramatically. Unlike in March in Tokyo and June in Bangkok, when Japan and Germany were still ahead in the war, at the end of 1942 the Japanese advance in Asia had been stalled by the US, Germany was retreating in North Africa and encircled in Stalingrad in Russia, so the Germany-Italy-Japan Axis was now on the back foot. British defeat did not seem that certain at all.

Tension between the Indians

Rash Behari Bose, the titular head of the Indian Independence Movement, was now in Singapore and urged Singh not to fret – his view was that Japan was clearly on India's side and no additional declarations were needed. He had in fact not informed the others that Colonel Iwakuro, who had taken over from Fujiwara and now in charge of relations with India had refused to forward to Tokyo their Bangkok letter saying nothing more formal was required to be said, knowing it would create a crisis, as indeed it did when he finally disclosed this. To add fuel to the fire, at this time Japanese officers in Bangkok told the Indians that they did not consider the INA or IIL equal nor worthy of forming an agreement with. At this critical juncture, the one person who could have kept things together, Major Fujiwara, was missing. A victim of his own success, very soon after Singapore's surrender, he was replaced by the more senior Colonel Iwakuro Hideo with a much larger staff, in the expectation that Indians could be wielded more successfully to Japanese objectives. Iwakuro was aware of Japan HQ's aim and knew he had to string along the Indians. He did not share the bond Fujiwara had with Mohan Singh, developed building the INA from scratch. Had Fujiwara been there, it may never have reached this stage, and even if it did, he may have been able to bring the two sides closer.[45]

Gill's Arrest

Then, on December 8, 1942, Lieutenant-Colonel Gill, the most senior Indian Army officer in Singapore, was arrested by the Japanese. Earlier in the year Gill had been tasked to arrange for contact parties to go to India to spread pro-Japanese propaganda, as had succeeded so dramatically in Malaya. While supposedly working on this, Gill's most senior aide, Major Mahabir Singh Dhillon, Royal Indian Army Service Corps (RIASC) had gone over to the British in late October 1942. Gill hid this from the Japanese who, when they finally found out, arrested him on suspicion of double crossing them. This was the ostensible reason for his arrest; In reality, Gill had been one of the key men pushing Mohan Singh to stand up to the Japanese and they wanted to get him out of the way.[46]

The End of General Mohan Singh's First INA

As far as Singh was concerned, Gill's arrest from his own bungalow where he was staying, based on a warrant signed by Rash Behari without any discussion with him, was the last straw. The entire Council of Action resigned, except for Rash Behari. At a meeting of senior officers around December 15, Mohan Singh laid out his concerns about Japan – after having known them well for a year, he now knew their declarations were not genuine and they wanted to use the INA for their own purposes. He accused Rash Behari of acting as a Japanese stooge stating that he had no right to remain head of an empty Council of Action. Mohan Singh said he would probably soon be arrested or even assassinated, and if that was to happen, all the officers and men must tear off their INA badges and refuse to obey Japanese orders[47]. Almost all the officers present agreed to do this and promised not to re-join the INA. One of the few dissenters was Captain Ehsan Qadir 5/2 Punjab, who, having burnt his bridges with the British after starting radio broadcasts to India from Saigon as early as February 1942, said the INA should consider itself like Vichy France* that was now allying with Germany and continue.

Mohan Singh's last attempt

Singh made a last ditch effort to come to terms with the Japanese. He felt that as the main force of the movement was the INA, and as he did not respect or get along with R B Bose, asked Iwakuro for independent control of the INA without any civilian oversight, and then they could work out an arrangement between themselves directly. Iwakuro knew he could not control Mohan Singh, so he refused.[48]

---

* The rump regime in France based in the town of Vichy that was collaborating with Germany and claimed to represent French interests.

Preparations for the Arrest

Expecting the inevitable, on December 21, Mohan Singh wrote out orders disbanding the INA if he was removed. Normally the head of an army cannot order its end, as the soldiers have sworn an oath to a country or a King. In the INA's case, as the volunteers had sworn an unconditional oath to him personally, he could. In it he said the INA needed to be disbanded as "Circumstances have arisen under which it is impossible to achieve the complete independence of India without any foreign control". He added that "Though we have not been able to achieve our final object, the movement has not been in vain. It has inculcated in us the true national spirit... brought a degree of unity among us unknown in the past...Remember our strength is in our unity and our life is for our country". He signed off:

INDIA FIRST AND INDIA LAST

LONG LIVE INDIA.[*]

The Arrest of General Mohan Singh

Early on December 29, 1942, Japanese Military Police arrived at Mohan Singh's bungalow and took him to Iwakuro's office where he was arrested. At 10.00am that day, as per his instructions, INA Headquarters issued an order disbanding the INA and the destruction of INA badges and records. Thus, what later came to be known as the first INA came to an end. The Japanese and Rash Behari refused to accept this and an interim INA remained for a few months, invigorated into the second INA, or as it was renamed, the Azad Hind Fauj (Army of Independent India), after Subhas Chandra Bose arrived in Singapore on July 2, 1943.[49]

"I love INDIA just as much as any Englishman loves ENGLAND. This is my only crime."[†]

So ended the brief Generalship of Mohan Singh. His story is remarkable, both for how incredible it is, and for how few people know of it. In 1942 Mohan Singh went from being an unknown Captain commanding a company of 100 soldiers, to being GOC of an army of 60,000 soldiers including many offices senior to him. He had indeed been anointed by Fujiwara, but had to earn everyone's loyalty which he did through his oratory, a brilliant propaganda program, empowering VCOs and also the concentration camps. His efforts at building communal harmony were revolutionary.

---

[*] MS-Toye App FF.

[†] MS-Toye App B.

{ 33 }

Commenting on the early months of 1942, Captain Pritam Singh, 2/16 Punjab, remarked that "It was he who brought the INA into existence. He is feeding it with his ideas and he is influencing it with his personality. He has got no weakness in terms of greed, lust, drink, women…there was a general feeling, among the officers, that right or wrong, one thing was certain, MOHAN SINGH was sincere and not acting a part".[*] Much was said about him by some of his fellow officers after the war that he was just average and not up to the job, but none of them dared stand up to him when he was in charge.[50]

A British assessment after the war said the first INA (referring to Mohan Singh) was largely a "one man" show. He "towered head and shoulders" over his colleagues, both civilian and military. However, the "wine of power" went to his head and he sought dictatorial powers. On the concentration camps, they said that despite them he had the "genuine & general esteem and admiration" of the men.[†] Major Hugh Toye, the British officer who probably knew the INA best, having interrogated most of its senior men, said of him that starting the INA was the only course of action open to him, and wondered if he would have the same courage had he been in that position.[51]

Finally, though he was brutal in his methods of recruitment for a period, once he realized he had backed the wrong horse (a Japan whose strategic goals did not include freeing India), he disbanded the INA at great risk to his own life.

---

[*] Pritam Singh Report 19.
[†] CSDIC (I) report see INA Chronology pg11/ INA 415.

Chapter 3

A DOUBLE CROSS OR A TRIPLE CROSS?

"An expert double crosser who double-crossed himself."[*]

In the pitch-dark pre-dawn hours of December 8, 1942, Japanese military police arrived at the residence of General Mohan Singh, GOC of the INA at Mount Pleasant Road, Singapore. They had with them an arrest warrant for Lieutenant-Colonel Narandar Singh Gill who was staying there. Mohan Singh protested strongly saying if there was any wrongdoing he would investigate and punish Gill if needed. Politely, but firmly, he was told to stand back, only being allowed to accompany him to police headquarters. From a comfortable bungalow bedroom, Gill moved to a 12 by 12-foot cell. He must have been terrified for he knew why they had come, and that the Japanese pulled no punches when facing an adversary. Had they discovered his double cross or was there another reason?[1]

Gill's privileged life began in 1906 when he was born into a prominent Sikh family of Maijtha, Amritsar with links to India's British rulers going back many generations. He graduated from the Royal Military College, Sandhurst in 1925 and thus received the King's Commission, giving him a very prestigious position in the Indian Army. With Indian nationalism rife in the 1930s, Gill was one of many officers who asked for guidance from Indian political leaders such as Motilal Nehru, Jawaharlal Nehru's father, on whether they should resign and join the movement. They were told – stay in the army and remain true to your oath, soon India will be independent and will need a strong army of loyal men.[2] While serving in the 4/19 Hyderabad Regiment, Gill was in Singapore in 1939 with his fellow Captains Satyawant Mallanah Shrinagesh and Kodandera Subayya Thimayya. In a twist of fate, they returned to India and later became Chiefs of Army Staff, while he stayed on and became a POW.[3]

---

[*] Major Hugh Toye on Gill, as recounted by Mohan Singh in a letter dated September 12, 1974 to KPK Menon. From Singh family archive.

By 1941, Gill was a staff officer of the 11th Indian Division defending North Malaya, where the barracks of the Indian troops were full of leaflets that seemed to appear out of nowhere. They attacked the rule of "English dogs"* over India, and their use of its fighting men for their own purposes, as in the case of the soldiers here. Japanese backed Indian nationalists in Thailand were spreading them through the granthis or priests of the predominantly Sikh units. The British were aware of this and had arrested some of the infiltrators,[4] but they wanted to know how well organized they were and the exact nature of their relationship with the Japanese. To investigate this Gill was sent on a secret mission to Thailand.[†]

Rajdhani Hotel, Bangkok

Despite having experience of politics in the army, Gill was a strange spy for this job. He was tall, imposing, upper-class, well-dressed and most comfortable only in English. His cover story of being a merchant selling cotton fabric made him even more unsuited. When his train steamed into Bangkok railway station in late November 1941 with dark clouds of war swirling overhead, he had two things with him – a list of pro-Japanese Indians known to the British and an introduction to one of them, Narain Singh Narula. Gill stayed at the Rajdhani Hotel at the station and was chaperoned by Narula. Gill soon found out about the Indian nationalist Giani Pritam Singh's strong Japanese connection and is alleged to have met him then. In an amazing coincidence, they were both treated by the same doctor at that time in Bangkok. The close connections did not end here – even a fictional cloak and dagger scenario could not have beaten the reality, as at this time the Japanese intelligence officer Major Fujiwara, in charge of dealing with Indians, was living in a bungalow adjacent to Gill's base, the railway station. It is tempting to imagine backroom meetings between Gill, Fujiwara and the Giani, but there is no evidence this happened. In fact, in the INA era that was soon to begin, the colonel was denounced as a British spy due to his Bangkok visit.[5]

Gill at Farrer Park, Singapore

Once back in early December, Gill's report said that most Indians in Thailand were not involved in politics except the Giani and Chanda Singh, another prominent Indian

---

* Leaflet text NAI, INA File 254 pg22.
† At this time the British Ambassador to Thailand was keen to observe their neutrality, but despite this Gill was sent – his visit is noted in a British CSDIC (I) report and by many witnesses (see notes). SOE also mounted Operation Cleeves in Thailand in 1941 (book by Kathleen Reid-Smith, Pen & Sword, 2024).

nationalist. Nothing much could have been done with this as the war began a few days later, on December 8, 1941. While retreating with the 11th Division, Gill was contacted by the Giani's men, but he did not trust them and declined their overtures.[6]

He next emerged at Farrer Park on February 17, 1942, as an enthusiastic and senior INA officer. Behind the scenes, delicate negotiations had occurred. Being the highest ranked Indian combatant in Singapore Gill had a prominent position, but the Japanese had chosen the much junior Captain Mohan Singh to head the INA, anathema in a highly hierarchical army. How then did these two men face off with each other? It was no surprise that their relationship was troubled and the accounts of what happened differed. Gill said he declined Singh's request for him to head the INA. Singh did not mention this, and instead said Gill told him he was the best man for the job. To add to these conflicting accounts, Gill is said to have asked Major Fujiwara to be made the INA commander. What really happened between them is not known. It is clear though, that at this stage it was vital for Singh to have him on this side without which "the whole scheme would have broken down".[*] When confronted with the INA after Britain's surrender, like many men, Gill remained loyal neither to the British nor India, but to himself. Joining the INA meant promotions, comfort and protection. And so, the privileged Lieutenant-Colonel from Sandhurst became the deputy of the captain from a humble background.[7]

Rajdhani Hotel Bangkok, again

Put in charge of all the Indian POW camps, instead of making urgent arrangements for their care, Gill flew off to Bangkok with Fujiwara to meet Indian nationalists there. Once again, he stayed at Hotel Rajdhani, and told those with him about his secret pre-war visit, even showing them the false name he had used in the hotel register. This trip was very strange. As Singh had been chosen as the INA commander, why did Fujiwara instead take Gill to meet the Indian leaders in Bangkok? He then took Gill to Saigon, and this next leg was even stranger, as there was no ostensible reason and it all seemed very secret and hush hush. In fact, the visit was a very high-level meeting with General Count Terauchi, the commander of the Japanese Southern Army, in charge of operations in Southeast Asia. He had met Giani Pritam Singh and Captain Mohan Singh in the early days of the war at Alor Star on December 15, 1941. Now that Singapore had surrendered, this meeting was to perhaps decide what next to do with the INA. Gill was considered more suitable for such a conference and went instead of Singh. At this early stage for Singh to succeed, he needed Gill more than Gill needed him.[8]

---

* Lieutenant-Colonel Deakin INA 403.

Back in Singapore in early March, a telegram awaited inviting Indian leaders to a conference in Tokyo which Mohan Singh and Gill were to attend. The days before they left were awkward as Gill was questioned by Indian officers about being away when he was tasked with taking care of POWs in Singapore. He had no reply other than to say he was ordered to go by the Japanese. Though the several weeks in Japan gave Gill a breather from the indignant officers, after returning he was disappointed and somewhat cast down. This was probably because he had kept hoping to become the INA leader, and in Tokyo that dream was dashed. He started a whispering campaign that in raising the INA, Mohan Singh was committing the Indians to an undesirable course of action. Hearing of Gill's intrigue and needing him less after Tokyo, Fujiwara had him sent him off to Bangkok. Gill wanted to oppose them but did nothing as he was not ready to face the consequences.[9]

Rajdhani Hotel Bangkok, once again

Besides their duel over the INA leadership, Gill and Mohan Singh had another tussle. They both wanted Major Mahabir Singh Dhillon, Royal Indian Army Service Corps, to work for them. Dhillon knew both but was closer to Gill, just a few rungs below him in seniority and a fellow Sandhurst graduate. He too became an early INA supporter as Mohan Singh's military secretary and represented him while he was away in Tokyo. However, soon unable to face living in his shadow, Dhillon switched over to Gill and went with him to Bangkok. Effectively banished, they arrived in early May and came under the tutelage of Colonel Iwakuru Hideo, who had succeeded Fujiwara and was aware of their issues with Mohan Singh. Gill was given a high salary with Dhillon as his deputy, tasked with uniting the two warring Indian civilian factions in Bangkok. They once again stayed at the Hotel Rajdhani, before shifting into a villa owned by Narula, Gill's chaperone during his pre-war visit. Armed with a large expense account, the two officers lived a comfortable life accompanied by Indian meals from their good friend Dr Jagdish Singh, who had treated Gill during this pre-war trip.[10]

Iwakuro to the Rescue

After a few weeks when the Bangkok conference began, the reality of being in Singh's shadow reared up again and so did Gill's politicking; their rivalry was noted by many of those present. Having set his eyes on being nominated to the five-member Council of Action, akin to a war cabinet, he was very disappointed at not making it. As Gill became more and more morose, he was rescued by an ingenious solution by Iwakuro. Seeing how successful the infiltration of Malaya had been, the same was planned for the impending invasion of India. In a diplomatic masterstroke, Colonel Iwakuro, then in charge of relations with the Indians, asked Gill to lead this mission to be based out of Rangoon, far away from Singh who would command the INA in Singapore. Gill and Dhillon jumped on this and decided to use the job as an opportunity to escape to India. The idea of the double cross was born, and the irony is that the Japanese gave them this gift.[11]

Recruiting Spies who could spy on spies

To kick off the recruitment of this elite force of contact parties as they were called, Gill arrived in Singapore around July 20. He needed a core team who were just like him – appeared pro-Japanese while the going was good and now willing to take risks to betray them. For this, he sought out his relative by marriage, Captain Tehl Singh, 1/8 Punjab Regiment, who in turn selected Lieutenant Jang Bahadur Singh Grewal, 5/2 Punjab Regiment, and Second Lieutenant Bakhtawar Singh, Bengal Sappers, who he knew well. Their pro-Japanese credentials were perfect. All three surrendered early once the invasion of Singapore began and were prominent in the INA from the start. Their personal links ensured that it was known they would be now willing to betray their masters. For the wider team, it was inevitable that Mohan Singh would include some of his men. After screening volunteers for loyalty to him, eleven were selected. A twelfth, Havildar Shiv Singh, 5/2 Punjab was included to serve as a spy on the inside. He was one of two men who ran Mohan Singh's secret service in Singapore, ferreting out those obstructing INA recruitment in full swing at this time, and knew the men well.[12]

Pritam Singh Musafir

Three Sikh civilians were recruited through Bakhtawar Singh's contact, Wazir Khan, a carpet merchant originally from Ludhiana and "father of notorious Wazir Mohd Khan & friend of even more notorious Osman Khan".* Two were policemen from Johore and the Singapore naval base. The third was the very interesting Pritam Singh Musafir, a 40-year-old from Bikaner, sallow, slim, five feet, six

---

* Dr Lee Interrogation, NAI's INA File 499 CSDIC (I) Report 952.

inches and with the letters PSM tattooed on his left forearm. Whilst a student in Jullundur in his early twenties, he joined the Congress Party to fight for India's independence and was jailed for distributing a *fatwa** that said working for the British was irreligious. After being released he found work with a construction contractor and after many years in the same line found himself in Singapore when war broke out in December 1941.

A few days after the surrender in February 1942, Musafir met Wazir Khan at the newly launched Singapore branch of the Indian Independence League he had started frequenting to "spend time in society and avoid questioning"[†] at Japanese checkpoints. In July when Gill's party was being put together, Khan recruited Musafir. When he reached Khan's home on July 29, the two policemen were already there. They were picked up in a truck and taken to a room in Tyersal Park POW camp[‡] where they joined many of the INA soldiers who had arrived the day before. Then Gill entered and all stood up out of respect. He told them they had volunteered for an important mission to spread propaganda and get military information vital for the invasion of India. He added they were to go to Bangkok under command of Bakhtawar Singh on behalf of the INA and gave each 20 ticals[§] with the officers getting 50. The military men were given civilian clothes and shoes, and Shiv Singh handed out beers welcoming everyone to the new brotherhood.[13]

Train to Bangkok

Gill's officers now had twelve INA men from Mohan Singh they did not trust but had no choice but to accept. They also had six reliable INA men known to them who were in on the secret from the start and employed in key positions later. Wazir Khan's three men that they could only hope were trustworthy, made a total of twenty-one. To manage this, the planning was meticulous. The next evening, on July 30, most of the new men took a train from Singapore with Bakhtawar Singh in charge to watch over and start assessing them. A few days later Gill, his officers and some of the reliable six left by car. The train party reached Bangkok on August 2 and checked into the Europe Hotel, with three men in each room. Later that afternoon Dhillon, who had been in Bangkok during the recruitment, came to ask after them and ordered that they

---

* *Fatwa* is a ruling on a point of Islamic law given by a recognized authority.
† Musafir quotations from his interrogation, CSDIC (I) Report 62 in NAI's INA File 499.
‡ One of several used for Indian POWs. The British were mainly in the Changi area and the Australians at the Selarang Barracks.
§ Tical was another name for Thai Bhat, equal then to 1 Japanese Yen.

must "take care of our character and refrain from alcohol". For five days they had nothing to do and during this lull and later, many of the men used their allowance to enjoy all that Bangkok had to offer. When Gill and the others arrived soon, he addressed them again in a deliberately vague way, saying "you may have some doubts in your mind about why I sent for you, but when the time comes, I will explain everything. Do not worry about it now. Just obey the orders of the officers."[14]

The Test

Of course, there was serious work to be done as well. The spies had a very difficult job – successfully infiltrate India, avoid the authorities, and unobtrusively gather army intelligence and send it back to the Japanese in Burma. Some were to also sabotage military targets, railway and telegraph lines after connecting with men in India. At the outset the objectives were explained and then the training began in earnest.

But first there was a test. The men were split into groups of three. Musafir's team had two days to complete their task. First, they were to ascertain the political leanings of the Indian Independence League clerks, but he failed to elicit any information. For their next task, enquiries led him to a Dr Kundan Singh. He seemed to be part of the group who were rivals of the IIL. Though anti-British, unlike them, they were also anti-Japanese and did not want their involvement in attaining India's independence. Musafir described him as a true nationalist, which tells us which way he himself was leaning. Dr Singh seemed to know of the men in Europe Hotel, but Musafir denied he was one of them. He mentioned thirty people conducting pro-Japanese propaganda with his opinion of them, often scathing. Musafir submitted a report listing them, leaving out the commentary. As Gill's men could easily have done this more easily themselves, he was puzzled by the exercise, and felt that the goal seemed not to collect information but to train and assess the men.[15]

The Training

Then the main lessons began, delivered by the officers in Gill's team. First, they needed to know Burmese as they had to pass through the British occupied parts of Burma. Grewal taught them the language and the geography, being born and brought up there. The engineer Bakhtawar Singh lectured on bombs, including how to disable explosives laid down by the British on bridges in the border areas, Tehl Singh spoke on politics, independence and unity across religions, and Dhillon on the mission objectives and difficulties. As most came from humble backgrounds and may later need to hobnob with gentry in India, they were taught deportment and good manners. They were trained on how to get information by entertaining military men or being coolies, slip past sentries and how to change military habits and live like civilians. They were taught how to use invisible ink – either onion juice or liquid soap and water followed by application of heat. Anyone who wanted to opt out was given that choice. None took it.[16]

Bangkok to Rangoon via Singapore

At the end of August, plans were made for the move to Rangoon, where Gill was to have his headquarters. The group was split, with one group being flown there and the second sent by train back to Singapore, from where they were to go by ship to Rangoon with Bakhtawar Singh, who was on a secret mission within a secret mission. He was sent back to collect documents about the INA organization to give to the British. The explanation to the Japanese for this roundabout route was that they had too much equipment to carry by plane.

By now Gill's officers had got to know the men and the reliable ones were sent to Singapore. Accompanied by a Japanese to watch over them, they boarded a goods train in Bangkok to remain hidden, emerging once they reached Japanese occupied Penang. In Singapore they were isolated in a bungalow in Bukit Timah occupied by the Japanese and ordered not to leave or contact any friends or relatives. Besides the INA papers. Bakhtawar Singh had another task, to recruit two reliable wireless operators for Gill to whom he had an introduction. Two others also joined, taking the Singapore total to twenty-five. Before they left, Iwakuro met the whole team, shook each one's hand and reminded them to spread anti-British and pro-Japanese feelings amongst Indians back home. They then sailed for Rangoon and arrived on September 16. Dhillon met them at the harbour and took them to the Suzuki Hospital at Stockade Road, formerly the Little Sisters' Home, where they met the others who had been flown from Rangoon.[17]

Chanda and Deb's Nationalists

To the twenty-five Singapore recruits and Gill's core team of five officers, were now added perhaps the most important members of the group, eighteen civilians. Several Sikhs were recruited by Chanda Singh who Gill had got to know during his pre-war visit. Deb Bhattacharia from Malaya added fellow Bengalees from Burma who knew the country well and spoke the language. Most were like Musafir, nationalists who after contact with the law left India when the embers were hot, to live with friends and family in Southeast Asia. Now that there seemed to be a chance again, they volunteered for this dangerous job, risking death by hanging if not being shot in an encounter.[18]

The Doublecross – an inspection and an escape

Once everyone had been collected, things moved fast, and Gill and his officers made their plans. From Burma, there were three main approaches to India, through Myitkyina* in the north, Kalewa in the centre and Akyab in the south. Each of these were to serve as bases for contact parties to cross over to India. Mohan Singh's spy Shiv Singh was to manage Akyab with an assistant loyal to Gill. The other two bases were to be managed by Dhillon and Grewal who were to go on ahead to report on their areas for which a coded signal was devised. Routes first class very good meant Gill could come and even if he had a Japanese escort, they would be able to go. Routes second class good meant they could go across the border, but no Japanese escort must be present. Routes third class, Bad meant they could not get across the border under any circumstances. Then Gill was to go to the better area for an "inspection" to escape with them. The reliable men knew about the real plan. The others were not to be told until they reached the border, and then only if they could be trusted.[19]

Gulab and Chameli[20]

Meanwhile three teams were formed, one to attempt each route. The first two were named after flowers, Gulab (rose) and Chameli (jasmine). The third was called Corop. To keep the pretence going, the team leaders were given typed instructions in English detailing the area they were to cover, information they were to collect and the role and alias of each person. They were also to explain this to their team members. To ensure it was clear, Gill spoke to those who knew English. Grewal spoke to the others, who were then taken before Gill, their instructions repeated and asked to take an oath. The Sikhs were told that, if necessary, they had to cut their hair, a very drastic step as it symbolized their religion. If arrested in India, they were to give their real address but not the nature of their work. A Japanese doctor and an Anglo-Indian nurse vaccinated them.

---

* Pronounced "Me-chee-na".

Gulab was headed by Havildar Kulkarni, a young Marathi, 5 feet 6 inches with a scar on the left size of his forehead. His team included Musafir who could not read English, so Kulkarni explained the instructions, telling him not to tell anyone. Attempting the central Kalewa route, they were to split up after reaching India. Musafir was then to go to Mymensing (Bengal), find a place to live and contact the local Congress and await orders. After spending half an hour talking over the plan, the team went to the bazaar to buy supplies with money given by Gill. For each one they bought a torch, an umbrella, a cigar lighter, a blanket and a haversack to store them.

The instruction not to talk to anyone was not strictly followed as Musafir knew about team Chameli, headed by Havildar Sumer Singh, IAOC, a tall, fair Rajput with a pockmarked face and a mole on his lower lip. To his team he explained their northern route through Mytikyina to survey Manipur* and gave them the location of British military units there. Once they reached India, he would finalize where they would stay and how they would operate. Later, when their route was found to be unusable, they switched to go through the central Kalewa area. Their new instructions were to get information on Assam (from Gauhati to Silchar). Once they had settled down, their rendezvous was the first-class waiting room at Silchar train station at 12 noon at dates to be fixed by them. When greeting each other, their hands were to be folded with thumbs inside palms, and the same signal was to be used for other Gill party members they might meet. The password when greeting was IG (pronounced eye gee, i.e. I for Iwakuro and G for Gill). Two men including Sumer Singh were to return to Rangoon with the information, while the other two were to remain behind gathering more and spreading propaganda. When returning to Burma, the password was Iwakuro, and if needed they could add they had information for Captain Sakai, who was the Japanese minder assigned to Gill.

Corop

The third team was Corop, headed by Warrant Officer Charan Singh, a young Sikh with a medium build. This was a larger team with six members, three military and three civilians. They were to go through the southern Akyab route, and two were to return from no man's land after reporting if the rest had made it across. The others were to survey Midnapore and Murshidabad in Bengal, and then two were to return to Burma with the information, with two others remaining behind. They were to choose who was to do what. Once formed in mid-September, all the

---

* In India bordering Burma.

teams were ordered to be ready to leave at short notice. The day before departing, each team leader was called for a private talk with Gill and given two revolvers, thirty bullets, money for all in the team and a Japanese pass to help them through checkpoints. The fourth and last team of six Bengalee civilians was led by Deb Bhattacharia. It was to accompany Corop through the southern Akyab route.

A Briefing by Udhe Singh

Before everyone left, Gill and Dhillon were briefed on conditions in the border areas by Havildar Udhe Singh, 5/2 Punjab, who was part of another group running teams into India run by Jemadar Ram Sarup. Seeing the success of the infiltration in Malaya when the war began, the Japanese collected a group of fifty-two Indian INA volunteers in January 1942 headed by Sarup and brought them to Burma to aid their impending invasion. Once this phase was over, they started sending infiltrators into India as Gill had been tasked to do and knew the border area well. It would have been very galling for Gill as Sarup was seven ranks lower in his own unit 4/19 Hyderabad, but now was his equivalent, being highly valued by the Japanese. It is not known if Gill attended the garden party hosted by Sarup for them at his bungalow.[21]

Dhillon and Captain Pritam Singh

The first team to leave was Dhillon's reconnaissance party seen off by Gill at Rangoon railway station on September 19. He was to scope out the central Kalewa route. Upon reaching Monywa on the way there, he headed straight for the gurdwara where he had been told a Sikh officer was hiding. Captain Pritam Singh, 2/16 Punjab Regiment, had escaped from Singapore in early May with two other officers. They had made their way through Malaya, Thailand and Burma, reaching Monywa in mid-August. There, their luck finally seemed to have run out as after a month of trying, they had been unable to get a permit to move on. To be less conspicuous they split up, with Singh deciding to go alone. The two other officers left on September 16 to try reaching India through another route, while he stayed on. A week later Dhillon arrived and said he could help him get to India.[22]

But there was a problem. Singh was too well known to the Japanese after his month in Monywa and would jeopardize the mission if seen with Dhillon. To take care of this, on September 26 Singh boarded a train leaving Monywa, got off at the next station, walked back and met Dhillon at a designated spot in the jungle. Then they went to the out-way house hired for Gill on his planned inspection visit.

To remain unseen, Singh stayed in the upper floor, only a few of Dhillon's men were allowed up to bring him his food, and he rarely went downstairs except at night. Then, on September 28, Pritam Singh's hair was cut and his beard shaved. This was anathema for him, a Sikh on religious grounds, and done purely to be less prominent in the long, dangerous journey ahead. A witness was the 38-year-old Dr George Muller Lee, an Indo-Ceylonese Christian who the men described as Chinese or "*Madrassi*".* Dr Lee was known to Gill and had accompanied Dhillon from Rangoon. From his base in Monywa, he would later shepherd the teams on their way to the next stage, Kalewa. When he saw Singh shaved and Dhillon taking his entire kit when leaving, Lee realized this was no reconnaissance but an escape.

The Steamer to Kalewa

By the time Dhillon and his men left Monywa on October 3, the Gulab team had caught up. On the boat, Japanese secret police asked the dressed down Singh where his master was, and he pointed to Dhillon. His shaven disguise had worked as they had not recognized him. Also onboard was Colonel Koba, who knew Dhillon worked for Iwakuro and was very friendly. Dhillon declined his offer of an escort saying that his work required them to be in disguise. After eight days of anxiety, they reached Kalewa on October 11 at 3.00am. It was full of more secret police. Dhillon explained that they worked for Iwakuro and were moving closer to the border to probe a route into India. The next morning, they left in a convoy consisting of the Fatima and two other steamers, loaded with Japanese troops and ammunition. Two miles out, as they crossed the Japanese outposts, Singh felt like he had awakened from a bad dream. Not only had he slipped through the Japanese net, but also missed possible death by friendly fire, for soon after they left, six Allied planes bombed Kalewa. Singh had escaped twice that day.

But there was far more to come. As they progressed, Dhillon gave precise instructions to Singh where a patrol would be waiting. A Captain Macdonald was expecting them and would take care of things. Parting from Dhillon on October 18, Singh hired guides and finally made it on October 24. Captain Pritam Singh had reached home after a 173-day ordeal. The toughest part had been his almost six weeks stay at Monywa, followed by the tension filled month with Dhillon. It had taken patience, courage, resourcefulness, ingenuity and the shaving of his hair to finally succeed.

---

* "*Madrassi*" colloquial for from Madras (now named Chennai).

Dhillon's Elephant Hunt[23]

Dhillon had stayed behind, waiting at a PWD Dak Bungalow* for Bakhtawar Singh who was close behind. Having hired as guides the cartman Lal Khan and a Manipuri on the way, he finally caught up on October 19. This was when he was able to tell Dhillon that the Japanese had not allowed Gill to leave Rangoon to come for his "inspection" to escape. They could either go back for him together, send Bakhtawar with the INA papers, or both go to India leaving Gill behind. Dhillon said he chose the last option as only he knew everyone and everything about the INA plans. This was a convenient but also a very human decision. He was almost across. It would have taken a superhuman resolve to go back for Gill now, an option fraught with great risk.

Bakhtawar went on ahead to arrange a patrol to capture the guides with Dhillon to prevent them from spilling the beans as their fellow officer Grewal was expected to reach soon. They did not know that he had stayed back and was not coming. On October 25, Bakhtawar reached the same Moreh post where Pritam Singh had reached just twenty-four hours earlier. As planned, he made arrangements for the guides to be abducted.

A few hours behind him, Dhillon set off on an elephant carrying all his kit and the precious INA papers. Such was his aura that in the retelling of his escape, this one elephant morphed into many, and even into an elephant hunt. On the way they came across Pritam and Bakhtawar Singh's guides who were returning. When asked, they said their journey had been smooth. The well laid abduction plan was spoilt as Dhillon's guides Lal Khan and the Manipuri refused to go up to the border. This would have severe repercussions later. They were paid off and returned with the elephant and the mahout. A few hours after Bakhtawar, Dhillon too reached the Moreh post, who now received their third group in two days.

Everyone who went through Dhillon's central Kalewa route escaped, including Gulab. Team Chameli also crossed a month later. Corop team also made it through the southern Akyab area. Bhattacharia's team were taken through a slightly different route from Corop, were unable to cross and returned to Akyab. Despite, this, twenty-two men had made it to India.[24]

Meanwhile, Gill Back in Rangoon[25]

After seeing off Dhillon on September 19, Gill could only wait for news. In a story within a story, that of the letters between them had a life of their own.

---

* Public Works Department (PWD) Dak Bungalow – these were rest houses built for officers on inspection routes as they travelled through their administrative areas.

Allowing Dhillon to take all the INA papers when he left Rangoon indicates that Gill had agreed he should go if he had a chance. However, the letters and their reactions to them show that it was not that simple. And the last letter had a special significance.

Dhillon's first letter arrived on September 29 telling Gill to reach his base of Kalewa in a month. Gill replied with instructions for Dhillon to remain there until he got further orders. But when Gill was denied permission from the Japanese to leave Rangoon, he sent Bakhtawar Singh on October 4 to tell Dhillon to escape without him. The next update Gill got a few days later was from Grewal in person. Having left Rangoon with Dhillon, he returned after discovering his northern Mytikyina route was unusable. It was decided to send the Chameli team intended for this route through Dhillon's area.

In early November, Gill got his next update, a letter from Bakhtawar Singh saying he was en route to join Dhillon who had gone towards the border and was hiring elephants. This was the first news about Dhillon since his letter five weeks ago, and the elephants indicated he was himself escaping. The time it took for letters to reach meant that Gill was unaware that Dhillon had already gone by the time he had received this letter. Finally, on November 8, Gill learnt that he had. Despite telling Dhillon to escape if he got a chance, he did not expect him to leave without him. When he heard the news, Gill lost his nerve, fearing the Japanese reaction. If they did not know already, they would find out soon. News was spreading and despite a strict gag order, soon all the INA men in Rangoon knew. In desperation Gill thought of going to Mohan Singh and asking him to tell the Japanese. Equally anxious, his officers Grewal and Tehl Singh begged him to get permission for them to go to India. Though they were meant to manage the teams and not themselves go over, the Japanese agreed.

"The bearer of this letter will explain"

For Grewal and Tehl Singh to carry to India, Gill wrote five letters – one addressed to the Adjutant General at Army Headquarters in Delhi, a second to his bankers Grindlays in Bombay, and three more to his family – his wife, his maternal uncle at Lyallpur and his brother-in-law Harcharan Singh. If the letters between Gill and Dhillon had a life of their own, these letters took on an almost supernatural power in later events. Writing them was very risky. The letter to his bank could be explained away as a personal affair. However, the family letters would make it clear he had earlier lied to the Japanese when he said they had been massacred by the British. Finally, his letter to the Army looked worst. It had reference to his temporary rank of Lieutenant-Colonel granted just days before the British surrender in Singapore on February 15. He said nothing more except the cryptic "The bearer of this letter will explain", making it sound very mysterious. What did Gill have in mind when he wrote this? His explanation was that he was informing the Army Headquarters of something they might have been unaware of – his promotion, so they could ensure his family allowance represented the higher rank. But to the Japanese it sounded like he was sending a message paving the way for his return to the British.

These dangerous letters were securely locked away in his safe when on November 24 Gill was suddenly called to Singapore by Mohan Singh, to help tackle the crisis with the Japanese described in the previous chapter. And in the safe they would have remained had it not been for what happened next. Before Dhillon escaped, he gave his guide Lal Khan a letter for Gill. It reached Udhe Singh, who instead handed it over to the Japanese. Though Dhillon had been missing for over a month by now, it was this letter that confirmed he had gone. The Japanese swooped down onto Gill's safe and then found more evidence, his five letters to India. Had Dhillon's plan to abduct Khan worked, he would have had no one to give any letter to. Without this smoking gun, Gill might have been able to convince the Japanese he was duped by Dhillon.[26]

Gill's Arrest

Unaware of all this, Gill was in Singapore with Mohan Singh. The Japanese planned their surprise well, arresting him on December 8, 1942. The reason stated was the letters found and Dhillon's defection. In his defence he pointed out how much he had supported the Japanese, and his only error had been trusting Dhillon. He stressed how well connected he was in North India, with the Indian Army and Indian extremists in East Asia and hoped to be used again by the Japanese. It did not move them, and he remained in prison for the rest of the war.[27]

However, the Dhillon defection was a smokescreen. The real reason for his arrest was that now back in Singapore he was stiffening Mohan Singh's back to stand up to the Japanese during his stand-off with them. With Gill gone, they hoped Mohan Singh would back down, but he did not. This can be seen by how lightly they treated Gill's team in Burma.[28] His remaining officers Grewal and Tehl Singh were in Rangoon and expected to spend Christmas in Delhi. That was not to be, for in a coordinated exercise all of his team in different towns were arrested on December 11. It started with Japanese policemen surrounding and arresting everyone in Gill's bungalow in Rangoon that morning. Their confinement was not strict, and all were released in February 1943, treated to a feast at the Bombay

Hotel in Rangoon, given a parting bonus, an apology and all re-employed by the Japanese. They were warned however that further misunderstandings might result in them being shot.[29]

"Half measures would be useless. He is much too clever to be taken in by eyewash"[*]

Now we must move back to India, where Dhillon's men were interrogated like anyone else coming from Japanese occupied territory. All were treated with suspicion, guilty until proven innocent. Captain Pritam Singh was soon identified as a genuine escaper as his two fellow officers who had gone their own way had reached India before him corroborated his story. The others were kept apart at the Red Fort in Delhi so they could not coordinate theirs. Their accounts matched in every detail on the escape, which was true. However, they all claimed to have joined Gill to escape. The interrogators knew that was not true and most had wanted to incite anti-British feelings in India.[30]

When it came to Dhillon he was treated differently, never interrogated and even sent on leave a few days after his arrival in Delhi. A well thought out British assessment dated November 11, 1942, says of Dhillon that he gave the impression he was entirely out to help. They did realize there was an element of whitewashing in what he said as they noted that "reading between the lines, he had been a big help to the Japanese during the last few months". It goes on to say that Dhillon himself was probably unsure at this stage what he wanted to do, and this would depend a good deal on the British attitude to him to whom he could be very useful. It ends with a clear warning, though they had yet to decide if he could be trusted, "Half measures would be useless. He is much too clever to be taken in by eyewash". That this may not just be a double cross as described by Dhillon, but possibly a triple cross, occurred to the British. The same assessment of him says that as his family had prevented him from marrying a woman outside his caste, this loosened his ties to India and made it possible for him to return to the Japanese.[†]

---

[*] All the quotes on Dhillon are from British Library IOR/L/WS/1/1711.

[†] Bakhtawar Singh's report described him as "honest, not highly intelligent & not subtle enough to carry out 5th column work…A likeable, trustworthy, efficient, but somewhat unimaginative officer". Bakhtawar was brilliant. They thought he could not do what he had just done, subtly and very imaginatively tricking them better than the suave Dhillon.

Dhillon's Deceptions[31]

Though the British knew there was an element of whitewashing, they did not realize how much paint had been used. Dhillon gave a very different picture of the relationship Gill and he had with the INA from what happened, but the British were used to this being downplayed once men reached India. His main deception was about the civilians who came with him. They were hidden in plain sight, passed off as servants or translators. In fact, they were all anti-British activists, and the main cargo Dhillon had been carrying. First was the already known Musafir who came out with Gulab. The second was the giant Sher Singh who was with Chameli. A 42-year-old, 5 foot and 11 inches Jat Sikh with a strong build, black eyes, *kes** and long beard streaked in grey, he was quite a sight. Given the role of an orderly, he was in fact Sardar Sher Singh who lived in the border area between Malaya and Thailand. When the Japanese were advancing from Thailand into Malaya at the start of the war in December 1941, he was sentenced to death for not allowing his truck to be requisitioned. Freed by Giani Pritam Singh he was one of the men who persuaded many Indian soldiers to join the INA in the first few days and weeks. His cover story was that he was a civilian who joined the team at the last minute to get help to go to India. Despite this he was recognized as the villain of the piece, but not as the even more prize catch he really was.

Besides these men who came with Dhillon, no mention was made of the fourth group composed entirely of civilians headed by Deb Bhattacharia, who like Sher Singh was a prominent nationalist and the recruiter of many Bengalees to the cause. They tried to make their crossing on the same day as Dhillon but several hundred miles away, so he was unaware they did not make it. Had he been truly pro-British, he would have given up all these men, but he did not.

So, which was it finally, a Double Cross or a Triple Cross?[32]

For Colonel Gill it was a double cross gone wrong as he got caught. Dhillon fared much better. Using Gill's position to create the contact group structure, he managed to reach a border area from where he escaped and left Gill behind. Dhillon double crossed the Japanese and triple crossed the British.

As advised, the British rulers of India decided not to take half measures and awarded Dhillon (and Bakhtawar Singh) the MBE.† Their investigation continued for months and when they discovered on April 17, 1943 that Dhillon had shielded

---

* The Sikh/Gurmukhi term for hair on the head.
† MBE = Member of the Order of the British Empire.

civilian infiltrators it was too late. Not only had his MBE been announced the previous month, but on that very day Dhillon married the Khatri Ms Urmila Khanna, the lady outside his Jat Sikh caste that his family had been opposing.

At the same time as Dhillon, Captain Pritam Singh was given the Military Cross, along with his fellow officers Captains Balbir Singh and Gangaram Parab. The three had been the first set of men who escaped from Singapore. Having drawn too much attention to themselves in Burma, they had split. Balbir Singh and Parab stuck together and reached India in early October, over three weeks before Pritam Singh. When they arrived, they found that though they had been the first group to escape, they were not the first to have reached India, for two other officers had arrived five weeks earlier. And it is to the escape of these officers that we now turn.

Chapter 4

THE GREAT ESCAPE FROM SINGAPORE[1]

"It is the duty of every prisoner of war to escape."[*]

When the British surrendered to the Japanese in Singapore on February 15, 1942, almost 100,000 Allied soldiers became POWs, half of them Indian. To most, becoming a prisoner meant they had no choice but to remain one but to some, captivity was unacceptable, an urge shared with POWs across the world. Beyond the duty that every soldier had to escape, the greater factor was their refusal to accept the restrictions of captivity – being enclosed, having to obey orders of those who were not their own superiors. In the confusion of the immediate surrender, some escaped and a few reached safety. But for most the shock of the surrender was overwhelming, and they stayed put.

Once things settled down, it became clear to British and Australian POWs that even if they managed to escape, once outside, they would stick out like sore thumbs. For Indians, there were two factors that made escape just about possible. First, they were not yet enclosed by barbed wire and guarded by Japanese soldiers, but in camps commanded and guarded by Indians. Secondly, they could melt into the large local Indian population. This was possible only if they dared, for being caught meant fierce retribution.

There were many who thought of escape from the beginning, some tried to reach India and were caught, some escaped and decided to stay on as civilians in Malaya. Only five officers were acknowledged by the British as genuine escapers in 1942. Captains Pritam and Balbir Singh and Parab were the first to leave and arrived in October, but Pillai and Radhakrishnan were there before them.

---

* *A Daring Journey to Freedom – Escape from a Japanese Prisoner-of-War Camp: Memoirs of Colonel Gangaram S. Parab, MC*, published 2014.

Pillai's early escape attempts

Lieutenant Markandan Mairugesan Pillai, Royal Bombay Sappers and Miners, was one of those who refused to remain a prisoner and thought of escape from the very beginning. He was wiry and determined, and it showed in everything he did – when he joined the army against his family's wishes and later when he refused to remain as a prisoner after the surrender. He waited for a chance to join the engineers, his preferred field, and the 29-year-old was commissioned on February 24, 1941. Soon he set sail for war from Bombay on the Royal Navy heavy cruiser HMS *Devonshire* that eventually took them to Singapore. During the battle in Malaya that followed, his unit spent most of their time blowing up bridges to hinder the Japanese advance, though that was not enough to stop them. They returned to Singapore on January 31, 1942, the day the causeway linking it to mainland Malaya was blown up. After a few days of being deployed in their trained role as engineers, they were thrown in to fight like infantry.

When the surrender was announced on February 15, with two colleagues he thought of taking a boat to Sumatra, but being far from the coast realized that was not feasible. That night he could not sleep, and his mind went back to some days ago when he had been cut off from his unit and wandered alone through Malaya before finding them. He had survived as he had been able to melt into the local population, many of whom were South Indians like him, and wanted to try that again. The next morning he mentioned this to his commander officer, Major R. Dinwiddie, Royal Engineers, who told him that Kirkee (the home base of the Bombay Sappers) was a long way away, and besides, as ordered by the Japanese he had already submitted a list of names in his unit that included Pillai. If he escaped now, he would be missed, hunted and those who remained would pay the price as well. Despite this dampening assessment, seeing his determination, Dinwiddie gave Pillai $30 to help, seed money that was soon to be used very effectively.

Deterred by Sharks

Later that day the Japanese segregated the races, with the British officers of the Indian Army being ordered to the Changi area, and the Indians to Farrer Park near Little India, where thousands started gathering. As there were no Japanese guards and hence no prison atmosphere, the determination to escape became stronger. Pillai was encouraged by Major Bhonsle* who also asked him to tell his own wife he was safe, in case he happened to succeed. That night Pillai tried his first escape.

---

* Major Jagannathrao Krishnarao Bhonsle, 5th Mahratta Light Infantry.

A strong swimmer, he went to the coast from where he could see islands nearby. Though Sumatra was 60 miles away, there were about 100 islands on the way, so he estimated there would be no more than a 1- or 2-miles swim between each. Many were uninhabited, but would be good resting grounds. He left his uniform on the beach, and set off in his underclothes with just Dinwiddie's $30 wrapped in the silver foil of a cigarette packet. After a quarter of a mile of breaststroke, he saw a splash about 150 feet away. Realizing these were shark infested waters he returned as quickly as he could. But he had lost his bearings and could not find the spot where he had left his clothes, so he headed stealthily back to Farrer Park and managed to rejoin his unit before dawn.

That morning, February 17, Pillai met Major Bhonsle again who was annoyed to see him back, and told him that now he would be unable to escape. Later that day he witnessed the Farrer Park handover ceremony,* and then moved with his unit to the Bidadari camp. There they soon settled down into a routine of poor food and medical facilities, overcrowding, hard labour and increasing restrictions on movement, a far cry from what was promised by the Japanese. Pillai was determined to escape. By March 1942 Sumatra had fallen to the Japanese, so heading there was not an option. Besides, the lack of boats and threat of sharks meant the sea route anywhere else was also out. The only option was the much longer trudge by land across three thousand miles of Japanese occupied territory. But for any plan to work, he needed help from the outside. This is when he thought of contacting the only person he knew beyond the confines of the camp.

The Second Escaper, Lieutenant V. Radhakrishnan, Singapore Volunteer Corps

Radhakrishnan was a 34-year-old Tamilian[†] engineer who had moved to Singapore in his twenties and started working in the Government Trade School as an instructor. His wife was from a Tamilian family in Ipoh, Malaya and they had two children. After World War II began in Europe in 1939, he joined the Singapore Volunteers,[‡] civilians who received military training and were called upon to fight when the need arose. In early 1941 with war clouds looming in the region, he sent his family to India. Shortly after, when Pillai was recovering from malaria after his arrival in Malaya, they happened to meet at a coffee shop in Singapore. Finding much in

---

* Covered in Chapter 1.
† Hailing from Tamil Nadu in South India.
‡ Radhakrishnan was a Lieutenant in the Cadet Corps in Singapore.

common, a friendship began that was to be pivotal in the escape in 1942. After the surrender the Japanese did not imprison Indian members of the volunteer forces, so Radhakrishnan remained free in his bungalow in McNair.

Eunos the Wine Waiter

As Pillai was in a camp, he needed someone with outside access to contact Radhakrishnan. Many Indian POWs planned to escape into the city and melt into the local civilian, as did Eunos, the wine waiter in the officer's mess of Pillai's unit. So, from Dinwiddie's $30, Pillai gave him $10 to find and ask Radhakrishnan to get in touch with him. They met in early April 1942, and he arranged for an Indian Independence League (IIL) card for Pillai that enabled free movement in the city. However, on the escape, he wanted some time to think about it.

Meanwhile, Pillai continued preparing. His men had given him two books they had found. One was called *On The Run*, stories of escape during World War I that provided inspiration. The other was an atlas of the region that he devoured. Always fond of maps, it fascinated him. By looking at areas in the map in Malaya and India that he knew well, he was able to understand the terrain of Thailand and Burma. He also prepared for the expected long walk back home by traversing the camp barefoot to get used to it. Soon his feet got hardened and he learnt to avoid the pitfall of stepping on thorns and ragged stones after accidentally doing so. Everyone who noticed him thought he was crazy. At times, Pillai himself agreed with them and realized he needed human companionship and could not do this alone. Radhakrishnan was an obvious partner.

The Third Escaper, Lieutenant Natarajan, IMS

To add to this, medical care was also key, so he started looking discreetly for an army doctor who also wanted to escape. He found Lieutenant Dr Natarajan, Indian Medical Service, also a fellow Tamilian. He was 33 years old, 5 feet 7 inches, bald, dark and clean shaven. The eldest of eleven children from Coimbatore, he followed his father and studied to become a doctor. After ten years of failure, ill health and a shortage of funds, he finally qualified. When the war began, he joined the army and was posted to Malaya. During the campaign he was wounded in his right foot by a shell burst which was to plague him and his mates later during the escape. Pillai met him in Bidadari camp and when Radhakrishnan had decided to join, the three Tamilians teamed up to escape. Radhakrishnan sold his possessions, bought provisions like cigars, butter, jam, Horlicks and milk and the remaining $500 was to finance their escape. Natarajan was able to collect medical supplies.

Escape on May 7, 1942

Radhakrishnan, Pillai, and Natarajan were ready to escape in early May. The timing was driven by many factors, including the fact that at this time Captain Mohan Singh was ramping up volunteering for the INA. PIllai did not want to sign-up, but knew that if he refused, there would be unpleasant repercussions.[2] He had already got himself into trouble by refusing to form the infamous 323 unit – the Japanese had asked for various work parties to be formed with this exact number of men. Suspecting it was the size of a Japanese unit and fearing they would be incorporated into their army if they did, Pillai and many others refused. But this would not be tolerated for long. He knew he had two choices – escape or face the consequences.[3]

The reversal on May 1 of the ban on civilians travelling to Malaya from Singapore, also made things easier as now they could legally travel even if disguised as civilians. At this very time when everything was set, the plan almost fell apart as Pillai was transferred to Tyresall camp near the Singapore Botanical Garden where all the engineers were being collected. So far Natarajan and he had been together in Bidadari camp, so this separation made things difficult. Fortunately, Captain Mohan Singh asked all officers to collect at Bidadari on May 7 for a speech. Camp discipline had become strict, but this order allowed Pillai to return there the previous day. Pillai also convinced his Tyersall camp commandant to delay news of his escape as long as possible. Natarajan also left behind what appeared to a suicide note in which he said he "could not stand mental tortures and mental games of MS and party and decided to put an end to his life".[*] On the evening of May 6, after a farewell party of mugs of tea sweetened with candy syrup, Pillai and Natarajan walked out of Bidadari. They were dressed in a dhoti, shirt, khadi Gandhi cap and a long towel left hanging round their shoulders.[†]

Closer to the city they took a tram when Pillai felt the eyes of everyone staring at them. That was just his imagination, as they reached Radhakrishnan's home undetected. The next day, a civilian friend gave them some money, taking the total to $600. The three headed to the train station and bought tickets for Prai, and arrived there without incident on May 9.

Passports from Penang

They then took the ferry across to Penang island and headed to the home of a Ramakrishna Iyer at Beach Road. Natarajan had got to know him during his service

---

[*] Lieutenant-Colonel Gopal Das Malhotra OBE, IMS, Report 1217/ INAI 499.

[†] Dhoti is a thin cotton garment worn mainly by Hindu men – tied at the waste and wrapped around legs. Khadi is the homespun cotton encouraged by Gandhi to be used instead of buying British manufactured cotton.

in the region some months back, and the others were Introduced as teachers from Singapore, all headed to India. He was very helpful and arranged accommodation in a South Indian Brahmin* hotel where they paid Rs 30 including food for the three days they eventually spent there. They were told the border was infested with bandits so sneaking across was not possible. Besides Natarajan had fallen ill and would not have been able to make it even if it was safe. To go by train, they needed passports issued by the Japanese. These officially cost 25 cents each, but they had to bribe the office clerk and the peon† $5 each. Their photographs were taken by a Chinese who had a shop opposite the office to whom they also paid $5. To help obscure their records, he promised that the photographs would fade within thirty days, making them unrecognizable. When filling out the forms they gave fictitious names, an address in a bombed out area of Penang that could not be verified, and claimed to be traders. They got the passports easily, left Penang on May 13 and later that day took the train to the border crossing at Pedang Besar. As they arrived in the evening, they spent the night at the station and the next morning went on a freight train to Haadyai, their first stop in Thailand.

(Another) Pillai's expensive surety

After having entered Thailand, they were told that to stay, someone had to guarantee their good behaviour. The border guards allowed Radhakrishnan to arrange this while the others had to remain at the station. He went in search for Sundaram Pillai, to whom they had been referred by fellow Tamilians on the way. He was a man of influence in the town and on his word the three officers were allowed to spend the night at his home. Radhakrishnan had told him they were traders and had $600. He asked to be paid the whole amount in return to stand surety, though reduced that to $450. After just one week, they had spent almost all their money and Pillai admonished Radhakrishna, telling him they must be frugal. Sundaram Pillai had been told by the Japanese that the three men could be communist spies, so he had two additional conditions – they must not get involved in politics and return to Malaya by the end of the month. In a craftily worded response, they promised to leave Thailand by then, which was quite different from what he had asked. While their host talked volubly, his petite wife fed them well. They were advised to go to Tap Tiang, 100 miles away, with an introduction to Valiappa Chettiar,‡ a money lender.

---

* Brahmin – the highest level in the traditional Hindu caste system.
† Peon is a term commonly used in British colonies for the assistant to an officer.
‡ Chettiars were a prominent money-lending community in South India, many of whom also operated in Southeast Asia.

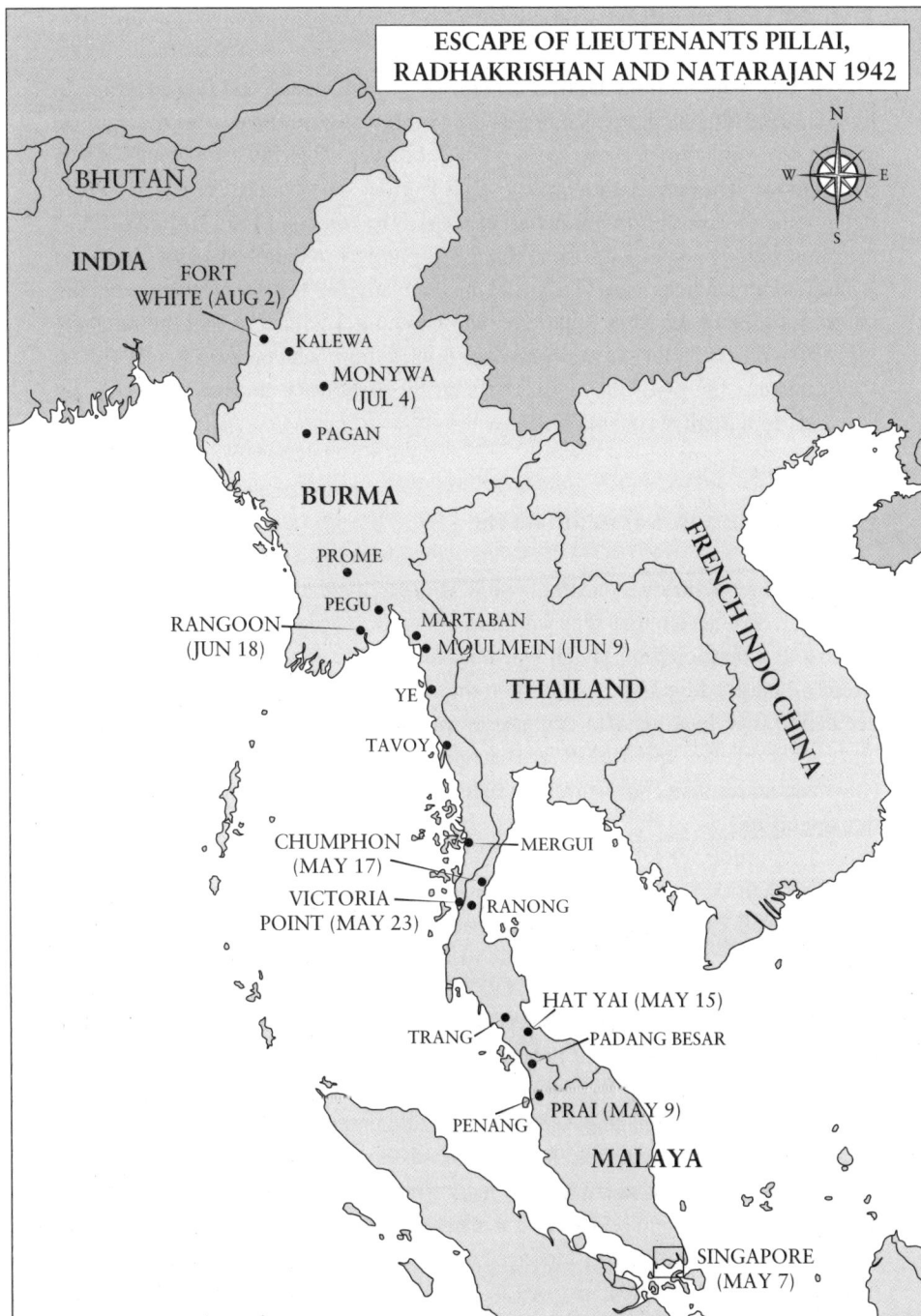

ESCAPE OF LIEUTENANTS PILLAI, RADHAKRISHAN AND NATARAJAN 1942

(SJmagic DESIGN SERVICES, India)

A night in a brothel

They left the next morning by train and met the Chettiar later that night. Getting to India through Thailand and China was a possibility, but as there were few Indians along their route and they spoke no Thai, this was discarded as they would be conspicuous. The best option was through Burma, where there were many more Indians and it was a shorter journey. They set off by train on May 17th and reached their first halt, Chumporn, the same day. As in every town they looked for any South Indians who may help them. They met one who advised they not roam around too much and hide themselves in a hotel. This was good advice as there were many Japanese soldiers about. As they had little money, they slept on the corridor floors. Unfortunately, the place they chose was an insect infested brothel, so customers and bugs kept them awake all night.

Radhakrishnan's fear of water

The next day on the way to their next stop Renong, they came across a half mile stretch of water that they could have swum across. It was here that they got to know that Radhakrishnan was not only unable to swim, but also mortally afraid of water. He gallantly told them they could proceed without him, but they decided to stick together. Radhakrishnan was sensitive and impulsive. He blamed himself for this lost opportunity and imagined his friends were very disappointed. However, at this stage not fearing being caught, the others were fine with missing this opportunity.

Abu Bakar Kaka and the Japanese Consul's Indian second wife

When they reached Renong on May 19, Natarajan was sick, so the others went in search of helpful Indians and came across Abu Bakar Kaka. The 45 year old was from Malabar in India, a rough diamond, a fair man of generous proportions, with strong likes and dislikes, yet had sterling qualities. He had lived here for decades, and spoke many languages. Taking charge of them, he arranged accommodation and introduced them to the few Indian families there, from whom they were able to gather information about nearby Burmese towns. Most importantly, Abu Bakar offered help to get passports to cross to Burma and took them to the Japanese consul, reputed to be the mastermind of the infiltration in this area. He said he would get back to them after a few days as he was busy on official tasks. They knew he was checking up on their poor cover story and their chances were slim. But luck was on their side. Though he was a 70-year-old pocket Mephistopheles, he had three wives. The second was an Indian, and hearing of their plight, she convinced him to issue the passports, granted on May 23. They left immediately.

An anxious border crossing into Burma

At the border crossing the Japanese guard laboriously went through their IIL papers in English, the visas in Siamese, other documents issued by his compatriots in Penang and Ranong. All this time they continuously repeated the two magic words, India and Gandhi. Finally, the guard let them through into Burma. They had kept their promise to Sundaram Pillai to leave Thailand by the end of the month and the papers they left behind had by now photographs that had begun to fade, so they would be unrecognizable. They felt a huge relief and wanted to run from the check post, but with great will power, to appear normal, busied themselves sorting out their papers and luggage near the guard, jabbering in Tamil.

Lambu Kaka

Finally, they moved on, climbing a steep path up to Victoria Point, their first stop in Burma. It consisted of one narrow street with houses and shops on both sides. They entered one store that was bigger than rest. This was owned by Lambu Kaka, recommended highly by Abu Bakr, an admiration returned in kind. He was thirty-five with a pock-marked face, and though brusque was kind. After he asked them a few questions, he went inside to get tea and biscuits. The rest of the day they sat there and watched people, and saw many Indians, a few Burmese and a small number of Japanese troops. Their host was a Moplah* from the west coast of India, given the nickname Lambu Kaka† because he was tall and thin. They did not get to know his real name. Whoever he was before the war, he was now a changed man. They watched the remarkable manner in which Kaka carried out his business, and making money certainly was not what motivated this towering figure. While people-watching, they were most surprised to see a couple of Australians, taken prisoner in Malaya. In a camp nearby guarded by Japanese soldiers, they were here on a construction project. The POW said they thought of escape but knew that chances of capture were

---

* Moplah's are Muslims from Kerela in India.
† Lambu is Hinduislang for tall and Kaka is a respectful term used for an elder man.

high, and that meant certain death. They bribed their guards[*] with 20 cents and were allowed out to get provisions, much of which Kaka gave free. Stories of him spread like wildfire. His generosity was not selfish. The escapees only saw him reducing his own wealth and could not understand why. All they saw was unassailable optimism and unparalleled kindness. He had no thoughts for his immediate future, let alone his distant future. Their sincere hope was that no harm came to him and he was able to "regain the wealth he had fed to the river of charity".[†]

Kaka asked them to stay as he needed clerks who knew English. They knew that was not true and it was his way of saying if they stayed, it would not be on charity. Pillai told him he was an escaped POW and the two others were civilians. They were desperate for money, but did not ask. Kaka reported that there were many Tamilians in Tavoy and Mergui who could help them on their journey. Despite the monsoon that made travel by sea tricky, he arranged for a fishing boat to take them to Mergui, accompanied by two of his men. The rough weather forced them to halt often, and though land was always in sight, it may have worried Radhakrishnan who was unable to swim. Each time they moored, they noticed apprehension from the locals who feared attacks. At the same time, Radhakrishnan was happy being on terra firma. While onboard the boat, they got soaked each time it rained. As they each had only one change of clothes, they were constantly wet and could have caught malaria but this did not trouble them much as they regularly took their anti-malaria pills.

The Long Walk from Mergui to Moulmein

Finally, when Mergui was in sight, they were alarmed to see a Japanese sentry, and decided their cover story in advance. Fortunately, he did not focus on them and their entry was smooth. Kaka's men arranged a hotel for Pillai and Radhakrishnan. Natarajan stayed with a relative, Natarajan Nair who warned them about the dangers of Burmese who had attacked Indians after the British left, resenting them for their dominance in trade and commerce. But they were not deterred. Radhakrishnan was also worried that this had resulted in too much loose talk about their escape.

---

[*] Japanese guards were of different types, some allowed them out without bribes knowing there was no chance of escape. Some took a small bribe and let them back in easily. There was one guard who was brutal – he would allow them out after a bribe, and when they returned, beat them up and took away any provisions they had. To offset this, there was one who gave them titbits to eat. He was nicknamed the "Sucker" not meant to be derogatory, but a way of the Australian POWs acknowledging him without being mushy. pg65.

[†] *Three Thousand Miles to Freedom*, Brigadier MM Pillai, MC, Lancer Publishers (India) 2009.

They stayed less than forty-eight hours there and left on the second morning for Tavoy. Though they walked all the 159 miles, they did not find it unduly alarming and talked and got to know more about each other. The taller Radhakrishnan walked fastest, then Pillai, followed by Natarajan whose old foot injury slowed him down. This time Pillai fell ill on the way. Natarajan cured him by pouring water from a well over him which made him feel better immediately. After having walked 29 miles without food, the pores on his skin dilated to keep blood warm and it was this that had made him ill. The cold water opened up the pores. They decided not to push too much – and have at least 1 cup of tea and walk no more than 25 miles in a day. That night was spent in a hut.

Further on they met some Indians who advised them not to go further as the area was infested by anti-Indian Burmese. One day followed the other, gradually reducing their funds and supplies and soon they were paupers again. Fortunately, they met a Tamilian from Coimbatore who was a rice contractor. As he was from Natarajan's district, he treated them as one of his own. Gorging on his food, they all had diarrhoea. But they had to keep going and when they finally reached Tavoy, spent four days there nursing their upset tummies. Here too they enjoyed the hospitality of another fellow Tamilian introduced by Nair of Mergui, and he arranged tickets for the next leg of their journey to Ye.

In the bus amongst possibly unfriendly Burmese, they were careful not to jostle their fellow passengers. When their bus broke down, all passengers had to get down and push. However now Radhakrishnan was quite unwell. Seeing him standing by and not helping, a Burmese with a gun threatened him and it took careful handling to calm him down. This was their first experience of anti-Indian Burmese that they had been warned about and it shook them. The bus however had to be abandoned and they continued the journey on foot, reaching their destination at dusk on the third day. In Ye, they came across another helpful Tamil who took them to the home of the banker Raman Chettiar. After dinner he took them to a farmhouse in the middle of the night where they slept. Next morning he returned and dropped them off by bullock cart near the railway line, and pointed the way towards Moulmein. They set off, accompanied by his son, who being fluent in Burmese was a great help on the way. This was a fortunately uneventful journey. It was still tough going as every day they covered 25 miles on just a plate of rice and a cup of tea. They reached Moulmein around 5.00pm.

Moulmein to Rangoon

When they reached Moulmein on the evening of June 9, they headed straight to the Bank of Chettinad's office. Knowing that it was the financial hub of Indian trade, they hoped to get some help there. With all the officials having fled, it was now being run by the secretary, Muthukumar. He advised them to go their headquarters in Rangoon to try to get some money. He also asked them to contact his elder brother Arumgam who was a member of the IIL there and could help. In return for this introduction, feeding and letting them spend the night there, Muthukumarh bought from them, at what must have been a knock-down price, a diamond ring for Rs 8 and a watch for Rs 3. These belonged to Pillai who considered him the most unsympathetic person they had met so far. To be fair, it seemed a reasonable trade.

After a month on the run, the three officers were worn out, but wanted to keep going. The next morning they set off by in a crowded ferry to Martaban, crossing the Salween river that was like a vast inland sea. When they reached the rail terminus, they decided to walk along the rail line to Rangoon 100 miles away as they were almost broke. On the way Pillai was gratified to see the handiwork of Allied sappers. With a fellow engineer's pride he noted that except for the one over the Sittang river, both abutments of other bridges had been completely destroyed and steel girders beautifully twisted and dropped into waterways.

After two days of walking, surviving on just peanuts and water, they came across a group of South Indian Muslim fishermen who took them in. They happened to be from the same area where Pillai's uncle, a prominent local personality, lived and knew of him. Invited to share in their meal of fish curry, the current (Radhakrishnan) and former (Pillai) vegetarians found this odious and declined. Instead of being offended, the kindly men provided them supplies and they cooked their own meal of rice and lentils. The vegetarians wanted to eat separately, but the others waited patiently while they cooked their meal and eventually all ate together. At night they were given the best places to sleep in their meagre hut. Though the fishermen commiserated with them for their situation, the soldiers did not forget the help such poor folk had given them.

Woken up at 4.00am they got onto a boat and by dawn approached the right bank of the Sittang river. The fishermen took care of them until they reached Pegu, then went their own way. By now Natarajan was unable to walk, so with the little funds remaining he went by bus to Rangoon and was to prepare for their onward journey once he arrived. They were to rendezvous at the Bank of Chettinad. Pillai and Radhakrishnan then crossed Pegu and at a Hindu temple heard worrisome reports of the onward journey to Rangoon, still 45 miles away, which they wanted to reach the same day. A Tamilian at the temple told them there were Chettiars at Hlegu 21 miles away on the Rangoon road who might help. They arrived that afternoon, and in the outskirts came across a temple where they met an employee of the local Chettiar banker. Piling them with questions, he fed them tea, dinner, gave them a place to sleep and saw them off the next morning after breakfast.

The long walk continued. By now the soles of their feet were covered with blisters the size of ping pong balls. At each step they felt the squish of the bulbous blister and it shifting away to the side as their weight bore down on it. Eventually they used thorns to puncture the blisters, careful to do so as far as possible from the ground to avoid infection. Squishing their blisters under them, they limped into Rangoon on June 18.

In Rangoon

Natarajan, who had gone ahead by bus, reached Rangoon two days before the others. He went to their rendezvous, the Bank of Chettinad, where he waited for them to catch up. There were many Indians and South Indians here and when they heard of their journey, as almost everyone had family or friends marooned in the region, met them to ask about their experience. For decades before the war as Burma was part of British India, almost all the business had been dominated by South Indians operated remotely from home. They would visit for a few months each year, keeping behind a fellow Indian as a permanent representative, who often married a local Burmese lady. One of them, the 50-year-old Nagappa Chettiar, hosted them while in Rangoon. These precious days were not like an actual luxurious Thomas Cook* vacation, but given what they had been through so far, it seemed like one.

When at Moulmein, Muthukuar had referred them to his brother Arumugam Pillai,† who they met in Rangoon. A lawyer of standing held in high regard by the Japanese, he offered them a chance to reach India in a Japanese submarine in return for carrying out anti-British propaganda. Though this came as a bombshell, they did toy with the idea. This, and other offers like going to Manipur by land to do the same were considered. They were sure that once they reached India, they could convince Army Headquarters they were not anti-British and had they taken up one of these offers, that it had been as a cover to get back home, just as Dhillon had done. Natarajan finally told Arumugam Pillai they were escapers and he then counter-offered by asking for a report on local conditions in Malaya. They knew if they agreed to this, they would not survive the certain interrogation that would follow, to vet their *bona fides*. So they decided against taking up his offer and readied themselves to leave Rangoon promptly.

---

* Thomas Cook, famous luxury travel company.
† Elder brother of the secretary of the Moulmein branch of Bank of Chettinad.

Onwards to Prome

When they informed their friendly Chettiar host of their intentions, he was very worried for them and urged them not to go beyond Prome. He cited examples of Indian officers who had stayed on, knowing the dangers ahead. Like at every step on their way so far, they decided to press on. The next morning he took them to a temple and proffered the offering box into which they placed a 4 anna coin he had given each for this purpose. They bid an affectionate farewell to this god fearing, gentle soul, and boarded a goods train bound for Prome with the money he had given them for their onward journey. There were many halts on the way due to Allied bomb damage that they were very happy to see. Pillai even yearned to witness an air raid despite the obvious risk to them. When they reached Prome, they found enough South Indians to help them and employed their now familiar modus operandi. They befriended them and waited for an invitation to a meal. With little to do since the war disrupted their busy business lives, many spent lots of time talking about the prevailing war. On routes back to India, the closer Akyab area had been recently heavily bombed by the Allies, was impassable with thick undergrowth, leeches, wild animals, many mountain passes and the 160-mile route was largely uninhabited. So they decided to take the route north through Kalewa, also used later in the year by Dhillon.

While they were in Prome, violence broke out with attacks on the Indians in charge of vast assets and money. The first target was the most prominent one, with his rice mills burnt, the iron safes in his home emptied, and he himself bayonetted in the belly and left for dead. Natarajan rushed to tend to him. On reaching, he immediately cleaned the raw wound oozing pus, with hot water and cotton. Amazingly, the victim recovered without further medical treatment, and said that if normalcy returned, he could recover his losses within a year. More importantly, Natarajan's effectiveness as a doctor became widely known. Besides running most of Burma's trade, Indians were also prominent in the medical profession. Most doctors had fled to India or congregated in large cities, so there were almost none left in places like Prome. The Japanese could provide medical supplies, but not doctors. So Natarajan's help could be vital if they stayed. He slipped easily into this role and his fame spread far and wide.

The Split at Prome

Weakened by the privations of their trip so far and hampered by his damaged leg that continued to trouble him, Natarajan wanted to stay and questioned the need to take the unquestionable risk of going on. He felt Pillai exaggerated the risk of capture and underestimated the risks of moving on. However, Radhakrishnan was not happy staying idle, and Pillai was worried that the Japanese would soon follow up on the report on Malaya expected from them. When Arumgam Pillai had asked them for this in Rangoon, they had left without giving him a clear answer. Not having heard from them for some days, he could have easily found out they were in Prome. If they were found, Radhakrishnan could have said he was the civilian he indeed was and Natarajan could have been protected by his doctor status and value as one. Pillai, being the only combatant officer amongst them, was most at risk, so wanted to move on as well. Had they listened to warnings of danger, they would not even have left their camps in Singapore, now almost 3,000 miles and two months behind them. Every warning had been dire and from a reliable source; yet, they had almost reached the last leg.

At this time in Prome occurred the second biggest event in their escape, after first deciding to embark upon one. They split up. Trouble had been brewing all along, specially between Natarajan and Radhakrishnan. They just could not get along* and Pillai had been the peacemaker between them so far. But by now the differences had become unbridgeable. Besides the personal issues, Natarajan wanted to stay and the others to go on. It is possible there was no one moment when they realized, accepted and discussed this. Natarajan started off on his local career as a doctor, visiting patients in and near Prome, while the other two remained there searching for a way home. After about ten days there, they found a boat going north where they were headed, negotiated a fare and were told to come that night as it was to leave early next morning. They could not say goodbye to Natarajan who was away tending to a patient.† It was hard to reconcile that Natarajan had dropped out, his steady presence had been a source of great strength. His decision to stay back also triggered doubts in their mind – would they reach the border, if they did, would they make it across? Nonetheless, they moved on.

Prome to Monywa

The journey by boat did not turn out as hoped. At a stop on the way, they shrank away in horror when they saw a Japanese soldier settle himself on. Fortunately they were not on board and had their meagre belongings with them. Now they had no choice but to walk. After more scares of Japanese soldiers and the help of South Indians on the way, they crossed Pagan, once the seat of the Burman empire, and its vast ruins told the story of its past glory that the grand architecture brought to life.

---

* Evident from their respective reports.

† Each of them gave a different account of the how they split: what is said above is Pillai's account which seems most likely. Natarajan said that when at Prome, he went to check the feasibility of an escape route and when he returned, the others had left. Radhakrishnan said they split as they disagreed on which route to take from Burma to India.

When they reached the Irrawaddy river they had no money to cross it. After wandering around for two days, they met a generous South Indian who gave them some money. First they indulged in a meal and then bargained for a boat. The river was like an ocean, a vast sheet of dirty brown water as far as they could see. The farther bank was so far away it seemed to have sunk into the horizon, yet they were elated at the prospect of crossing. Unfortunately, one of their fellow passengers was a drunkard who brandished a knife at Pillai and screamed "Chetty* are you still alive?" To escape him he jumped into the river. Before doing so, he signalled to Radhakrishnan that he would find and meet him ashore. After he swam to the other bank, he reached a road and while he walked down it, met a truck driver who needed help. Using his engineering skill he fixed the truck and in return was given a lift.

Pillai now had to find Radhakrishnan, and fortunately stumbled upon him further along the road. While waiting, Radhakrishnan had come across John Babu, a frontier Muslim from India who was sympathetic to them. He treated them like royalty and advised them what route to take. They chatted for a long time and the men could not bring themselves to tell him they were broke. He gave them clothes and probably would have given them money had they asked, but their false sense of pride left them penniless. Next morning they set off, and after having trudged 30 miles reached Yesagyo that night. They easily managed to find South Indians and one of the first was the wealthiest in town. He took them home, fed them well and they stayed a day longer to recuperate. When they set off again, their destination was Monywa.

After a journey by boat upriver, arranged by their generous host, they were set down on the right bank the next day, from where Monywa was a two day walk away. Setting off on foot that afternoon, gnawing with hunger, they lay down to rest near a stream. They fell asleep and when they woke up later decided to take the easy way out and continue their slumber. Early next morning after a breakfast of water, they began the long last leg to Monywa. Talking was an effort but they persisted, speaking about anything to keep their spirits up and energy going – the prospect of a meal in Monywa, conditions in India when they reached, what it would be like in no man's land at the border crossing. They sighted the town at 3.00pm on July 14, and entered it an hour later.

At Monywa

Here too they needed food, shelter and information, but unfortunately had no introductions to help them get any of these. After wandering about, they sat at a bench outside a tea shop, happy to be just resting. The kind shop owner gave them tea and they slept that night on the bench. The next morning they bathed in

---

* A pejorative term for the prominent Chettiar community of moneylenders.

the Chindwin river and while walking back met a Tamilian who painted a gloomy picture of conditions there. The tea shop owner was a Moplah from South India who gave them more tea and information that confirmed what they had just heard. He directed them to a South Indian colony where the few who had not left for India remained. There they met the most prominent person, who brusquely told them not to expect food from him. Perhaps too many refugees had sponged off him. He saw through their disguise, identified them as escaped soldiers and advised them to return to southern Burma. They knew they could get no help from him and left.

At midday, they met some Manipuri* Brahmins. Though they appeared to be headed to India as spies for the Japanese and may have known the soldiers did not share their enthusiasm, nonetheless shared their lunch. Despite this welcome feast, the two were despondent. Their next objective was Kalewa, 200 miles away. Going over land meant encounters with wild animals that they were willing to face. The greater danger was dacoits who preyed on any Indian, all of whom were reputed to be wealthy. The steamers going up the Chindwin river were controlled by the Japanese and used only for troops, and even fishing by locals was not allowed. The only Indians on the river were those who helped the Japanese navigate it and power the boats. But the Manipuris gave them a vital piece of information – they might get a permit to travel as these were granted on occasion.

The Coffee Shop Disguise

Armed with this information, the next morning they went to Japanese headquarters to apply. There they found one Japanese officer, a Burmese and a Manipuri official and decided to pretend not to speak English. Radhakrishnan spoke in Hindustani to the Manipuri who translated into English for the Japanese and through this laborious process they were interrogated. Their story was that they were new to Burma, hence did not speak the language. Radhakrishnan's brother had run a coffee shop in Chauk (a town they had passed through) and while escaping to India had fallen ill and was now stranded in Kalewa. They were headed there to rescue him. This indeed did happen to many refugees, so was a plausible cover story. The Japanese contacted Chauk and heard there was a coffee shop that had shut, but the locals there did not know who the owners were. After just three days, they got their pass. In an incredible spirit of hutzpah, they declined the pass when told it did not include food. In an equally benevolent spirit, the Japanese officer amended the pass to include meals. The kindly tea vendor let them sleep on the bench again that last night.

---

* From Manipur in India.

The Steamer to Kalewa

In the morning they went to the jetty where they presented their pass to the Japanese officer on board. To their horror, he just tore it up and threw it away, telling them to go away. Not knowing what to do, they just stayed there. It was lucky they did, as that morning some of the staff for the steamer did not come. The Japanese asked if they could run engines and cook. Pillai was an engineer, so they said yes, and were immediately employed. Despite a lot of zig-zagging as the navigators did not seem to know their way around well, they reached Kalewa in three days. There the soldiers were told they would be needed for the return journey, but as that was four to five days later, they were allowed to go and look for the fictitious sick brother.

Pillai's Snake Trick on Radhakrishnan

Getting the chance to leave the steamer, they started off towards Tamu, the border crossing. This area was full of small and large streams, always difficult for Radhakrishnan who could not swim. The first impassable one was 100 feet wide that, luckily, a Japanese soldier who was fishing on a boat took them across. They crossed many other streams where Pillai had to wade around to find a ford shallow enough for Radhakrishnan to cross. Finally they reached one 30 feet wide but 8 feet deep at the centre. Here occurred an event that might have split them further. Pillai convinced him he could pull him across and they tore two dhotis into thin strips and tied them together to use as a rope. Pillai took one end and swam across, and asked Radhakrishnan to tie the other end round his waist. He did, but when he entered the water, had cold feet, rushed back to land and refused to budge. Pillai saw that cajoling was of no use as Radhakrishnan held onto a thick bush for dear life. So he decided to trick him, and shouted out to watch out for a snake near his feet. As expected, he jumped, let go of the bush and Pillai dragged him across. Radhakrishnan was sputtering with all the water he had taken in and though all right, was furious. After he was more comfortable, he berated Pillai for trying to drown him.

The Kind Couple

There was an uneasy truce between them as they returned to the task at hand, getting back home. After this crossing, they continued walking and soon came to a village. They met a man with a pretty young wife and asked for water and directions to the village resthouse. He told them where it was but as they started walking away, heard the couple talking. The man came back and asked them to join them for a meal, sumptuous rice, dal and bamboo shoots. It was almost dusk after the meal and as they started walking away, were called back again and allowed to sleep in the verandah of their humble hut. After this unexpected hospitality, at night they heard strange noises, peered inside and saw the husband sharpening a *dah*.* Expecting an attack, they waited anxiously. Soon the door opened, but instead of a fearsome knife attack, they saw the couple bringing out a mosquito net to make their sleep more comfortable. The next day, the couple fed them again. They learnt that the resthouse would have been a death trap, as some time ago, South Indians sheltering there had met with violent deaths at the hands of villagers as they hated Indians with a vengeance.

The husband told them they did not need to go to Tamu, as Indian Army patrols came nearby and they could try to approach them. Japanese patrols too came close as this was in effect no man's land. During one such conversation, a villager rushed in and said one was in fact almost upon them. They were quickly and carefully hidden behind sacks of rice in the hut. After the all clear, great care was taken to feed and protect them. They did what they could for each other – a better hiding place was made for them and the soldiers helped the couple's sick child with the few medicines they had left. After this, the villagers said the soldiers must go as their presence was a danger for everyone. Their host was the headman and rejected this, but as another Japanese patrol was expected any day, Pillai and Radhakrishnan decided not to impose on him any longer. After what seemed like a long and eventful stay, but was in fact just three days, they left. The young villager's parting gift was some money to help them on their way.

Home, at last

When they set off, once again they came across a water obstacle, a river 150 feet wide in the middle. To cross it they constructed a raft made from cloth and timber salvaged from a dilapidated hut nearby. Pillai was to haul Radhakrishnan across on it, but again he was hesitant. Fortunately, they soon met a passing boatman who took them across and even returned half the fare he had taken at the start. They did not know it then, but they had almost reached their destination. They knew when a few miles down they came across a sign for Fort White, a British camp.

---

* Dah is a large sharp knife.

When they stumbled across an Indian Army patrol headed by a Sikh Havildar, they must have thought their troubles were over. They told him they were Indian Army officers who had been fighting in Burma and had got lost – they decided not to say they were from Singapore as they would not have been believed. Seeing their bedraggled appearance, the Havildar did not believe the Burma story either, and told them to move back. Frustrated, Pillai shouted abuse in army Hindustani back to the Havildar. Knowing that such language could only be known to a real Indian Army man, he relented and took them to his camp. It was August 2, less than three months since their escape on May 7. After 3,000 miles through enemy territory, they had finally made it. They had covered roughly 1,000 miles each on foot, boat and train. Bullock carts, the tops of buses, motor boats, canoes, sampans, mules and ponies had also been used. But eventually they had arrived, so it was all worth it and so not such a bad journey after all.

Their unexpected arrival created quite a stir

They were passed from company to battalion to brigade to division, and moved onwards through Aizwal, Silchar, Calcutta and finally reached Army Headquarters in Delhi on August 25, 1942. The British had so far no reliable information on what was going on in Singapore, Malaya, Thailand and Burma and Pillai and Radhakrishnan were the first officers who could inform them of conditions there for POWs, civilians and the Japanese. Military Intelligence debriefed them, and even General Wavell, the Commander-in-Chief of the Indian Army, sat in on some of these. After the debriefs, Pillai had an interview with Wavell who told him his was a story to be repeated to grandchildren and worthy of a book, but advised him to write it after the war. Five days after they reached Delhi, Wavell recommended both for a Military Cross, the third highest decoration British medal for valour in the field.

Chapter 5

THE RASH BEHARI BOSE ERA

Japan Rampant[1]

While Pillai and Radhakrishnan made their way from Burma to Assam and onwards to Delhi in August 1942, the war in East Asia reached a turning point, with the first land invasion by the Allies of Japanese occupied territory, the small island of Guadalcanal to the north-east of Australia. In the last 8 months the Japanese advance had been incredible, leaving the Allies and the locals reeling, so at that time this invasion did not seem like a turning point, but it was the first step in what was to be a 3-year long slog of rolling back their advance.

The Japanese Blitzkrieg had begun on December 8, 1941, with simultaneous attacks on Hong Kong, Malaya, Singapore, the Philippines and the US naval base at Pearl Harbor in Hawaii (on December 7 local time). It had taken the Allies totally by surprise. In rapid succession, Thailand agreed on December 10 to their territory being used for the invasion of Burma, Hong Kong fell on Christmas Day 1941, the Malayan peninsula on January 31, and Singapore on February 15. The next round of invasions led to the fall of Rangoon on March 7, Java on March 12, the Andamans* on March 23, and Sumatra on March 28. Only the Philippines took months and not weeks to collapse, with the Americans finally surrendering on May 8.

Besides the petroleum, rubber and palm oil in Southeast Asia that the Japanese sought,[2] they also wanted the rich mineral and agricultural resources of Australia, and to deny it from being used as a base for an Allied counterattack. Moving south on the way there, in what is today Papua New Guinea, Japan captured the strategic base of Rabaul and parts of the island of New Guinea in January 1942. Then they brought the war to the Australian mainland with bombing raids on Darwin on February 19.

Meanwhile the Imperial Japanese Navy ventured on a raid in the Indian Ocean, bombing Colombo and Trincomalee in April 1942. They seemed everywhere and unstoppable. By now, the extent of their attacks spread from Ceylon in the west to

---

*   The Andaman and Nicobar Islands are an archipelago in the middle of the Bay of Bengal and part of India.

Hawaii in the east, and from Aleutian Islands in the north to Darwin in the south. At this time, India and Ceylon were wide open and had they invaded then, would have faced little resistance. But the Japanese followed a plan, and they had none to invade India then, so did not. But these attacks certainly alarmed Britain, India and Ceylon, creating widespread panic.

A Last Gasp

However, though it did not seem like it at that time, these attacks were a last gasp in the initial phase of the war in East Asia when they had succeeded beyond their wildest imaginations. For very soon the Japanese and US navies fought two battles, in the Coral Sea to the east of Australia in May 1942 and off Midway Island in the central Pacific the next month. They were the first naval battles where opposing ships did not see each other, and all the combat was by planes attacking the enemy at great distances from the aircraft carriers they were based on. The Japanese lost the bulk of their carrier fleet, that served as the backbone for shielding invasions and keeping the Allies at bay in the vast Pacific Ocean. The ships and the men who died were irreplaceable, and the Japanese lost the tactical advantage they had so far. Strategically of course, by attacking the USA with its vast industrial might, they had bitten off more than they could chew. It was only a matter a time before the tables would be turned.

Allies regroup in Australia

Australia was indeed used by the Allies for a springboard to launch a counterattack. General Douglas MacArthur had been the Commander of the United States Army in the Far East based in the Philippines. Forced to evacuate to Australia in March 1942 before advancing Japanese forces, in April he was appointed Supreme Allied Commander of the South West Pacific Area (SWPA). His job was to roll back the Japanese advance, island by island, until they eventually reached Japan. After a few weeks spent building up reinforcements, on August 7, 1942, he invaded Guadalcanal, captured by Japan just three months ago in May. It was an iconic six-month long struggle that lives in the annals of war as one of the most fiercely fought battles, forcing the Japanese to finally evacuate on March 9, 1943. To use Winston Churchill's famous words after the Battle of El-Alamein in North Africa that marked a turning point in the war in the west, Guadalcanal was "not the end. It is not even the beginning of the end. But it is, perhaps, the end of the beginning".*

---

* Speech at the Lord Mayor's Day luncheon, November 10, 1942.

The War with Hitler

Using this opportunity to see what was happening in the western sector of the war, El-Alamein had stopped the relentless advance of the German Field Marshall Erwin Rommel who had almost reached the gates of Cairo in North Africa. The oil fields of the Middle East vital for Hitler's war effort had been almost at hand. In Russia, despite being stopped within eyesight of Stalin's Moscow in December 1941, Hitler had launched a summer offensive in 1942, and his forces were driving south towards the oil fields of the Caucasus to meet up with Rommel who was expected from North Africa. German U-boats were winning the Battle of the Atlantic, sinking over 6 million tons of Allied shipping bringing badly needed food, raw materials, equipment and US soldiers and airmen to reinforce Britain, the last man standing next to Nazi Germany. Despite the first Allied victories at Guadalcanal and El-Alamein, at this stage both the wars – against Germany and Japan – were poised at a razor's edge.

The Aftermath of Mohan Singh's Disbandment of the INA

With this background, we now head back to Singapore. Mohan Singh was arrested on December 29, 1942, for defying the Japanese order to send INA troops to Burma. He had done so as they had so far refused to formalize the alliance between them. With his arrest, the First INA, as it came to be called, was no more and his absence left a huge void. If 1942 was the Mohan Singh era, the next few months of 1943 were that of Rash Behari Bose. Despite being the formal head of the Indian independence movement in East Asia since March 1942, the main force so far had been Mohan Singh and his INA. Now, RB Bose had to take on the mantle of being the leading Indian, and he did.

Varied Emotions

Away from the politics between India and Japan, what did the disbandment of the INA mean for the Indian POW? Reactions varied. Some were relieved they would not have to fight again, those who had been coerced into volunteering were happy. Some officers senior to Mohan Singh were glad to see him gone. But despite such positive emotions, there was an underlying uncertainty – what was to happen now? Were the Japanese just going to let them remain as POWs working in Singapore? Or were the rumours that they were going to be sent to hard labour camps in New Guinea true? Things were back in the melting pot just like after the fall of Singapore almost a year ago and the suspense left everyone insecure.[3]

Once again, there were those who wanted to restart the INA and others who wanted nothing to do with it. The main in charge, Colonel Iwakuro, was clear. It must be reinstated. There was no officer who could take on Mohan Singh's mantle, and besides the Japanese did not want another strong man, so they turned to RB Bose, and it was his valiant effort that prevented the INA from disintegrating. Using a set of officers who supported a second INA,[4] he played on the fears of the men. Initially the disbandment by Mohan Singh was considered valid as they had sworn a personal oath to him and so he had the right to do so. Now they were asked whether it was right for them to have sworn such an oath and was it legal for him to have disbanded the INA? Just because of a difference with the Japanese, should the independence movement be stopped? Most importantly, as the Japanese refused to accept former INA men as POWs, what would happen to them?[5]

Iwakuro meets the Indians

Removing all uncertainty, these questions were clearly answered by Iwakuro. At an address to 300 officers at Bidadari camp on February 6, 1943, he criticized Mohan Singh's actions and said the Japanese government did not recognize his dissolution of the INA. One of the concerns was that the Japanese only wanted a small INA force in Burma that could not be an invasion force and only for propaganda. To brush this aside, he said that for freedom a big army was not needed, just 5,000 patriots. His most important statement was that reverting to POW status was not possible and if they persisted, they would be shipped off to labour camps in the Southwest Pacific Area. He ended by saying that as they had enjoyed Japanese hospitality with better food and living conditions by being in the INA, if they left they would be treated worse than POWs. The implications were clear – they had to choose between directing their energies in the lusty renaissance of the INA, or being dispatched as fatigue parties to the SWPA.[6]

Rash Behari Bose labours on

While Iwakuro played bad cop, Rash Behari Bose donned the role of good cop and worked hard to get the INA back. He published a short pamphlet "Our Struggle" where he outlined the imperatives of fighting for India's independence and doing so now when the British were under attack. He also expressed his shock at discovering the atrocities of Mohan Singh when soldiers were shot, tortured, humiliated and sent to concentration camps. Though he had been fully aware of this and did nothing earlier, he promised that there would be no more coercion. Inviting officers individually and in groups to his bungalow in Mount Pleasant, he tried to get them on his side. To address the men, he went from camp to camp where he was often insulted but laboured on. There were questions about him that he was forced to address, such as why was his son fighting in the Japanese Army? He explained that as he had settled in Japan, his son had to follow the rules and join the army, and that when the time came would fight in the INA. He said that Mohan Singh had been removed as he had defied the civilian leader of the movement (himself). He tried to brush aside the concern about Japan's true intentions about India, stressed that the issue was not confidence in them but in themselves as Indians. Though he had to face great indignity to keep the INA alive, with great patience the old revolutionary was able to revive it.[7]

Community driven decisions

Despite all his efforts, there was one factor that he could not do much about, the community feeling that seemed to be predominant. Most Sikhs stayed away due to their loyalty to Mohan Singh. Punjabi Muslims, many of whom were in the Sikh dominated Punjab regiments, decided to follow their comrades and stayed out, as did most Dogras, and others who felt forced into the First INA. The Garhwalis, Jats and Kumaonis largely decided to stay. The Gurkhas were again approached by the Japanese claiming a racial affinity. Most had not joined the first INA and decided to stay out.*[8]

The Questionnaire

To the INA officers, RB Bose sent a questionnaire asking for their views on Indian independence, if they wished to rejoin the INA and if not, why. He was very irritated by those who said no. Calling each one for an interview he asked why they had joined in the first place? He also told them if they persisted to stay out, he would have to hand them over to the Japanese. Iwakuro was more direct. He visited the camps again and told the recalcitrant officers they would be sent to the SWPA to be bombed by the Allies in the front lines, and wither away with malaria and dysentery. Despite this, 50 of the 190 INA officers decided to stay out. Then, taking a leaf from Mohan Singh's book, they were segregated, first in bungalows on Orchard Road and Bukit Timah, and then taken to the police barracks in Johore Bahru, guarded by the same men who had been at Mohan Singh's concentration camp. After visits by INA supporters to

---

* Dogra's, Gurkha's, Garhwali's Jats and Kumaoni's were from North India and Nepal, many of whom traditionally served in the army.

convince them, when they remained adamant, they were asked if Mohan Singh was released would they stay? About half agreed.[9]

Mohan Singh was certainly not going to be freed, but after all these shenanigans, about 165 out of 190 officers of the First INA decided to join the Second. All were asked to sign a volunteer form. It asked one question to which a Yes or No answer was needed – "Are you prepared to remain in the current INA under the conditions issued?" The conditions were a one-page note that stated the goal of independence and stressed obedience to the civilian leadership. It included many aspirations, that the INA would be considered an allied army by Japan, would be used only to invade India, and upon freedom, the Indian government would be asked to retain the INA as a nucleus of the future army of India. As the Japanese had not yet agreed to formalize the arrangement, all of this was wishful thinking. Most had already decided which way they would go. But if anyone needed a nudge this aspirational document helped.[10]

Bhonsle and Kiani

From the officers who rejoined, a new command structure was announced on February 20, 1943, splitting control between two men, Lieutenant-Colonel Jagannath Rao Krishnarao Bhonsle, 5/5 Mahrattas, appointed as Director Military Bureau, with a role like a Minster for Defence, and Lieutenant-Colonel Mohammed Zaman Kiani, 1/14 Punjab, as Chief of Staff of the INA, with both reporting to RB Bose. Bhonsle, was a well-respected Maratha from Sandhurst and one of the most senior officers in Singapore. Kiani was from Mohan Singh's old unit and the second most senior Muslim officer present.[11]

What were they thinking?

Meanwhile, with the recalcitrant ringleaders kept away in Johore, RB Bose asked the soldiers for a clear decision. After earlier playing good cop, he removed the velvet glove to show his iron fist. He told them that anyone who stayed out would be shipped to the SWPA, and that the convoy they had left last month had been sunk with many deaths. Ships were coaling in the harbour waiting to take them away if they did not rejoin. The Sikhs were taunted – they were told they had saved the British in 1857* and were doing so again. Despite this, 5,000 of the 16,000 INA

---

* In 1857, Indian soldiers had risen against their British masters who were saved by a force of largely Sikhs who helped them regain control.

men refused to rejoin. They were all moved to the Seletar POW camp and stripped of their belongings, most remaining in just the clothes they were standing in. After a last-ditch effort of scaring them, a few decided to remain, leaving a final total of 4,500 holdouts.[12]

These men who had been in Mohan Singh's INA and decided to stay out had been offered a clear choice – rejoin the Second INA where they would have a chance to fight for India's freedom with Japan's help and return home as heroes, or be treated worse than POWs, get shipped to the SWPA to face horrible conditions. And even then, only if they arrived, bearing in mind that the last convoy had been sunk. They made an incredible choice. It was not that they had suddenly realized a loyalty to the British, or did not want India's freedom. It was a feeling of distrust about the Japanese and of loyalty to Mohan Singh. For this they decided to give up the chances of their own survival, despite all the odds being against them.

A Hole that could not be filled

To fill the gap, the INA was forced to spread its net wider. A recruiting team was sent to the Malayan mainland in March 1943 where there were an additional 8,000 Indian POWs who had been largely left out of the recruitment in 1942 as there were more volunteers in Singapore than the Japanese were willing to arm. They were falsely told that half of the recalcitrant lot in Seletar had rejoined, and more were coming across every day, when in fact only 10% did. The team going from Singapore was prepped on what questions to expect and the best answers to give. On the overall pool of POWs, initially the focus was on the traditional martial races (as defined by the British) of Sikhs and Punjabi Muslim's, but as that well dried up, they decided to recruit Gujjars and Ahirs. By the end of May, 2,500 more had joined, but a gap of 2,000 remained and it was acknowledged this was difficult to fill[13].

All this time, Rash Behari was the only Indian who the Japanese allowed to wield any authority. A conference was held in Singapore at the end of April 1943, to formally anoint him as all-powerful. In the words of the INA Diary, "Mr. Rash Behari Bose is the constitution (Dictator) of the Indian Independence Movement in the Far East".* But he was just a placeholder, and a powerful replacement had been on the way.[14]

---

* INA Diary pg28, INA Papers File 161 in National Archives of India.

Chapter 6

THE SYMBOLISM OF SUBHAS CHANDRA BOSE*

Mohan Singh's arrest in December 1942 created a void that could not be filled by anyone then in Singapore. For the time being, the Japanese propped up Rash Behari Bose who valiantly tried to keep the INA alive. However, a more dynamic leader was needed, so it was then that the Japanese arranged for another Bose to be brought to Singapore. He was Subhas Chandra Bose, one of the most well-known Indian nationalists.

Born on January 23, 1897, into a prominent Bengali family, in 1921 he was selected as a Probationer into the Indian Civil Service, the most prestigious job in India. Instead he joined the Congress Party to agitate for India's independence, becoming its President in 1938. After differences with Gandhi on how to oppose the British, he left and continued his activities through other means. A little over a year after World War II began in Europe, Bose escaped from under the eyes of the British in Calcutta in January 1941. During what would be the last of several times he had been imprisoned by the British for his agitations, he threatened to go on a hunger strike. His jailers decided not to risk turmoil in case he died and released him, but kept him under close watch.

Bose and Bhagat Ram Talwar

However, the British did not watch Bose closely enough and he slipped their net and made his way west across India towards Afghanistan. He was helped out of India and aided in Kabul by Bhagat Ram Talwar, a Hindu Pathan, who guided him on how to purport himself as a Muslim to fit his disguise. Rebuffed by German and Russian diplomats there, Bose was aided by the Italians, given a passport in the

---

* In *The Lost Hero* pg381, Mihir Bose also refers to Bose's symbolism.

name of Orlando Mazottab and taken to Moscow. Once again he reached out o the Russians, who showed no interest.[1]

Frustration in Berlin

Once Bose left Kabul he made his way through Russia and reached Berlin on April 2, 1941. Bose believed that India would achieve independence only by fighting for it, and needed outside help to do so. It was curious that he chose to seek the aid of the most racist leader in modern history, Hitler, who had written very derogatory things about Indians in *Mein Kampf*.[2] He would have also known that if he did agree to help, Hitler would extract his pound of flesh. Perhaps he thought, first let us get to Delhi and he would handle that problem then. Nonetheless, Bose was aware that working with Hitler would not look good and for over a year did not declare his presence there to the press. He had arrived hoping that a proposal to thwart their common enemy, Britain, would be appealing, but his stay in Berlin was very frustrating. He got no real support and was kept waiting for months to meet Hitler. However, he did get permission to raise an Indian Legion from soldiers fighting in North Africa with the British and captured by Germany. Eventually, of 17,000 POWs, 3,000 volunteered. But the Legion was very different from the INA, as it was commanded and armed by the German army, with each man being vetted and trained by them. When they joined, they took an oath in German to Hitler and Bose. They wore German uniforms with a patch badge of a springing tiger, representing Tipu Sultan, the biggest thorn in Britain's flesh in the late eighteenth century. Eventually the legion was not used for its original purpose as the hoped-for German advance towards India did not materialise.[3]

Bose's Sole Meeting with Hitler

After a long wait of thirteen months, Bose finally met Hitler in May 1942. Hitler spoke for most of the hour long meeting, and Bose was hardly able to get in a word. He asked Hitlerto support the announcement of a provisional government of free India. Hitler said that doing so was pointless now as India was too far away from where Germany was fighting. What was unsaid is that he admired Britain, despite bombing her every day, and retained a romantic notion of the two nations ruling the world together, of course under his control. He did not want India to be free, but remain under Britain.[4] Even in the short term, he did not see any benefit for Germany.

Bose was so disappointed that he did not discuss what happened with his team. He later told his inner circle that Hitler was "Buddhpagal" (in Bengali, mad in the head).[5]

The Windfall from Mohan Singh

Bose then switched his focus to Japan. While he had been in Europe, the war in East Asia had begun with them capturing vast territory and supporting the formation of the INA. Despite having spoken to RB Bose by phone in January 1942 and radio broadcasts and messages to the movement in Asia, he had little control over them. After his failed meeting with Hitler, he was desperate to go east. But despite earlier having asked for him to be sent to Asia, at that time the Japanese did not want him. They already had their more amenable RB Bose and knew that Subhas Bose could not be controlled. It was only when Mohan Singh disbanded the first INA that they asked for him in January 1943. RB Bose was not respected due to his long association with Japan, and was unwell. They needed someone else. Even if it was the uncontrollable Subhas Bose, it had to be him.[6]

On the *U180* from Kiel

Arrangements were made quickly and on February 8, 1943, Bose left the German port of Kiel in the Baltic Sea in the German submarine *U180*. His only companion was Abid Hasan, who he had come to know in Germany and now served as his secretary. Luckily for them, Hasan managed to find some rice and lentils and made daal-baht* that they survived on. Threading its way through waters controlled by the Allies, *U180* rendezvoused with the Japanese submarine *I29* off the coast of Madagascar on April 27. Each submarine had valuable cargo to be exchanged. The Germans had to handover Bose and Hasan, samples of weapons and documents from the Japanese Embassy in Berlin. The Japanese had to pass on 2 tons of gold to pay for military equipment, plans for their aircraft carrier, sample weapons and also had two senior naval officers tasked with examining the U-boat. The seas were too rough for the submarines to come close enough for the valuable cargo to walk across, so eventually two Germans swam across to the Japanese and then came back in a rubber dinghy hauling a thick rope with them. Bose and Hasan then stepped into it and hauled

---

* Rice and lentil soup.

and paddled their way laboriously towards the Japanese submarine, sometimes disappearing from view in the rough swell of the sea. Exhausted, they finally reached the submarine and were dragged on board. As the rest of their cargo was exchanged, the submarines were sitting ducks but their luck held and both reached home safely. *I29* did not return to its base of Penang as rumours had been swirling. The flotilla commander had personally been on board and watchers noticed Indian food including curry powder being loaded. Immediately word spread like wildfire that Bose was coming as had been expected. The Japanese were worried British intelligence may have heard about this, so headed instead to Sumatra, anchoring at Subang island on May 6, where Bose was greeted by his acquaintance Colonel Yamamoto Hayashi, formerly the Japanese Military Attaché in Berlin.[7]

Bose and Hasan

Throughout the three-month long journey, Bose had been reading, making notes and preparing for what was to come next. He made Hasan perform role plays, as the Japanese Premier General Tojo. Bose knew this meeting had to go better than the one with Hitler. He reviewed what little he knew about what happened in 1942 with the independence movement. He had heard that Mohan Singh had lost patience and resigned. He felt that perhaps with some perseverance he could have got what he wanted, and this act may have been short sighted. After all, Bose thought, how did it matter if the INA did something that helped Japan but not India, if it eventually achieved its own objectives as well? Bose agreed with the Japanese that as the Indian movement was not a government, it could not be treated as one. He would approach things differently. He would demonstrate that the movement was not just useful for intelligence, but for its overall propaganda effect. At this stage, slogans were more important than action. He would form a provisional government as Japan itself had proposed earlier, be a dynamic leader and mobilize men and money to be independent. He was confident of himself. Mohan Singh had asked for him as early December 1941 and so had many others later. His welcome was assured.[8]

The British knew Bose was coming, having decoded *U180*'s messages. He could not be dismissed as a tool of the Japanese and had considerable influence on Indians inside and outside India, as well as on Indian soldiers. However, at this stage (early 1943) they felt morale was high in India, and there seems to have been no concerted effort to sink the submarine and stop him from travelling.[9]

Bose Impresses Tojo

When he reached Sabang, Bose was ready to go to Tokyo immediately, but due to military delays arrived ten days later in a torpedo bomber. He was anxious to meet Tojo, but the war was going badly for Japan and he had a lot on his plate. Besides, he had nothing specific to say about India, and so far the independence movement had just been a headache with their incessant and unrealistic demands. The collapse of the first INA in December 1942 had also left a bad taste in his mouth. But Bose was used to this, having waited thirteen months to meet Hitler. He changed tack and by impressing other Japanese leaders, was able to get Tojo to change his mind. Even then, when they met on June 10, Tojo had planned to just get it out of the way. After all, he had invited him to Tokyo and he must meet him as a courtesy. Bose surprised Tojo with his charm and force of personality and they had a second meeting on June 14 when specifics were discussed and commitments given. The deal was done and on June 16, in Bose's presence, Tojo announced in parliament the unconditional support for India's independence. It was a great achievement. Bose had managed to get more from Japan in one month than Mohan Singh had failed to in six months.[10]

> General Mohan Singh's sacrifice and Rash Behari Bose's patience
> gave us Netaji, a unique leader.[*]

The other consequential meeting Bose had was with the elder Bose, Rash Behari, who had come from Singapore. Handing over to the younger, more vigorous and well-known Bose was a foregone conclusion, decided before he was invited. They spoke about the events of the last eighteen months and all the personalities involved. RB Bose's greatest contribution was that he handed over a fully functional though depleted INA and a civilian organization operating in Southeast Asia. The Second INA that Bose inherited would not have been possible without the First INA of Mohan Singh and RB Bose's valiant attempts to keep it together in the interregnum.[11]

There is only one Netaji

The two Boses flew down together to Singapore and on July 2, 1943 a large reception committee was at Kallang airport where they were expected. They waited

---

[*] *From My Bones – Memoirs by Colonel Gurbaksh Singh Dhillon of the Indian National Army*, Arya Books International 1998, pg199.

for hours, no plane came. Unknown to them, due to rain earlier in the day, the plane had been diverted to Seletar airport. When it landed, there was no one to greet them. Gradually, as news spread, people started arriving one by one and when there were enough to make a procession they made their way to Kallang where the formal reception happened with an INA guard of honour. From there the entourage drove to 61, Meyer Road, a bungalow that was to be Subhas Bose's residence.[12]

There was an immediate change in tone and atmosphere. Bose was not just any leader but Netaji.* In Hindi "neta" means leader and "ji" is a sign of added respect, so Netaji literally translates into respected leader. It was a term of respect and affection chosen by the Indians in Germany and Bose wished it to be used in Asia. The title stuck and even today, though there are many "neta's" in India, there is only one Netaji, him.

Cathay Cinema

Bose gave his first public address on July 4 at one of the most prominent buildings of Singapore, the Cathay cinema. Crowds lined the streets waiting for a glimpse of him and ignored the drizzle. The 1,300 capacity hall was packed. On the dais were the Japanese flag and the Indian tricolour. Addressing the crowd, RB Bose said he had told them he was getting a present, pointed to Bose, said here he is, and handed over to him. Bose accepted gracefully and then exhorted the crowd to see his vision for India's independence and how they must fight for it. At this and other speeches, he stressed that if any had doubts about Japan's sincerity they should put their trust in him. A total mobilization of men, money, material and the raising of an army of 300,000 including a women's regiment was announced. Finally, he said he would form the Provisional Government of Free India (PGFI) to formalize the movement. His talks left the audience spellbound. He could go on for hours, in English and

---

* The first ref to Bose in the INA Diary is on July 4, 1943 when he is called Srijut (Bengali for sir). On July 5, he is Netaji Srijut. INA Papers File 161, pg34–7. Other steps to fire up patriotism were the use of the greeting Jai Hind. While in Germany, Bose had asked his secretary Hasan to think of a phrase that would appeal to all Indians. From an amalgam of greetings used by the soldiers of the Indian Legion he came up with this catchy greeting that means Long Live India (His Majesty's Opponent, Sugata Bose pg211). Once in Singapore, Hasan also worked with Syed Mumtaz Hussain and Major Aziz Ahmed, Kapurthala Infantry to translate into Hindustani a Bengali song by Rabindranath Tagore which became Jana Gana Mana, now India's national anthem (Hasan). This replaced *Saare Jahan Se Accha* (India is the best place in the world) in use in Mohan Singh's time, still a patriotic Indian song.

Hindustani, and even if they did not understand him (as many Tamilians could not), his tone converted many.[13]

The Caesar at Padang

A flurry of activity followed. The next day, Bose inspected the INA at the Padang, the field before the Singapore City Hall and addressed them with their new name, the Azad Hind Fauj (Army of Free India in Hindustani). The slogan *Chalo Dilli* (Onwards to Delhi) made its debut here. The following day, there was a repeat performance, this time with Tojo standing next to him. Though Tojo had come for other purposes,[14] the timing was fortuitous and getting him there, a huge diplomatic coup. On July 9 at the same venue was a mammoth public rally with over 50,000 civilians, almost all the Indians in Singapore. It started raining heavily, and when he brushed aside an umbrella offered to him, the crowd roared in appreciation. Asking for donations, women rushed to give him their *mangal-sutra** and other jewellery. When he announced the launch of the all-female Rani of Jhansi regiment, the crowd erupted in a hurrah. Bose was described by some as a Caesar, conquering all before him.[15]

The PGFI

The most significant step was the proclamation of the PGFI on October 21, 1943. This was aimed at giving the so far informal movement official status. But what was a provisional government of free India that was still under British rule? It was a strange animal, a "government in waiting" formed by Indians outside India. Torturous negotiations preceded this announcement. The Japanese in Singapore had been aghast when they first heard of it. Tojo must have consented earlier, but had not thought the details through nor passed it down the chain. Tokyo eventually decided to recognize it for its propaganda benefit, but not formally exchange ambassadors. Bose would have to continue to deal with the army's Colonel Yamamoto. But these were irrelevant details to him. What mattered were the headlines when the PGFI was announced and recognized by all the Axis powers, their satellites, and Ireland. Bose made himself Head of State, Prime Minister, Minister for War and Foreign Affairs and took an oath to India, and the cabinet ministers he chose swore one to him. It was clear who was in charge. His first action was to declare war against

---

* *Mangal-sutra* is a necklace representing an Indian woman's married status, and considered the most emotionally valuable jewellry they possess.

Britain and the USA. When questioned by one lone cabinet member whether there was need to include the USA as their fight was only with the British, he replied it would be neither ethical nor expedient to exclude them. The unpleasant reality was that there were US troops on Indian soil who would fight with the British to ward off a Japanese invasion, so if the INA came along, they would have to fight and defeat the Americans as well.[16]

The Rani's and Dr Lakshmi Bai

The day after the action packed launch of the PGFI was the start of what was Bose's greatest brainchild. It was October 22, the birthday of the Rani of Jhansi, Lakhsmi Bai,* and on that day the Regiment named after her was inaugurated by him. An all-women's unit, the first set of recruits paraded in sarees with their rifles. Its commander was Captain Dr Lakshmi Swaminathan. From a prominent family in South India, Dr Swaminathan had moved to Singapore in 1940 and was one of the most well-known Indians there, a natural choice for the job. Recommended to Bose for this role, she was awestruck after meeting him and took to her role like a duck to water. She was full of regard for her women (and girls as some were still in their teens), and they considered her not just their commander, but a sister, guardian and guide. Captain Dr Lakshmi Swaminathan had the incredible coincidence of sharing a first name with the famous Rani Lakshmi Bai, and her role and fame was ubiquitous. Juxtaposing the two, many called her Dr Lakshmi Bai.[17]

Bose had asked for INA soldiers to train them, with only one demand – no swearing, endemic on army parade grounds all over the world. The Pathan and Sikh soldiers training them were hence heard shouting, "Theek Nahin, Jawan, Akal Se Kaam Lo, Jawan, Hasna Nahin Jawan", (not right soldier, use your brains soldier and no laughing soldier). This was one of Bose's most popular ideas as it galvanised one half of the Indians, women, in a way that had not happened earlier. Many of the Ranis, as they were called, recalled this period as the greatest time of their life.[18]

Bose and the Indian POWs

Besides the feel good work, there were difficult tasks for Bose, such as recruiting more men. When he arrived in July 1943, there were 42,000 Indian POWs in

---

* Rani of Jhansi is a famous heroine in Indian history. As the Regent for her infant son, she led her army against the British in 1857 and died in battle.

Singapore and Malaya, 15,000 in the INA and 27,000 outside it.[19] Many of the latter had volunteered for Mohan Singh but had not been armed by the Japanese, and he turned to them. All had the threat hanging over the heads that if they did not join, they would be shipped off to islands like New Guinea (referred to as the South West Pacific Area or SWPA).

So far, they had only feared what would happen. But on July 10, a few days after Bose's arrival in Singapore, 600 men who had been sent to Timor in January that year returned. They were in a pitiable state, most of them hospital cases. They told horror stories of what they had endured and how many of the 400 others with them had died. Everyone now knew that the reality was worse than their darkest fears.[20] Bose toured the camps and touted the inevitable victory of Japan and freedom of India. He did not mention the threat of being shipped to the SWPA but added one of his own. After independence, anyone who had not joined him would be sent off to Britain. This may not sound so bad now, but in 1943 being separated from one's family and dumped on the British was not an attractive prospect.[21]

Only a Fraction of the POWs join Bose

These 27,000 men faced the same choice as the 5,000 at Seletar during the RB Bose era did – join the INA or be shipped off to the SWPA. This time the person asking them was no less than Bose, but only 2,000 joined.[22] Compared to the total control of the mind Bose had over the INA men,[23] their reaction seems strange. Bose also asked the Japanese to bring back those already sent to the SWPA so he could recruit them, but they refused[24] and instead sent 2,200 more off in August 1943.[25] He could not stop this, or perhaps did not even try as they had not joined him and so did not interest him. His focus was solely on Indian independence and those who agreed to follow him in achieving it.

Civilian response to Bose

Rejected by most of the Indian Army, Bose shifted focus to civilians. Under Mohan Singh, many volunteered but the Japanese had not agreed to arm them. But Bose was able to get a commitment to do so, and though eventually very few were armed and fought, the euphoria of being recruited was immense.[26] In some cases, a whole family joined, such as that of Abdul Wahab Khan, a doctor in Thailand. He became a Medical Officer, his two sons started training as officers and his wife and daughter became Ranis.[27] For some civilians though, joining the INA was an escape from the lack of food and the threat of being shipped to the SWPA as many had been. It was a difficult time and survival was the priority.[28]

Bose and the INA

Though Bose was clearly in charge of everything from the moment he arrived, he technically became Supreme Commander of the INA only on August 25, 1943. On the advice of his officers he decided not to have a rank. Commanding 15,000 men, a division in most armies, he would normally be a Major-General, but for a person of his stature, even the highest rank, Field Marshall, would not suffice. Bose did not need a rank as he was their Netaji.

The Japanese View of the INA

At the first meeting with his officers he had good and bad news. The bad news, which they probably already knew, was what the Japanese thought of them. He had recently met the commander of their Southern Army in Southeast Asia, Field Marshal Count Terauchi, and had asked for a fighting role for the INA in the vanguard of the impending invasion of India. The Japanese had a low opinion of the INA. Not only had the men surrendered, they had also agreed to fight alongside their erstwhile enemies. Given the code the Japanese lived by, this was incomprehensible. Besides, the INA officers had so far commanded companies of 100 men in the Indian Army, and now led regiments of 3,000 in the INA for which they had no experience. So Terauchi said they would be used in the propaganda role as in the Malaya campaign. Bose told him it was a matter of honour and Indians had to be seen fighting to reclaim India.

The Subhas Regiment

The good news was that Terauchi finally agreed that one regiment would be allowed to fight, but under Japanese command. If it worked well, more would be used. This was a happy compromise for Bose. As he had told the Ranis, it was not the number of rifles and how many times they fired, but the moral effect of them fighting that was important. A crack unit with the best men was formed, named Subhas. The INA was very poorly equipped by the Japanese – the rifles rusty, the machine guns had few spare parts and ammunition, the mortars and cannon unusable without optical sights, and the armoured cars fit only for ceremonial parades. So, the rest of the INA was cannibalised to equip the Subhas Regiment as best as possible.[29]

Bose and Mohan Singh

A connection with the past that Bose eventually had to encounter was Mohan Singh. One could have expected a meeting with the founding INA commander to have occurred as soon as Bose arrived, but it did not. Even though Mohan Singh was no Bose, he was still a threat, especially with the widespread support he had from the powerful Sikh community. Bose did not want anyone else to detract from his cult-like status. Soon after he reached Singapore, Bose was approached by Sikh civilians asking for Mohan Singh's release, to whom he replied it was not possible then, but he would try. He gave a similar answer to Sikh officers. In fact, Mohan Singh had also been wary of Bose when he was in power. Had Bose come in 1942, he would have been eclipsed. Having become all powerful, he did not want that. Despite calls in public for Bose, in private he said it would be easier to get Nehru from Delhi to Singapore than Bose from Berlin. However now things had changed, and the power was with Bose.

The Intermediary, Dr Raju

When Mohan Singh heard of his arrival, he passed on a message through Major Raju who had been his personal physician and was now Bose's, that he was keen to meet. Bose sent him a questionnaire, including whether he would accept him as his leader, here and inside India. Singh baulked at answering this, especially the second part. After holding out for six months, Bose's hand was finally forced by the Japanese who wanted a rapprochement.

The one time the two INA Commanders met

The two met just once, at a bungalow in the east coast of Singapore at the end of December 1943. At first the two spoke alone, and later Raju joined them. Bose did not acknowledge his role in the movement and told him that he had been impatient in disbanding the INA. This offended Mohan Singh, but he offered to work in any capacity, but outside the INA. Bose then said that he had many detractors and his coming back now would be bad for the movement. When asked again if he was willing to accept him as his leader, Mohan Singh replied that in Singapore he would, but in India his leader would be Nehru. This was probably what Bose expected but did not want to hear. They did not meet again, and Bose did not try for his release, though he arranged for him to be taken to a better climate as he was unwell – the next month Mohan Singh was taken to Sumatra where he remained until the end of the war.[30]

Shaheed, Swaraj and Symbolism

> It is not the number of rifles you may carry or the number of shots you may fire which is important. Equally important is the moral effect of your brave example.[*]

The last event of a dramatic six months after Bose's arrival was a visit by him at the end of December 1943 to the Andaman and Nicobar Islands in the Bay of Bengal. The Japanese had announced their handover to the PGFI, the first former Indian territory under their control. The previous month, Bose had returned to Tokyo and had alarmed Tojo by asking for these islands to be handed over. They had been captured in March 1942 and were the first Japanese line of defence for any invasion by the Allies from India. There was no question of handing it over. Once again, Bose succeeded in getting a symbolic concession from the Japanese. They agreed to announce a handover but told him clearly this was for propaganda purposes only. He could visit it, but in secret and news was to be released after it was over. This was enough for Bose – the press in Japanese controlled areas splashed the news of his visit and the renaming of Andamans as Shaheed (martyr) and Nicobar as Swaraj (freedom), a wonderful combination of slogans as well as the use of Urdu and Hindi that appealed to Hindus and Muslims.[31]

As in this case, much of what Bose did was symbolic. As indicated in the quotation above, the image is what he pushed for. What mattered was that there was a PGFI, not that it was just aspirational. What mattered was that there was an INA, not that it was small and ill equipped. Yes, he had declared war against Britain and the USA, but he did he really expect to defeat them? He said he would, as the Indian Army would join him once he reached India. He expected them to behave like the 100 men who had gone to arrest Napoléon and ended up joining him instead.[†] He described it colourfully in speeches to soldiers when he thanked Wavell for expanding the Indian Army, who would join him as soon as he asked, and looked forward to inspecting all of them at the Red Fort in Delhi. But he himself confessed to Mohan Singh this was unlikely, and his officers also told him it would not happen. They were right, and when the time came it did not.[32]

But the slogans and headlines were what Bose was pushing. And he was not wrong about their symbolism, as despite failing in its military objective, the

---

[*] Bose in a speech to the Rani of Jhansi Regiment, *The Indian National Army – Second Front of the Indian Independence Movement*, K.K. Ghosh Meenakshi Prakashan, 1969, pg181.

[†] See *The Indian National Army: Towards a Balanced and Critical Appraisal* published July 25, 2015 in *Economic & Political Weekly* 2015 by Chandar Sundaram (article sent courtesy of the author).

headlines and emotion were dramatic, and the INA's greatest achievement was how it enthused the people of India after the war. More on that later.

The year 1943 ended with a high for Bose. In just six months he had taken over complete control of the INA and the civilian movement, got Japanese support for his Provisional Government of Free India, and galvanised Indian civilians, especially women. Parts of the INA had moved towards Burma and the Japanese were expected to invade India soon. Within a year he might well be raising the Indian flag and taking the salute at Red Fort in Delhi. While that was the image he was trying to convince his followers was in their grasp, what was happening to the POWs? Over 16,000 had been shipped off to the SWPA and it is to their fate that we now turn.

Chapter 7

IN HELL SHIPS TO TORTURE ISLANDS

The Sinking of the *Buyo Maru*

The first set of torpedoes struck the Japanese freighter *Buyo Maru* at 10.47am on January 26, 1943. The ship had left Singapore on January 6 with 497 Indian POWs and 629 Japanese soldiers and crew on board. At first, she was damaged but afloat. But then, forty-eight minutes later, another torpedo hit and "a tremendous explosion blew the structures aft of her bridge as high as a kite" and created "a gigantic hole on her side as big as a Mack truck".* As the ship started sinking, Captain O.A.V. Sen 5/2 Punjab Regiment in charge of the Indians said "The hooter blared, the decks were full with shouting men; the Japanese started jumping overboard and we followed suit".† Four barges and some boats were afloat, and everyone tried climbing aboard. There was not enough space, and the Japanese forced out Indians to make space for themselves. Fortunately, everyone had life vests. Despite this, being marooned in the sea would have been petrifying for even those who could swim. For those who could not, it was a nightmare. For everyone, there were immediate dangers, another torpedo or being sucked into the wake of the *Buyo Maru*. It was not the *Titanic*, but at 5,500 tonnes big enough to take down men with it when sinking. The men tried to hold onto anything they could find – planks of wood, lifeboats or each other.

Cheering in the *Pacific Maru*

The *Buyo Maru* was part of a convoy that included the *Pacific Maru* with 1,500 more Indian POWs. One of them was Jemadar Diwan Singh of the 1st Heavy Anti-Aircraft Regiment who said "we saw two Japanese ships sinking before our own

---

* Wahoo: *The Patrols of America's Most Famous World War II Submarine*, Rear-Admiral Richard H. O'Kane, Random House 2009, pg150.
† Sen AWM 54 1010/4/170, pg47.

eyes and out of joy we gave three cheers". They may or may not have known that fellow soldiers had been on board. Irrespective, it cheered them but infuriated their Japanese guards who shoved them into a smaller area. Already overcrowded, now Singh said "we could only stand like marble pillars". Access to air and light was shut off, the already sparse food and water was reduced further.[*]

Inside the USS *Wahoo*

Underwater, Lieutenant Richard H. O'Kane, the Executive Officer or XO of the submarine USS *Wahoo*, watched the devastation through his periscope. Before the torpedo hit "The fire control party was cheering it on as if it were a horse with their money on its nose".[†] The men aboard the Buyo "commenced jumping over the side like ants off a hot plate. Her stern went up and she headed for the bottom".[‡] There was no time for celebrations as the Wahoo was steered by her Captain, Lieutenant-Commander Dudley Wesley "Mush" Morton to its next target in the convoy. They sank two ships including the *Buyo* and damaged two others including the Pacific. After so much action, Wahoo had to surface at 1.10pm to charge her batteries, and Morton took to the bridge to survey the destruction. What he saw was many boats full of men and hundreds more floating in the water. There were Japanese flags on the boats to attract attention from passing friendly ships. Unfortunately for them, the first vessel to reach them was the *Wahoo*.

"We proceeded to have a field day"[§]

When Morton gave the order for battle stations and to man the guns on the *Wahoo*'s deck, he saw the look on O'Kane's face, and said to him, "Dick...the army bombards strategic areas, and the air corps uses area-bombing so the ground forces can advance. Both bring civilian casualties. Now without other casualties, I will prevent these soldiers from getting ashore, for everyone who does can mean an American life."[¶] He instructed the 5-inch cannon on the *Wahoo*'s deck to fire at the boats and machine gunners to drive the men into the sea. Morton reported that after the first shot, "Our fire was returned by machine gun...Therefore we considered free game to fire not only at the boats but the troops also. We proceeded to have a

---

[*] Jiwan Singh AWM 54 1010/4/164, pg96.
[†] O'Kane, pg150.
[‡] Morton Report, US National Archives, NAID 74859023.
[§] Morton narrative, US National Archives, NAID 278490254.
[¶] O'Kane, pg153.

field day for about an hour". He did not know there were friendlies, Indian POWs in the water too. Sen said, "many of us waved our hands, towels and handkerchiefs, shouting that we were Indian POW, but the submarine was too far off, and did not hear us".

"SHOOT THE SUNZA BITCHES"[*]

Morton was one of the most successful US Navy submarine commanders in World War II, and his attitude towards the Japanese was indicated by 8.5 by 11-inch placards put up all over the *Wahoo* stating in bold letters SHOOT THE SUNZA BITCHES. When he returned to Pearl Harbor on February 7, he flew a flag emblazoned with these words. The shooting of men in the sea was banned by The Hague Convention and this incident created some controversy, but the US Navy backed him up. He led three more missions on the Wahoo and was killed in action on October 11, 1943.

After being caught in this unfortunate crossfire, Sen and his men remained in the sea all that day and most of the next, when they were finally rescued by Pacific Maru that returned, accompanied by a Japanese naval cruiser. Their focus was on picking up the Japanese and they told Sen later any Indian left behind was because they could not swim to them. Sen said, "Some men had died before the rescue, but many were left to their fate". Though some Indians may have been hit by Morton's gunfire, most of the 195 who died in the sinking of the *Buyo* were left behind by the Japanese.[†]

Their troubles did not end there. The Japanese who had been in the sea with them were furious at the Indians for having waved at the *Wahoo*. Besides, drowning Indians had been seen dragging down the Japanese with them in revenge. The exhausted and terrified Indian survivors were ill-treated by their rescuers because of this, all the way back to port, though Sen was better treated in the naval cruiser than those of his men picked up by Pacific. Sepoy Abdullah Khan had been accused of having fought with and killed a Japanese in the sea. When he stepped off the Pacific, he had a rope round his neck and was beaten badly. He died a few days later.

After a brief rest, they boarded another ship and reached their eventual destination, Rabaul on the island of New Britain, north of eastern Australia on February 19, 1943. After one sinking, two ships and a forty-four-day journey through hell, they hoped for a reprieve, but that remained distant.[1]

---

[*] US Naval Institute, July 2003, Proceedings, Vol. 129/7/1,205, O'Kane pg117 says "Shoot the Sons of Bitches".

[†] Of the 195, 72 were 5/2 Punjab, 80 from 2/16 Punjab and 43 from RIASC – Sen INA109.

What did the Japanese want to use Indian POWs for?

Sen's men found themselves in this predicament as the Japanese had very different plans for the Indians from what they originally declared in 1942. They had no intention of arming the INA as an invasion force and used the Indians for their own purposes. Soon after the fall of Singapore, to free up as many Japanese soldiers as possible, 3,000 Indians were used as gunners for air-defence, drivers, mechanics, guards for British POWs in Changi, and engineers to repair oil wells in Borneo destroyed by the Allies. Most of these men were effectively part of the Japanese Army. This was banned under international law, and many resisted, especially the gunners, who were forced into it by Mohan Singh and his men.[2]

The biggest need the Japanese had for Indian POWs was as labour to fortify the vast areas they had conquered in 1942, primarily in Papua New Guinea. To enable this, in October 1942, Colonel Iwakuro took over all the Indian POWs who were not in the INA, including thousands who had volunteered but not armed by him. This was one of the reasons Mohan Singh broke with the Japanese. The first group to be shipped were 500 men, mainly Gurkhas, under Lieutenant Samuel Joseph Talibuddin, RIASC* and Lieutenant Abrar Hussain, 2/10 Baluch Regiment. They left on December 1, 1942, and had a relatively short journey, arriving at Rabaul on December 12. That month 5,500 more Indian POWs were readied to be shipped out. Groups of 500 were formed with a commander assigned to each. In the topsy-turvy world of the INA where Captains became Generals and Majors became Sepoys, many of the leaders were senior to others in the group. To reduce resistance, they were told their destination was the safer Malayan mainland or nearby Java.

Sen was part of this large group. On January 5, 1943, he collected his men and when marching out of camp the Japanese refused to let the last 3 men pass as they said the required 500 were present. Sen protested saying they were only 497, but to no avail, so he was forced to leave with 3 men short. They boarded trucks, but instead of the railway station to take them to the expected destination of Port Dixon in Malaya, they headed to the port. There he was beaten by a Japanese officer for having brought three men less. His protests went unheeded. They boarded the Buyo Maru and Jiwan Singh's group the Pacific Maru and sailed away to the fateful encounter with USS *Wahoo*.[3]

---

* As in other cases of split families, his brother Captain A.B. Talibuddin, IMS was a prominent and early INA supporter.

Captain Patel's Diary

For the next few months in 1943 the Japanese waited for the crisis, after Mohan Singh disbanded the first INA, to settle down. By March 1943, it was sorted with the 4,500 who refused to rejoin collected at Seletar camp. We can live through the fears and pressures these men faced in the month before they left, through an astonishing wartime survival, the diary of 33-year-old Captain Jaganath Haribhai Patel of Ahmedabad.[*] He was a doctor with a degree from Grant College Bombay who joined the army in 1940, soon after the outbreak of the war in Europe. Posted to Malaya, he joined Mohan Singh's INA and left when it was disbanded.

April starts on a happy note with "Fun and fooling during April 1" and "Baisakhi[†] celebrations".

On April 16 rumours swirl of them being handed back to the INA, then the opposite of being shipped out in seven groups.

The next day, Captain Asiruddin Jahangir, 1st Bahawalpur Infantry, a 6-foot tall, 31 year old from Loharu in today's Haryana in India came to the camp. An early and staunch INA supporter, haranguing them he said "you are the worst enemies and (so) you can keep only one pair of shorts, one shirt, one blanket and ground sheet", so people hid their clothes.

To prevent resistance the comfort was offered that "some will be taken to mainland" referring to the nearby and comparatively comfortable Malaya, "some overseas" referring to the scarier unknown of the far islands in the South West Pacific Area.

April 19 – He heard one Indian Colonel was to be sent, so many of them reported sick.
In an example of how rumours spread, he wrote that Unny said Richard said that Major Ogawa said, "previous INA non-volunteers were cowards, and new INA non-volunteers are our enemies, therefore they should get the worst treatment". It is very likely this was true.

April 21 – To rejoin the INA, he was bribed with a promotion "tried to persuade me to become a volunteer…good chance of becoming Major".

April 22 – Told that "Japanese will go to India. No intention of conquering whole of India. Will take Assam and Bengal".
"Heard that 26 people will not go for fatigues (overseas)"

April 24 – "said to be going in warship, but when and where unknown…People got worried. Says 10 days in ship – got frightened but nobody became volunteer"

---

* Patel Diary, INA 225 pg165 onwards.
† Baisakhi is the North Indian name for the spring harvest festival, celebrated across the country with different names.

April 25 – "Heard one Colonel was detailed for overseas", so many of them reported sick to avoid being picked "and therefore Col Chawla detailed"

"Unny said Richard had been to HQ" where he met Major Ogawa who said, "previous INA non-volunteers were cowards, and new INA non-volunteers are our enemies, therefore they should get the worst treatment".

April 29 – heard a ship that left a few days was torpedoed 50 miles away "thought it to be a rumour to frighten people".

"PUNASWAMI…Refused to take a lift" in car with 2 INA Colonels who asked him why "he had got out of the INA…replied even if he died would never (re)join". One of the Colonels "said he joined to save a few families. PUNAWAMI said troops would be 300 miles ahead of you and what would you people in HQ do if you wanted to save some families? Why are you trying to be in HQ? PUNASWAMI told about a Japanese NCO beating IMAMDIN ... party commander an Indian then how can you prevent a Japanese soldier raping?" The Colonel: could not reply".

April 30　"Heard that there will be 20,000 in the convoy, 12,000 Indian, 4,000 British and 4,000 Japanese…Instead of SUMATRA…going to Java". The men wanted news to be broadcast to the Allies, expecting not to be attacked if that was done – they were unaware of attacks on Buyo Maru and that any Japanese ship was fair game, even if it had POWs.

Jemadar Sharma, IMS, was asked by Rash Behari Bose why he had joined INA last time, and replied "I was a bloody fool last time, I don't want to be a bloody fool now".

The various nicknames of INA were "Indo Nippon Army, Indian Nutritional Army, I Never Advance Army".

May 2 – "heard the rumour of Bose's arrival for the third time".

On May 4, the day before Patel was to be marched out, he escaped to town without permission to get his teeth cleaned – he had been denied permission all month.

May 5 – they leave camp in trucks at 5.00am to go to the harbour.

Patel and all the men at Seletar joined thousands from other camps in the biggest shipment of Indian POWs to the SWPA in early May 1943. At the last minute about 50 men at Seletar got a reprieve, some being kept back for special treatment, others as they were ill or too old. In the confusion of boarding, the Dogra Sepoy Fejoo Ram, 5/14 Punjab, a wrestler, was jostled by a Japanese guard and struck back at him grabbing his bayonet. He was in turn bayoneted (not fatally) by other guards and forced to board. It was a time of great worry for these men and there were similar incidents. Eventually that week, two convoys left Singapore with 8,000 Indian POWs as well as Asian civilians forced to share their plight.[4]

The Lush Jungles and Isolation of the South West Pacific Area

These unfortunate men were taken to various islands such as New Guinea, New Britain, New Ireland, Bougainville, Manus, Palau, Guadalcanal, Solomons, Timor in the Pacific and Java, Sumatra, Borneo and Bali in Southeast Asia. The latter are parts of modern Indonesia, Brunei and Malaysia. The Pacific islands are all clustered north of Australia and had been captured as a base for the expected Japanese invasion of that country. New Guinea, over 300,000 square miles, is the third largest island in the world. At that time, the western half was part of the Dutch East Indies, and the eastern half a former German colony administered by Australia after World War I, as were New Britain and New Ireland. The others were under a mix of French, Japanese and British control before World War II. Lush tropical islands, they held horrible memories for the Allied POWs and Asian civilians made to labour in harsh conditions to fortify them for the Japanese. Eventually, over 17,000 Indian POWs were sent to the SWPA, but only 7,000 survived.[5]

Can Inferno be Worse?[*]

The voyage out was described as hell, torture or inferno by all aboard. Crammed into suffocating holds with just crouching space, little food and even less water, no fresh air, they endured voyages of up to two months without knowing where they were going and when they would reach. Scores died on the way. The journey is best described by Warrant Officer Clerk John Baptist Crasta, RIASC, a 31-year-old Indian Christian from Kinnigoli near Mangalore. After he arrived in Singapore in 1941, he witnessed the chaos of the campaign, and then the uncertainty of 1942, when he stayed out of the INA. One of the unlucky ones to be shipped out, he sailed on May 2, 1943. Crammed into the freighter Victoria Maru with 3,000 Indian POWs in holds divided with planks of wood into spaces three feet high, one could enter and exit only by crawling. He called it a "Torture Ship". The floor space for each man was 3 feet by 1 foot, so they could not sleep. It was suffocating, dark, stinking and hot with the boiler nearby. "Could Inferno be worse?" he asked.

The convoy sailed slowly south, and they were given a handful of rice, some dry fish and a cup of water twice a day. The Japanese said as they were resting, they needed less food. Crasta did not mind the meagre food, but with two cups of water a day "one might die of thirst". If they tried to go on deck, they were beaten.

---

* Inferno – from *Eaten by the Japanese*, John Baptist Crasta, 2013 edition.

On May 4, the Japanese asked for stool samples. With such little food, it was difficult to pass motions. Besides, with 6 latrines between 3,000 men, it took too long. The Medical Officers were thrashed for this delay. Someone had a brainwave and asked the sweepers to collect whatever was in the latrines as material. The Japanese were pleased at getting the samples, not knowing how they had been made. Due to this random sampling, many fit men were marked as sick and offloaded at the next port. Unfortunately, the sick ones had to stay on.

On May 12, they docked in Surabaya in Java and were allowed to disembark. They could bathe in the sea and a nearby swimming pool and buy food at cheap prices from the locals. They hoped they would stay on, but when they once again refused to join the Japanese, were shipped off again on May 14. The water ration was reduced to one cup per day. Crasta asked "Could humanity be degraded to such an extent? Could providence be so cruel?"

The queue for water started at 6.00am and took hours. One day when his turn came at 10am, the water was over. Crasta went begging all day for a sip of water. He could hardly speak. The next day, he lined up early, but the queue was huge. In desperation, he hoped for an Allied attack by plane or submarine so he could die, and his misery would end. While he was thinking this, a pipe in front of him sprung a leak and water poured out. Providence had sent him water instead of a torpedo. Before a huge crowd collected, he had his fill. Then, dysentery broke out in the ship and men died every day. Wrapped in a worn-out blanket they were lowered into the sea, unsung. He said "The scene was pitiful…Brave, virile soldiers were now helpless like babies".

On they went, with no timeframe or destination being told to the Indians. On May 28 they reached Palau, an island north of New Guinea. Hoping to be allowed out, they were kept on board for twelve days, sweltering. Then they got the welcome order to disembark, but after just 200 men had got off, the order was reversed. The lucky 200 were able to bathe in the sea before returning. For another week they stayed put. Conditions got worse. The Japanese said just wait for ten days and you will get good food. Fortunately, water was increased to three cups daily and they were given a sea water bath on deck – the first in one and half months. It was heavenly. Finally, on June 26, 1943, after one month and twenty-six days of this misery they reached Rabaul in New Britain.[6]

Torture Islands[*]

Once they had arrived, there was no rest. The men had to unload the ship, back-breaking work with heavy loads that took days. Then they had to walk to their camps, often miles away. There they had to make their own huts with little or no

---

[*] Title from Crasta.

material provided. Ants, mosquitoes and earthworms became their companions. It rained incessantly, without warning and sometimes for hours without stopping. They were always wet, and malaria became endemic. Food, drinking water and medicines remained as scarce as before. Crasta had malaria in July 1943, soon after arriving. When he shivered with cold, he only had a thin cotton blanket. When he burned with heat he would pass out and wake up in a sweat. There were few to tend to him as all the fit men were working.

The sick were treated with great suspicion and disdain by the Japanese. In the diarist Captain Patel's camp one day the senior Japanese commander, Colonel Takano, inspected them. Most were barely able to stand. Touching each one's forehead, if he found it hot, he slapped them and sent them back into the sick hut. If not, he kicked them and sent them off to work. This camp was 3 miles away from the work area at the Wewak aerodrome, so the men had to walk 6 miles a day, besides doing the harshly disciplined work. They left at 5.00am and returned at 6pm. Some of the sick forced to work took much longer.

In Crasta's camp on October 12, 1943, they witnessed their first major Allied air-raid. After running away to hide on a hill, he saw hundreds of bombers pounding the harbour and the town for an hour. The earth shook and he wondered if the "Day of Judgement" had come. After it was over, when he returned to camp, he found men running helter-skelter rescuing dozens buried in collapsed trenches and huts. Soon air-raids happened day and night and they just had to get used to it.[7]

As 1943 ended, the Indian POWs were desperate

So far, they had largely seen only the might of the Japanese empire, and though the incessant bombing indicated the strength of the Allies, so far it had only meant death and horror for them. In fact, some referred to them as enemy planes. There was no sign of any Allied invasion of the islands they were on. But unknown to them, a strategic shift had occurred. 1942 had seen the Japanese rampant over Asia, but starting from February 1943 when they had to evacuate Guadalcanal, the first territory they lost, they were on the backfoot. The US war machine had sprung into action and millions of men were armed and trained, thousands of planes and hundreds of warship were built. The Allies began their island-hopping campaign with the first strategic goal being the Philippines, attacked in 1944. Then they were to move north to Japan, island by island. But first, they cut off the SWPA from the Japanese supply route so they could not be attacked from behind, which meant that for Indian POWs things would get worse before they got better.

With supplies cut off, the already precarious food and medical situation only got worse. Nothing they needed was available here except coconuts, and now the

Japanese forced the men to improvise and somehow live off the land no matter what. With dysentery treated by chewing burnt copra ash, malaria untreatable with little quinine, fermented coconut oil and water used for beriberi, jungle rot just swabbed with mercurochrome, and bandages reused multiple times until they just fell apart, the situation was dire.[8] Rice rations became even smaller, and the men ate grass and chewed leaves just to fill their stomach. The 35-year-old Naik Gopal Pershad Jha from Banka in Bihar, who served in the Indian Army Ordnance Corps and was in nearby Bougainville with similar conditions, "carefully documented the diminution in rations. In Malaya in 1942 he had received 16 oz of rice or wheat a day. In Bougainville...from November 1943 the ration gradually fell, to 9 oz in May 1944, 4 oz in July, 2 oz in August until in 1945 the prisoners were surviving on plants they could forage from the jungle".[*]

Another result of this was that the Japanese resorted to cannibalism. Patel noted in his diary that on June 14, 1944, Havildar Sohanlal and Sepoy Hansraj of 3/17 Dogras were "taken away by two armed Japanese saying that if anybody (PW) accompanied them anyone who came will be given rice. They never returned, probably ate them". Later when more were invited, no one went. This act was not witnessed, though others were and taken to trial after the war. For the moment, the POWs were living through hell.[†]

A Beheading

On the vast island of New Guinea, the Americans were attacking on many fronts. In Patel's camp near Wewak, Captain Nirpal Chand, 2/17 Dogra had already alienated the Japanese in 1943 when he had led a hunger strike demanding better conditions. In April 1944, apprehending an invasion there, the Japanese decided to move to Hollandia, 300 kilometres away. With the men already emaciated, it was a death sentence for most. When they reached But, one-third of the way there, Chand refused to allow his men to move any further as they were getting further away from the Americans and rescue. After much tense negotiation and threats, he refused to budge, so the Japanese commandant, Captain Mitsuba, decided to execute him.

What happened next is from Japanese evidence provided after the war for a trial held to hold Chand's killers to account. Chand was taken away from the other POWs

---

* *Remembering the war in New Guinea – Where most of them perished: Indian POWs in New Guinea*, Professor Peter Stanley (Australian War Memorial), henceforth Stanley

† Another impact was the complete control of the sea by the Allies. Havildar Karim Illahi of the 1st Heavy Anti-Aircraft Regiment survived being bombed and torpedoed six times between July and November 1943. Report 15, AWM 54-423/11/51 – part 1.

by Mitsuba and three other Japanese. While one of them kept watch to ensure the Indians did not witness what happened, the second sat on his stomach, while Mitsuba held is hands down. Then the fourth, using Mitusba's Samurai sword, thrust it into Chand's throat and withdrew it. Chand died a few minutes later and they buried him there. There was nothing more to it. Chand was gone and of course his men never saw him again. There was to be justice, but only after the war.*

A Massacre of 291 Men

Almost exactly two months to the day later, another massacre occurred at But. If being shot or blown up by grenades is less scary than being beheaded, then the 291 Indians massacred had a better time of it. It was terror, nonetheless. There were many Indian POW camps, including one with 275 men close to the shore, and another half a mile away with 58 Gurkhas.[9] In May 1944, American planes started flying overhead regularly and the Indians signalled to them by spelling out "Indian POW" using strips of cloth. After first growing in frequency, the Japanese noticed that the planes suddenly stopped coming, and grew suspicious that the POWs had done what they indeed had. Then on June 26, 1944, fifty American planes flew overhead and one of their torpedo boats came close to the shore. Some Gurkhas from the neighbouring camp swam out to it, but were too weak to reach and had to return. The Japanese guards in the main camp of 275 had seen the boat but not the Gurkhas trying to swim to them. When the Americans left, at 8.00am the Japanese asked the two senior Indians, Captain Kishen Singh and Jemadar Adhin Chand, 3/17 Dogra, if they had seen the Americans land and if there had been any contact between them. They said no.

Unknown to the Indians, a Japanese observation post on top of a nearby hill had seen the Gurkhas swimming out. At 11.00am, the guards opened up with machine gun fire, followed by grenades to finish off any survivors. Of the 275 men in the main camp, only 42 escaped alive. The fate of the fifty-eight Gurkhas is not known.

Sepoy Lachman Singh's Diary

The Japanese had wanted to kill all the men in the 275 and 58 camps but knew some had escaped. They had earlier issued ID discs indicating the camp's name, and knew the discs would identify any survivors. Knowing that these men would discard their discs, they said anyone without one would be shot on sight. The forty-two survivors were in

---

*   See the later chapter on trials on the differing evidence and outcome.

three groups. The fate of one group of eleven is recorded in detail by Sepoy/Clerk Lachman Singh, 5/14 Punjab who was in another camp 7 miles away where these men headed. They hid in the jungle nearby during the day and came to the camp at night for food. After over a month of hiding, on August 5, one of this group, the same Jemadar Chand who had been questioned by the Japanese, had taken shelter in the camp to dry himself after a downpour. A Japanese soldier saw him under a mosquito net without his disc and took him to his commandant. The senior Indian, Captain Mohan Harish Chandra Hanowar, 5/14 Punjab, of Matunga, Bombay,[10] told the Japanese that Chand was from another camp, had lost his way as well as his disc, and had stumbled into this camp. He had ordered Chand to dry himself before being presented to the Japanese when he was caught. It was Chand's lucky day and the Japanese let him remain after he signed a bond swearing not to contact any of the local inhabitants or the Americans. After this, Hanowar told the remaining ten of the group to head to the Americans and not return here as it was too risky. Seven of these ten men left and were not heard from again. Two Dogras were allowed back in, taking the discs and identities of those who had died in camp. The tenth was Sepoy Kali Das, 3/17 Dogras. He remained close-by, but probably died of beriberi and wounds from the massacre. The two who had joined camp were too sick to accompany the rest when they escaped later. Chand did join them, but died after eating wild fruits. There was no one left alive from the eleven group, and it was from Chand's account of what happened before he died, noted down by Lachman Singh in his diary, that we know so much about this tragic event.

In the Hanowar camp of 171, when the Japanese ordered a move inland away from advancing Americans, eighty escaped, who later split into smaller groups. Eventually only thirty-nine of them reached the American's including Lachman Singh. While none of the group of 11 escapers from 275 camp survived, some of the 31 others did. But they had a very bad time and hid in the jungle for almost a year, being rescued by Australian soldiers in April and May 1945.[11]

The First Rescue

Depressing though all this was, a happy event occurred that unfortunately was unknown to the thousands suffering as they were so scattered. On Manus, one of the Admiralty Islands just north of New Guinea, were seventy-one Indians mainly from the 5/11 Sikhs. From Singapore they had reached Rabaul in July 1943, and Manus on October 14, 1943. The Americans landed on February 29, 1944, and quickly fanned out. On March 7, Havildar Baghel Singh, 5/11 Sikh and Sepoy Dalip Singh, 35 Motor Ambulance RIASC were sent to contact them. Unfortunately, in the dark of the night, they were mistaken for the Japanese and killed. The next day, bravely, Sepoys Warnam and Harnam Singh 5/11 Sikh tried again. This time they went in daytime and were successful, and all the remaining sixty-nine were recovered. They were led by the 36-year-old Jat Sikh from Hoshiarpur, Subedar Gulzara Singh who spoke English with an Oxford accent. Taken to Australia for a rest and debrief, they reached India in October 1944. This was later recorded as the first recovery of Indian POWs in the SWPA, but there was another, just a day earlier. When the Allies had landed on New Guinea, on March 7, Havildar-Major Ali Mohammed, 2/16 Punjab contacted them and they rescued the others in his camp. They left two days later for Brisbane and arrived there on March 15 for well-deserved rest.[12]

Subedar-Major Baboo Ram and his men

A few weeks later, a rescue by air occurred. Near Hansa Bay, New Guinea was the 40-year-old Baboo Ram from Hoshiarpur in Punjab. He was the Subedar-Major in Mohan Singh's unit, 1/14 Punjab the most senior man below officer rank. In armies across the world those in this position are held in high esteem. In the Indian army they had an even greater position as most units had no Indian officers so they were the senior most Indian, looked up to by the men and consulted by the officers on important matters. Even though there were Indian officers in 1/14, the traditional respect for the rank remained. So, Baboo Ram was one of the most prominent Indian POWs and as an early supporter of Mohan Singh was able to get most Dogras to join him. When the first INA was disbanded, he refused to rejoin and was shipped to New Guinea. Fortunately (if one can use that word given the deprivation they faced), he and 500 other POWs were near Hansa Bay, a part of the island that was another target of US attacks in 1944. Once this started, Baboo Ram and other men prepared for their escape. So far when they went out daily to work, they trudged like automatons, but now with the thought of escape, their keen eyes familiarized themselves with the terrain. He had with him a compass and binoculars and copied a map of the area through one of the Indian POWs who worked at the Japanese office in Hansa.

With the US coming closer, the Japanese decided to move the camp away in stages. Baboo Ram was in the last group to move out on April 24, 1944. Unfortunately, twenty-nine men too sick to move were left behind under Subedar-Major Bhai Kartar Singh IMD who bravely agreed to look after them. Their chances of survival were minimal and their fate remains unknown. Four days later Ram's group was further split into three, with him leading thirty-one men guarded by three Japanese. One morning the Japanese moved on ahead and Ram told his men to take the chance and scatter, but they were too scared. He had to stay on with them and on May 6 contrived to delay their departure while the Japanese moved on to a river 2.5 miles away to arrange boats to cross it. This time the men agreed to scatter. When they had left Hansa, Havildar Shankar Singh was one of the sick who had wanted to accompany them and four men volunteered to carry his stretcher. At this point they were too tired to move and in an incredible act, five more men remained behind to carry the Havildar in turns. After giving them rendezvous instructions, Baboo Ram and the rest left.

An Air Evacuation

They stumbled around in the morass for a month, barely alive. Towards the end of May, hope flickered in the form of an American flying boat overhead. The men quickly wrote out a message "INDIAN POW", but the plane flew away without any acknowledgement. They were horribly disappointed, rescue seemed so close but had evaded them. But unknown to them they had been spotted. A few days later a small plane returned, circling over them to ascertain if they were indeed what they claimed to be. It was piloted by Sergeant James L. Henkel of Pomona, California, an insurance salesman before he joined the army. He dropped food and medicines down to them, but in a cruel twist of fate, the food was tinned beef and pork that none of them could eat, though they were starving. Henkel dropped instructions asking them to head towards a clearing a mile and a half away and landed there. With him was Sergeant Ray Gregory of Victoria, Australia, an army medical orderly. There was no sign of the Indians and courageously the two men spent the night there, despite it being enemy territory. The next morning the Sergeants went looking for the POWs. They heard a whistle and headed towards the sound – one of the men had kept this simple yet vital device with him hoping to use it for exactly this purpose – attract help. When the Indians first saw Henkel, their hearts sank as his cap looked Japanese to them, but then they saw Gregory's distinctive Australian slouch hat and they ran towards them, shouting "Brother, brother". They were bewildered by the sudden change in their fortunes. At first they were incoherent, unable to realize they had been liberated and were once again back to civilization. Unfortunately, due to bad weather the evacuation took many days. Meanwhile, Gregory gave them medical aid and a few days later Baboo Ram who by now was at death's door was the first to be flown out by Henkel. Miraculously Havildar Shankar Singh and his stretcher bearers arrived, alas without Sweeper Harnam Singh who had died. Even with rescue already at hand, Lance-Naik Udham Singh and Sepoy Madru Ram, 1/14 Punjab died. We will never know if they were sad to have just missed being evacuated, or happy that they died once again free men

The journalist who wrote this account said that when he went to meet Baboo Ram in hospital, he was playing chess. After the rest had been taken to safety, Gregory went on leave and only Henkel remained. The men shared their hukka with the man they idolized, and told him that when they reached home, would compose and sing songs in his honour. Henkel said "their gratitude has given me the biggest kick in my life I have ever known".[13]

Right: Backroom Intrigues in Bangkok – The Indian nationalist Giani Pritam Singh and Major Fujiwara of Japanese Intelligence. (Giorgio Albertini)

Below: Giani Pritam Singh's men with loudspeakers at the front addressing Indian soldiers when war began in December 1941. (Giorgio Albertini)

Captain Mohan Singh's speech to Indian POWs at Farrer Park Singapore on February 17, 1942. (Giorgio Albertini)

Above left: The Indian guards over the British in Changi, Singapore by Ronald Searle. (Wikicommons)

Above right: Nationalist plays staged by Capt. Mohan Singh in Singapore 1942 – TODAY'S FEATURE MILAP (UNITY). (Giorgio Albertini)

The banner "Ghulam Rahne Se Marna Behtar Hai" means it is better to die than live like slaves referring to life under British colonial rule. This issue is dated 18 August 1942 (shown in the Japanese style used throughout the war). This is days after Gandhi asked the British to "Quit India" and the headline article says everyone in India is behind him

AZAD HINDUSTAN (Free India) newspaper started in Singapore 1942. Published in many languages, this is version in Roman-Hindustani. (National Archives India)

Above left: After the air crash that killed 4 Indian delegates from Malaya, the 5 survivors in Tokyo March/April 1942 – Standing S.C. Goho, K.P.K. Menon, Seated Capt. Mohan Singh, N. Raghavan, Lt.Col. Gill. (National Archives India)

Above right: Capt. Mohan Singh being greeted by Maj. Fujiwara on his return to Singapore, April 1942. (Wikicommons)

Above left: Captain Mohan Singh speaking in Bangkok June 1942 when he was formally appointed GOC (General Officer Commanding) INA. (From a British report in Singh Family Archives)

Above right: The daily flogging in the "Nimbu" parade in Singapore 1942 – by INA soldiers of Indian army men who interfered in recruitment. (Giorgio Albertini)

Left: Arrest of General Mohan Singh by the Japanese on 29 December 1942 for refusing to cooperate with them after their duplicity became known to him. This was the end of the First INA. (Giorgio Albertini)

Below left: Instructions being given to leaders of Teams Gulab, Chameli & Corop in July 1942 for their mission to India – part of Lt.Col. Gill's Double Cross of the Japanese. (Giorgio Albertini)

Below right: Major Mahabir S. Dhillon on his elephant on the last stretch of his journey from Burma to India – he escaped but Lt.Col. Gill could not. (Giorgio Albertini)

SRI. RASH BEHARI BOSE IN STRIKING APPEAL TO EAST ASIA INDIANS

Above left: Lt. M.M. Pillai, MC, Bombay Sappers, who escaped from Singapore in May 1942 and reached India in August 1942 – the first to bring news of Singapore and Southeast Asia. (Giorgio Albertini)

Above right: Rash Behari Bose recreated the INA after Mohan Singh's arrest. (National Archives India)

Subhash Chandra Bose took over from Mohan Singh/ Rash Behari and raised the movement to new heights – here he is speaking at Cathay Cinema Singapore 21 October 1943. (National Archives Singapore)

In this holy war for India's liberation, we ask for your blessings. Good wishes.

MAHATMAJI-FATHER OF OUR NATION

RANI OF JHANSI REGIMENT

RANI OF ZANSHI

(A PLAY IN THREE ACTS)

by

P. N. OAK, M.A., LL.B.

The entire proceeds of the sale of this booklet go to Netaji's Fund.

Above: Bose and other patriots seeking the blessings of Mahatmaji (Gandhi). (Wikicommons)

Left: Play Rani of Zanshi performed first on October 22, 1944, the first anniversary of the formation of the all-women's Rani of Jhansi regiment. (National Archives India)

The Japanese ship Buyo Maru seen through the periscope of the USS Wahoo 26 January 1943, carrying 1100 men including 497 Indian POWs. (US Naval History and Heritage Command)

As Indian survivors of Buyo Maru drown, they drag Japanese soldiers down, near Palau islands on 27 January 1943. (Giorgio Albertini)

Above left: Indian POWs like Warrant Officer John Baptist Crasta who was on the Japanese ship Thames/ Victoria Maru on a hellish 55-day journey from Singapore to Rabaul in Papua New Guinea May-June 1943. (Giorgio Albertini)

Above right: Life and Death under the Japanese in the Torture islands of Papua New Guinea – an American bombing raid. (Giorgio Albertini)

The beheading of Captain Nirpal Chand by the Japanese on April 27, 1944, in New Guinea. (Giorgio Albertini)

Above left: The rescue of Subedar-Major Baboo Ram, 1/14 Punjab Regt and his men in New Guinea, May 1944. (Giorgio Albertini)

Above right: Indian POWs fought back when they could, with only the barbaric options available – Havildar Rattan Singh 3/17 Dogra beheading 2 Japanese soldiers on 25 September 1944 in New Guinea, to prevent them from reporting their escape. He was awarded a Military medal for his services in the war. (Giorgio Albertini)

A Troop of the Gwalior Lancers, Indian Army join the INA and salute its flag – Lt. Bishambar Nath Bali holds the flag as Major L.S. Misra looks on. (Giorgio Albertini)

THE BRIEFING OF "MALIK BUTAI" BEFORE THE JAPANESE OFFENSIVE OF 1944.

The photo depicts Capt (Lt Col) S.A. Malik (B1316) briefing the subordinate commanders of the composite group of "I", "Bhdr", and "Rft" Group personnel who spear-headed the Japanese advance through the Chin Hills to Imphal in March/June 1944. The photo is a Japanese propaganda photo taken at Mutaik in Feb 44, just prior to the opening of the campaign.

Identity of the figures are (left to right)

1. Capt S.A. Malik   (B1316)

2. Sub Man Sing Bhandari   (B1334) (obscured by serial 1)

3. Hav Bachan Singh Negi   (B1334)

4. Hav Sher Bahadur   2/9 Gurkha (dead)

5. Hav Bhawansing Khandeka   2/9 Gurkha

6. Hav Hari Singh   (B993)

7. Jem Dilmansing Thapa   (B585)

8. Hav Narain Sing Rawat   18 R Garh Rif.

9. Jem Khuda Bakhsh   1 Bahawalpur Inf.

10. Not identified.

11. Jem Sham Lal   9 Jat (in foreground)

12. Jem Natha Singh   (B1321) Only white pugree
                                                            showing.
13. Hav Durgabahadur Chettri   (B761)

14. Jem Nanak Chand   RIASC

15. Hav Ram Sarup   (B461)

16. Not identified   (extreme right of photo)

The briefing of "Malik Butai". Col. S.A. Malik was the senior officer in the INA Propaganda units that screened the Japanese advance into Manipur in early 1944. (National Archives India)

Right: Major Pritam Singh and his INA men approaching Palel airfield defended by Gurkhas of the Indian Army, May 1944. Their attack failed. (Giorgio Albertini)

Below: The INA retreat in Burma May-July 1944. (Giorgio Albertini)

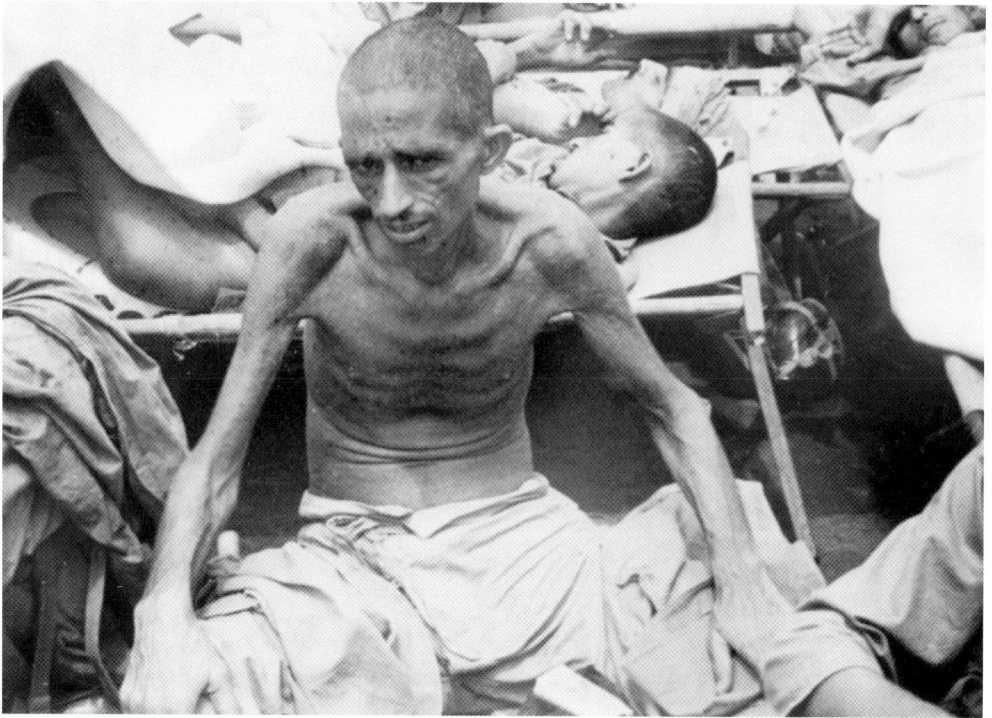

Indian POW survivors, September 1945. (Australian War Memorial (above) and Wikicommons (below))

Justice in Rabaul – Sub.
Chint Singh, 2/12 Frontier
Rifles, giving evidence at
the command trial of Lt. Gen
Adachi Hatazo, April 1947.
(Giorgio Albertini)

Telegram from Colombo
25 October 1945,
Thangamma hears from
her husband Jemadar
Uthaiah, 1st Mysore
Infantry after 5 years –
he is alive and coming
home. (Giorgio Albertini)

Left: Mariammal's wait is sadly over when she finds out in 1946 that her husband Sapper Marimathu who did not return, had died in Singapore in 1942. (Giorgio Albertini)

Below: The 100th birthday on 7 September 2024 of Lance-Naik Charan Singh, RIASC (seated middle) commemorated by the Indian Army and his family. He had fed the Indian troops who had liberated Singapore in September 1945. (Charan Singh Family)

Havildar Rattan Singh Beheads the Japanese

Alas the life of most on New Guinea was not as uplifting. It is a huge island, much larger than all of Japan, and camps faced different experiences. In August 1944 our diarist Patel was in a camp in Nuguluwela when the Japanese ordered a similar move away from the Americans as in Baboo Ram's case, this time to Maprik, 120 kilometres away. The sick would be left behind and it was suspected they would be killed as it happened in many cases. On August 19 they got orders to be ready to move out on September 9. Patel and the 28-year-old Havildar Rattan Singh, 3/17 Dogras, hatched a plan to escape. The night before the planned departure, they invited the eleven Japanese guards to a tea party with the aim of drugging them with soporifics. Though one did not turn up, they went ahead with the plan and 70–80 of them escaped. Ten to fifteen stayed back as they thought the plan too dangerous. What they expected the Japanese to do to them when they woke up is not known, neither is their fate. Those who escaped split up and fixed a rendezvous point nearby, with the aim of moving towards the Americans. Eventually, Patel was with a group of twenty-eight. Rattan Singh had a compass and led the way and was the main driver behind this escape. By September 20, whatever food they had been able to hoard was gone, the men were sick with malaria and dysentery. Two men ate poisonous fruits and died, and two others were so tired, they just gave up and also died.

On September 25 they stumbled upon two Japanese soldiers who started stripping them of their possessions. While they were engrossed in this, at a signal from Patel and Rattan Singh, four Indians grabbed the Japanese. With a *dah**, Rattan Singh beheaded them both. Despite this, the men were at their wits' end and even considering giving themselves up to the Japanese. Thinking they would not reach the Americans and the miseries would continue, Havildar Jai Singh and Sepoy Maher Singh cut each other's abdomens. Their apprehensions may have been right. On September 27 at 8.30am the twenty-two survivors saw a patrol of men in green uniforms. As in Baboo Ram's case, from a distance they looked Japanese and as they had been sighted, everyone dreaded what was to happen next. When they turned out to be Americans the nervous tension was so great, many fell ill.[14]

Gratitude to the Papuans

At the same time as Patel's escape, another Indian Army doctor succeeded. The 32-year-old Captain Valaudhan Krishna Pillay from Malabar in India had been taken from Singapore to Rabaul, and then further east to Bougainville, and arrived

---

* *Dah* is a large knife, a term used in east India and Southeast Asia.

on September 29, 1943. After the Americans landed here in October 1943, there were some approaches to the Indian POWs through the Papuans to escape that had ended in them being caught and killed, and it was suspected that the local Papuans had double crossed them. When a message was received in Urdu in August 1944 urging them to escape, as it came through the Papuans, there was suspicion that this was a trap. After discussions with Pillay, Naik Jha, who had recorded the reduction of the rice ration over time, decided to test out if this message was genuine. He escaped with Labourer Balla Samu, and luckily for them it was. Helped by the Papuans from one village to the next, they reached the Americans on September 7, 1944. Two men, Wanabis and Tomio, were especially helpful to him and other Indians. Emboldened by this, Pillay also escaped on September 17, and in a similar manner reached the Americans. He sent a message back to the camp which encouraged other Indian POWs to escape, and so there is much that they owed to the Papuans. An unfortunate result of this is that Japanese commander Captain Ikeba Toma came down heavily on the remaining Indians, and had at least one who was caught, shot.[15]

Though heartening, all these escapes netted barely 400 Indian POWs. Thousands had already died, and most of the others remaining on the Torture Islands. Deliverance was to come, but it was still a year away.

Chapter 8

THE INDIAN NATIONAL ARMY IN BURMA

While the few POWs still alive in the Torture islands desperately hung on to life, far away in Burma, the INA faced its tryst with destiny. It was from here that they were to accompany Japan on an attack on British India in early 1944.

The Japanese had captured Burma during their 1942 Blitzkrieg in East Asia and chased the Allied army that defended it into neighbouring Assam and Bengal. There was a large Indian civilian population in Burma then who were unpopular with the Burmese,* and so over half a million fled, the largest mass migration in history at that time. They had little support from their colonial masters and thousands of men, women and children died on the way. At that time Japan could have almost walked into Assam, and possibly Bengal. It was very lucky for India they did not, and instead spent time to consolidate their gains. This allowed the British to catch their breath and they then built a vast new army with millions of Indian recruits. The fall of Burma had also cut off the Allied supply road running through it to Japan's enemy Chiang Kai-Shek in China. It was replaced by one that started in Assam, from where dozens of Dakota transport planes flew every day over the hump of the Himalayas to deliver this aid.[1]

In 1943 the Allied build-up in India was complete, and to pre-empt their expected invasion of Burma, the Japanese decided to attack first. In one fell swoop they would also capture the air bases aiding Chiang. To supply their own army, they built the Thailand-Burma Railway with 60,000 British and Australian POWs and over 180,000 mainly Indian and Malay civilians who toiled on its 420-kilometre-long line. It was called the death railway as a fifth of the POWs and two-thirds of the civilians died during its construction.[2]

---

* Burma was part of British Indian until 1935, so many Indians migrated and were prominent in trade and other professional jobs. This aroused Burmese resentment.

Major Misra and the Gwalior Lancers

The main Japanese attack began on India March 9, 1944, with the aim of capturing Imphal and then advancing across the Brahmaputra* valley into Assam. To confuse and hopefully outflank the Allies, on February 4 a diversionary raid was launched in the Arakan Hills south of this area. It was here that for the INA the campaign started with a spectacular success. Not a military one, it was even better, a propaganda victory. It had been drilled into the INA that as soon as the Indian Army encountered them, they would join it. On February 5, 1944, on a remote Arakan hill, this is exactly what happened. Major Lakhshman Swarup Misra and his INA men approached the A troop† of the 3 Gwalior Lancers headed by Jemadar Gajendra Singh. This was the Lancers' first experience in this war and most of them had not heard of the INA, news of which had been suppressed by a rigorous British censor. Getting them to switchover was perhaps more dangerous for the INA men than fighting as they could be shot at when they tried to get close enough to speak. However, Singh had already been contacted and decided to join. It was unsafe to discuss this with others unless one knew their predisposition, but Singh had one of his section commanders, Anirban Singh, with him. What the others thought was not known and the plan remained between the two Singhs.

With the troop commander on his side Misra, his Japanese minder Captain Hattori, two INA officers Piara Singh and Bishamber Nath Bali, and about thirty-five men, approached the Lancers confidently. Piara Singh and Bali went down to a nullah‡ at the bottom of a hill where the Lancers were posted. They were dressed in bush shirts and khaki drill trousers and, in case anyone else saw them, had no INA rank badges on to make them look like civilians. They shouted out asking for water, and the two Singhs went down to speak to them. The two INA officers took them to a secluded spot nearby where Misra was waiting. He was the ringmaster, and after speaking to him the two Singhs returned to their men and said they had been surrounded and had no choice but to surrender. Everyone followed the troop leader's order. Either they believed him or suspected what had happened and decided to go along with it. Gajendra Singh had also arranged for a group of other Lancers to come at that time to reinforce them with food. Misra's men had been told where they were coming from and accosted them, and they surrendered as well. Bali dramatically unfurled the Indian tricolour and everyone saluted it.

---

* Brahmaputra river starts in the Eastern Himalayas, flows through Arunachal Pradesh, Assam, Bangladesh and into the Bay of Bengal.

† Lancers were originally horsemen who fought with a lance. In modern armies they were equipped with tanks and armoured cards. A troop is equivalent to an infantry platoon, normally about thirty-five men.

‡ Nullah is a watercourse or ravine.

Without a shot being fired, in a matter of minutes, Misra and his men had captured an entire Lancer troop. The INA men had been told this would happen, but how easy and quick it had been, and how large the bag was, dumbfounded them.

That night the lancers cooked the food they had brought to supply Singh's men and fed everyone. Around the campfire they sang *Vande Mataram*[*] and Misra lectured them. He used his Muslim alias, Mirza Bahauddin, adopted as the area had many Muslims. He said that all Indians should unite to liberate their country, passed around a photo of Bose and eulogized the saviour of India. They were told that under his banner lakhs had flocked, poised to strike. Nineteen of the thirty-five Lancers agreed immediately to volunteer. The next day Misra, guided by Gajendra Singh and four other Lancers, returned to contact their B troop but this time the attempt failed and they were fired upon. That night, three of the A troop who had surrendered fled back to the Lancers. Nonetheless it was a valuable haul and as he had enabled it, Jemadar Gajendra Singh was promoted three ranks to a Second Lieutenant in the INA.[3]

The INA's Bahadur Group

Misra's team was part of the INA's Bahadur Group.[†] Their job was to screen the Japanese Army and get as many Indian Army men as possible to join them. Though some had done so in 1943, there was not much publicity as it was a chaotic time for the INA after Mohan Singh's arrest. This incident when the Japanese were beginning their assault on India was capitalized on swiftly. Misra was brought to Rangoon and on March 18, 1944, given the *Sardar-e-Jung*, one of the INA medals introduced by Bose. At the award ceremony, he was also given a silver sword, cigarette case and matchbox cover. In the intense rhetoric of those days, the civilian who donated them explained that the sword represented death to their enemy, the British; the cigarette case meant they would be locked up in cages and the match box represented fire that would destroy their homes and businesses.[4]

Ram and Lakhsman

Misra from Mainpuri in North India was a Captain in the 5/17 Dogras. He was not taken prisoner in Malaya as most in this book were, but in Burma. He became a

---

[*] A patriotic Indian song.
[†] There were many such small units named Bahadur, Intelligence, Reinforcement, Special Services, and will be referred to as Bahadu.

POW on February 24, 1942 on the Sittang river when Japan was sweeping across the country. At first he resisted, but in July joined the INA, becoming one of its most fervent supporters. Jemadar Ram Sarup, 4/19 Hyderabad, who we met in the chapter on Dhillon and Gill's double cross, took him under his wing. Though Misra was five ranks higher in the Indian Army hierarchy, in the new democracy of the INA he became Sarup's understudy. Together they trained a new group of Bahadur's, Misra was to build-up their spirit, while Sarup focused on skills. They were known as the duo of Ram Lakshman, their first names, who would vanquish the evil Ravana (the British).* To ramp up the men's spirit, Misra lectured them on the concept of nationhood that many were unaware of. To them their village and battalion was their country. He explained what one's country was, what freedom meant, why it was everyone's birthright and must be fought for. Sarup and others taught them how to read maps, manage explosives, disguise themselves as sadhus, women in burqas and men in western suits, depending on who their mark was.

Latif Trains the Bahadurs on Disabling Airfields

They got specialist training on how to attack Allied aerodromes by Flying Officer M.M. Latif, Royal Indian Air Force, a 26 year old from Gurdaspur. His squadron flew in support of the Indian Army in Burma, and while on one such mission on May 12, 1943, he landed his plane at a paddy field and soon joined the Bahadurs. He taught them how to attack an aerodrome. He explained how to set fire to planes by gasoline, disable them by pouring grit into engines or sugar in petrol tanks and cutting wires. They were to lob grenades into hangars, plant landmines in runways and grab log books from controls rooms. If they could not read, they should just smash everything up.[5]

Leaflets and Loudspeakers

Besides the face to face talking as with the Lancers, the main way of spreading the INA gospel was through leaflets. In the multiple languages spoken by the diverse Indian Army, they spoke of freedom, how good the Japanese were, how bad the British were and exhorted men to join the INA to overthrow them. Besides being dropped by Japanese planes, the Bahadurs left them near Indian Army units, shot them across using bows and arrows, or handed over to villagers to pass on.[6]

Then there were the loudspeakers. The Bahadurs would speak for ten to fifteen minutes on similar lines as the leaflets. Duos would act out a short

---

* Ramayana is an Indian epic where the good Ram and Lakhsman vanquish the evil Ravana.

skit of a few minutes. An English-speaker would play a Briton, the other an Indian. It would be an argument over freedom which of course the Indian would win. The Bahadurs did what the Japanese really wanted the INA for, and were well equipped with portable printing presses, batteries, handheld loudspeakers and script writers in different languages. Most of all, their spirit was built up by men like the Ram Lakshman duo. It was a dangerous task in the front line where they had a loudspeaker in their hands instead of a gun and could be shot at any time.[7]

The Japanese almost at Imphal

The main Japanese thrust towards Imphal began on March 9, 1944. They advanced rapidly and a Japanese officer records seeing India on March 17 and entering it the next day at 10.00am. Along with him were INA propaganda units similar to Misra's. News spread and Bose was ecstatic, it was "a matter of days" before his dream would be fulfilled. In fact, he was not prepared for how quick the advance had been. The men he had trained to administer occupied India were still in Singapore. He hastily arranged the Azad Hind Dal, mainly Bengali civilians from Burma, to do this. Lieutenant-Colonel A.C. Chatterji, IMS, was appointed as the Governor and arrived in Burma in April. Currency notes and stamps were designed, laws drafted, and policemen recruited.[8]

What Japan had planned for India

Before the war began, Japanese right-wing groups had grand plans for a great empire that included carving up India, but this was not official policy. In 1944, though the Japanese had said they would free India, their plans were quite different. They openly told some Indians not to worry as they would leave fifteen to twenty years after the British were thrown out, as if this would give comfort.[9] Immediately upon arrival they were to retain control of airfields, industry and communications and Japanese specialists were at the front to do so. Whether this was agreed with Bose earlier is not known, but when told about it, he refused to worry about Japanese intentions. He had full faith in his power to sort this out later. His message was that once the tricolour was unfurled on Indian soil, the people and the Indian Army would flock to him. When that happened, the fact that the 4,000 INA men involved were a fraction of the 87,000 Japanese troops would not matter. Many in the INA believed him and prayed that rape and other Japanese atrocities witnessed in Malaya would not happen on their soil. This was one of the main reasons many had joined. In the longer term they hoped that Gandhi, Nehru and Bose would be able to negotiate favourable terms with the Japanese.[10]

The Euphoria Continues*

However, all this was in the future. For the moment, the news was that the Japanese and the INA propaganda units were almost in Imphal. The Japanese commander, General Mutaguchi, told the Indians not to worry: "My officers are doing everything. I just tend my rose garden". Everyone was ecstatic. In April a play was staged in the INA forward HQ at Maymyo "Confusion in British High Command". INA officers played the role of Britons such as the Viceroy and Commander of the Indian Army, and the laughs brought the house down. A similar military tattoo was organized by Colonel Bhonsle who headed the INA Rear HQ in Singapore on the impending fall of Imphal – the drama showcased an attack by INA troops on the Red Fort in Delhi and the Viceroy being arrested and sent by third class to Britain.

The Euphoria fizzels Out[11]

The INA did unfurl Indian flags before Imphal and Kohima, but the Indian Army and people did not react as expected. Some Naga Chiefs were excited and said they awaited their "king" Subhas Chandra Bose, but there was no wholesale flocking to the flag. The Japanese officer quoted earlier said in his diary:

> 24 March propaganda broadcast, difficult to win over Indians due to their national temperament.

> 26 March feeling of the population is uncertain, but they tend to be anti-Japanese.

Days turned to weeks with no news, suspicion grew that Imphal would not fall. The same Japanese officer said in his diary,

> 23 April general attack unsuccessful.

> 24 Apr Made decision to return to Rangoon.

> 2 May the confusion in the Japanese army and the contradiction in our operative work are enough to make me weep.

---

* Mutaguchi roses and satire Toyepg109, satire Reports 975/978 INA499, Singapore see HOME_POLITICAL _I_1945_NA_F-21-6_KW-1 p127 in NAI.

Euphoria to Retreat – General Slim and his Fourteenth Army

Soon, the suspicion of failure grew into a certainty for the Japanese had miscalculated badly. They had fought British and Indian troops in Malaya and Burma in 1942 when they won easily. They had captured vast "Churchill"* supplies, and thousands of Indians had joined Mohan Singh's INA during the battle. They expected to face the same army here in Manipur in 1944, but instead found the Allied Fourteenth Army of General William "Uncle Bill" Slim.[†] After the disastrous retreat from Burma in 1942, Slim gradually built up a new army of well-trained, well-equipped and well led men. Two-thirds of his 155,000 men in this sector were Indian, Chin Levies from Burma, the others British and West African. Other than a handful of cases like the Gwalior Lancers, few of his Indians joined the INA.[12] Despite initial setbacks, the Fourteenth Army soon forced the Japanese back. Unable to capture Churchill supplies, their own ran soon out, then in the steamy, hot, Burmese jungle with little medicines and food, chased by Slim's men, thousands died like flies.[13] Faced with this, Bose, who had been waiting at the INA Forward HQ in Maymyo in Burma for his triumphant entry to Imphal, returned to Rangoon in May 1944, his hopes dashed.[14]

The Severely Hobbled INA

If the Japanese were badly off, the INA never stood a chance. Not only were they poorly armed and supplied but also poorly used. What happened was this. After Bose's arrival in 1943, the Japanese had reluctantly agreed to use one INA unit to fight, and the Subhas Regiment was raised under Colonel Shah Nawaz Khan. When Bose and Khan met the Japanese in Rangoon in January 1944, they were told the regiment would be split into small groups to fight alongside them. Bose wanted it to fight as one unit and lead the attack so the first drop of blood shed in India would be INA blood. But it was too late for that now. The Japanese agreed to use the regiment in battalion strength, but in support roles. Once again, after wringing a hard fought concession from the Japanese in 1943, Bose found that they lived up to it only in word, not in spirit.[15]

---

* "Churchill" supplies were those left behind by the Allied army in Malaya, mockingly named after Britain's wartime Prime Minister as a "gift" from him.

† According to Robert Lyman and others, possibly Britain's Greatest General (https://www.nam.ac.uk/whats-on/slim-britains-greatest-general).

Arakan

Of the regiment's three battalions, one was asked to support the Arakan. For the umpteenth time, the Japanese played foul. Before the Arakan operation began in February, they had ensured that the INA propaganda unit they really wanted, Misra's Bahadur's, was in place. They had not wanted and so not asked for Khan's Arakan battalion. When it was forced upon them, they took a month to arrange transport and it left Rangoon on February 4 and reached its position in March, a month after operations began. In a support role in a subsidiary area, it did not have much military impact. But the men were happy as a company under Captain Surajmal was able to keep the tricolour flying in Mowdok in India from July 1944. The Arakan operation fizzled out and Surajmal was ordered by the Japanese to withdraw in October 1944. During his stay there he had the honour of being the only Indian to command Japanese troops.[16]

"The Japanese are using the crack INA regiment as labourers"*

Khan also left on February 4 with his two other battalions who were also given a support role, tasked with defending the rear of the main Imphal attack. They too were not provided transport and reached their positions over a month later after the attack had already begun. Soon Khan found to his horror that his men were being used to build and repair roads, and drive bullock carts for supplies.

His diary for March 30 says; "Booby returned from Kennedy Peak, his report is distressing. The Japanese are using the crack INA regiment as labourers…I wonder what is going to be the outcome of this one sided co-prosperity". In late April he was told by the Japanese to stay where he was and suspected they did not want the INA present when entering India. As he had no wireless, he complained in a letter to Bose and, perhaps due to that, was asked to support a Japanese attack on Kohima in mid-May. Khan's men were happy, and many came out of hospital to fight, but it was too late. Though some of his men were able to unfurl a flag overlooking India, the closest he got was the 24th Milestone marker from Kohima. When he arrived, the Japanese retreat had begun.[17]

---

* Khan Report 1002 INA File 499 (henceforth SNK), Booby is the nick name of Lieutenant Mehboob Ahmed 1/13 Frontier Force Rifles, reference to co-prosperity is a pun on the Japanese Greater East Asian Co-Prosperity Sphere.

The INA First Division at Palel

It was going to get worse. Though the Japanese had agreed to use only one regiment as a test case, Bose had brought forward the rest of the 1st INA Division to Burma. Without any transport, they had to march hundreds of miles from Malaya. Lieutenant-Colonel Inayatullah Jan Kiani, formerly of the 5/2 Punjab Regiment, who commanded the Gandhi Regiment of the division, said half his men were barefoot and badly deficient in equipment. However, the mood was still jubilant when they reached in March 1944, so the Japanese agreed to use them. As it was expected that they would reach the front line too late for the battle and could at best line the roads as Bose would drive triumphantly into Imphal, they were ordered to leave their equipment behind, carrying just a rifle, fifty bullets and a blanket.[18]

So far, the INA experience in battle had been Bahadur units suborning Indian Army men, and most of Khan's men mending roads and driving bullock carts. Only his Arakan battalion had seen action, but that was far away in a subsidiary area. This newly arrived division had the first real combat encounter in the main battlefront, when its Gandhi Regiment was tasked to attack Palel airfield near Bishenpore. Three hundred men were picked to fight under Major Pritam Singh.* On the night of May 2, they approached confidently, talking and smoking cigarettes, sure that the 100 Indian Army men defending the aerodrome would not fire at them, as had been drilled into them for over a year. Misra had lectured them before they left Rangoon – the Indian Army was weak; they would not fire back and instead join them instantly. This made them willing to attack even if their kinsmen could be on their other side, as they expected it to be a token battle.

Major Singh is surprised

When the defenders fired at them, they were all taken aback. Singh thought it was a misunderstanding and managed to speak to them to try clearing it up. He explained they were INA men and urged the defenders to join them, but when they refused to back down, gave the order to fix bayonets, shouted *Chalo Dilli* (the INA battle-cry meaning onwards to Delhi) and led a charge at them. It failed, but as his men were enthused, he led six more charges before he called off the assault. The seven charges he led were extolled up and down the line, but the realization that the Indian Army would not only refuse to join them, but also fire back came as a big shock.[19]

---

* Formerly Captain, 1st Kapurthala Infantry.

"The British have tied our wrists, but our hearts will always be with the INA and Netaji"[*]

The next morning one of Major Singh's men, Havildar Shiv Charan Singh, a well-built 33-year-old Rajput Sikh from Jullundur, led a team of thirty-two men out on a patrol. When they stumbled upon six Indian Army men, he repeated the major's message of the night before, but they insisted all thirty-two INA men surrender. They parleyed for an hour. As both sides refused to budge, he suggested they part ways amicably, but with guns drawn, they insisted upon a surrender of the thirty-two to the six. Then the Havildar suggested they take him prisoner and let his thirty-one men go. They refused. So far it was David vs Goliath, so the Havildar kept on arguing. But then the six were reinforced by eleven and it became seventeen Indian Army vs thirty-two INA. Finally, Havildar Shiv Charan Singh slapped his forehead in despair, cursing his fate and agreed to surrender. The tense stand-off must have scared many of his men and they must have been glad it was over, but not him. Later, when under arrest, he said "The British have tied our wrists, but our hearts will always be with the INA and Netaji".[20]

The INA fought well when they had a chance. A later British intelligence report said, "A measure of courage cannot be denied to the leaders of INA front-line units in Burma in 1945 when…they faced up to British equipment, tanks, guns, and aircraft with rifles and bullock-carts and empty stomachs".[†] However these were minor engagements that had no impact on the overall battle.

Hamara Hindustan

When the Indian Army had fired at Major Singh at Palel aerodrome, they debunked one myth that they would not fight the INA. There was another belief, equally deeply ingrained, that if the INA deserted or surrendered, they would be shot. At this time, leaflets titled *Hamara Hindustan* (Our India) were dropped on INA positions that said:

> *Hindustanion ko ghar aane ki daawat*
> *Tumhare saath koi bura saluki nahe kia jaayega*
> *Tum log apne baal bache ko mil sakte ho*
> *Tum log jaise bhi ho sidhe aao.*

---

[*] Havildar Shiv Charan Singh, 5/2 Punjab Regiment, Report 612/INA 499.
[†] Gordon pg513.

(Indians are invited to come home
You will not be ill-treated
You can go and meet your children
Come, just as you are now.)

These leaflets in four languages signed by General Auchinleck, the Indian Commander-in-Chief, had a remarkable impact on the men as it debunked the second myth about being shot. For many tired, hungry, sick and fed-up men, it solved a torturous dilemma – the fear of being shot against the loathing for the Japanese and the desire to go home. Hundreds took the plunge.[21]

"The military debacle in Imphal was followed by a harrowing retreat"*

Their fellow soldiers spent months more trying to fight with few weapons, little food and medicines for the sick and injured. Shahnawaz Khan recorded in his diary in July

"Number of sick still mounting – men's rations are one mess tin of daal for five days...saw some of the horrors of war, men eating dead horses...men going down with malarial dysentery...men just about starved...men dying like flies...some are committing suicide".

He arranged for the return of the survivors of the division. There was no transport available, and he hired bullock carts for the long journey. Of his own retreat, Colonel I.J. Kiani, said the men were more dead than alive, and despite being a regimental commander himself ended up barefoot. When the sick reached the hospital hastily prepared for them, the doctor said he had 1 bedpan for 700 men. There were no medicines, and they had to improvise just like in the Torture islands of the SWPA. Neem leaves were used for skin disorders, charcoal for dysentery and diarrhoea and his own concoction of jaggery and yeast for vitamin B. There were no anaesthetics, little quinine and bandages had to be reused many times. Of the 6,000 men of the division, 715 had deserted, 400 died in battle, 800 surrendered and 1,500 died of starvation. Of the 2,600 survivors, 2,000 were hospital cases.[22]

The Aftermath of the Debacle

When Bose had returned to Rangoon earlier in May 1944, he tried to keep morale up and condemned those who mentioned any debacle. He said the battle was still

---

* Sugata Bose, pg280.

on, and the public was re-assured. At auction, garlands worn by him went for large sums. But the truth could not be hidden. The INA's morale and belief in their leaders was badly shaken.

After the defeat, the Japanese had stayed where they were, but the INA was withdrawn to reduce desertion and demoralization. Besides the two myths already debunked, there was a third, that the Allied were finished and Japanese victory assured. Seeing the Japanese successes in 1942, little activity from the Allies in Burma in 1943 and hearing of the initial advances into India in 1944, they believed it. They were shocked by the reality. The conversation in the officers' mess was all about the unexpected recovery of Allied strength. One of them Lieutenant Wazir Mohammad Khan said, "He was fed up w everything, he cursed Bose, the INA, the Japanese and everybody else. He had been at the front for over a year, but the Japanese and the INA had made no proper preparations for victory".*

The Tamil Mutiny

There was another voice of dissatisfaction. After Bose gave up on recruiting more POWs into the INA when only 2,000 from Singapore joined after his return, he turned to civilians from whom he received a much better response. In the final INA total of 40,000, civilians amounted to 18,000. But the army men did not respect them. They were "*Madrassis*", not considered a "martial race"† and ill-treated as they were less fit to begin with, and ill-treated. In turn the civilians complained that though in many units they were the majority, almost none were NCOs. Finally in September 1944, when a fresh retreat was announced, as they had no food, they refused to move unless Bose spoke to them. He did meet the ringleaders, and they did acquiesce, but the antipathy remained. In a way they were more loyal to the cause. By now, some of the former POWs in the INA just wanted to get home and were willing to make tactical retreats so they remained alive. On the other hand, the civilians always wanted to move forward. This was a remarkable feeling amongst these men of Indian origin in Singapore, Malaya and Burma, most of whom had never lived in India. Even if their home was Southeast Asia, they wanted to free their homeland, India. This was very much like the feelings of the local Chinese towards their own homeland, whose struggle against the Japanese they supported.[23]

---

* Khan in Report 770, and more of the same in reports 888, 1013, 1023 in INA 499.
† "*Madrassi*" was the term used for people from Madras (now Chennai) used by people from the rest of India to refer to those from South India, martial race is a British term referring to those they considered fit for military recruitment given their preconceptions. INA numbers see INA 415.

Bose's Last Birthday Celebration

The pitiable condition of the INA was due to the lack of supplies from Japan, upon whom they depended entirely on. Relations had reached rock-bottom with each side blaming the other. The INA called the Japanese "*Murgi*" or chicken, for taking all their food. In turn, the Japanese name for the INA was "Hands-up" due to the numbers who surrendered.[24] After waiting for months, Bose was finally invited to Tokyo in October 1944 to tackle this. The Japanese once again made promises that, as usual, they did not fulfil later. He returned to Rangoon in January 1945, when for his forty-eighth birthday, a grand spectacle was organized on the 23rd. Much to his distaste, he was weighed in gold like a Mughal emperor, and the suicide *Jaanbaaz* (brave) squad paraded before him. The recruits included young women from the Jhansi regiment, young boys and other civilians and some INA men. Each one of them walked past him, saluted and with the blood running from their right thumb pricked with a needle, signed their name on an oath with their blood. A great battle with the Indian Army pursuing them after the debacle at Imphal was expected shortly.[25]

The Irrawaddy – it was like "fighting a sword with a needle"[*]

As the 1st INA Division had been badly mauled, the 2nd Division had been called up from Malaya. In January 1945, Bose addressed them in Rangoon. Jemadar Iltaf Razak from Hazara recalled him telling them the INA had done well in 1944, and now it was their turn. Bose apologized that they had to make the long journey of over 1,000 miles on foot, and would have to continue to the front the same way. But he promised better food and conditions than in 1944. Razak found him uninspiring and unconvincing. The division moved towards the front.[26]

Defending the Irrawaddy crossing were two Japanese armies and with them were 800 men of the INA Nehru Regiment, commanded by the INA's Nehru Regiment, was Major Gurbaksh Singh Dhillon.[†] Close to the front line on January 29, his dilemma was that he had no information on the Allied, Japanese or even other INA positions. That day he got a Japanese order to be in position on the river bank on the 20th, 9 days ago. When he asked why he wasn't told earlier, there was no reply.

---

[*] From My Bones, Dhillon, pg263.
[†] Chapter 2, The Changi Guard Commander.

There was no transport and he had to hire bullock carts. Soon after they arrived, the Allied attack began and he said it was like "fighting a sword with a needle".

After shelling, bombing and skirmishes that lasted a few days, the main river crossing took place on February 14, 1945. The vastly superior Allied forces were too much and by 4.00pm the exhausted, hungry, sick and poorly armed INA men cracked. In different groups 285 of them decided to surrender. The officers amongst them met at a temple on the river bank to discuss exactly how to go about this. They sent a boat across with a white flag with a message to the Indian Army announcing their intention and the next morning crossed the river in small groups as instructed.[27]

The Escape of the 2nd Division Staff Officers

Dhillon took his 500 remaining men to Mount Popa, where the 2nd Division had been asked to congregate. It was an extinct volcano that he said "rises suddenly and steeply out of a plain country".[*] Colonel Shahnawaz Khan was in charge, and the other unit there was the INA 4th Regiment under Colonel Prem Kumar Sahgal[†]. When he arrived he found that chaos reigned. Five of the division's HQ six staff officers had escaped on the night of February 28, 1945. So far, hundreds of men had deserted and even many officers, but for almost the whole officer staff of a division to do so in one go was unprecedented. The five were Majors Mohammad Sarwar, Mohammad Riaz Khan, Shanti Nath Dey, P.J. Madan and Lieutenant Mohammad Bux. Since the surrender of Singapore, the four INA Majors, who had been Second Lieutenants in the Indian Army, had got to know each other well. Three shared a house and the fourth lived nearby when they were in Malaya. When the Imphal campaign failed, they decided to escape but had to be cautious. While waiting in Rangoon to go to front, they started practicing not eating for a day and waking long distances just like Lieutenant Pillai had for his own escape. Most importantly, they managed to arrange for transfers to the same unit, the HQ of the 2nd Division.

An Ingenious Ruse

When they reached their allotted front line at Mount Popa on February 21, Sarwar wanted to escape immediately but Riaz Khan suggested they map out the area and see where the Indian Army, to whom they were headed, were. Sarwar told a trusted

---

[*] From *My Bones*, Dhillon, pg299.
[†] Formerly a Captain of the 2/10 Baluch Regiment.

soldier that if he came across any British, to tell them five Indian officers wanted to escape. Colonel Shahnawaz Khan had come for a few days to take over command of the division and then returned to Rangoon, so the coast was clear. The ringleader was Riaz and he realized it was impossible for five staff officers to escape together in normal circumstances. So he came up with an ingenious plan. At that time only Sahgal's regiment was at Popa. Riaz proposed that given this, the normal role of the HQ company of coordinating the action of three regiments when the division was at full strength was not required, and it could be better used instead to fight. And to prepare for this, undergo some training. This plan was agreed. Having already mapped out the area by now, Riaz proposed a night march along a route that would take the men closer to the front. Once reached, he hoped to escape. As part of the exercise he ordered that important documents and Rs 10,000 in cash be carried so they could practice protecting them.

The Trial Run

The entire HQ company set off at midnight on February 27, but they could not escape as Riaz felt his clerk had been suspicious. Besides, they had started too late and had still been too close to Sahgal's troops. He had also not outlined roles to the escapers so they could not separate from the rest. Undeterred, he took this as a good rehearsal. He told all the men this was a trial run and they would repeat it properly the next day.

To make it realistic, in the morning Riaz called the officers and NCO and criticized their performance last night and insisted they do better today. He assigned roles – for juniors to practice command instead of the officers, he appointed NCOs in charge of the two platoons. Two of the escaping officers were to be with him as his deputies and the other two were to go ahead, inform forward units a practice march was happening and locate important landmarks along the route.

The Real Thing

At 8.30pm the officers who were to go on ahead left, then Riaz and the rest followed. They met at a pre-agreed spot a mile beyond other INA men. Now all together, they marched some more until they reached a junction where the two platoons were to split and follow a route prescribed by Riaz. He then told the platoon commanders they should continue on their own and report to HQ the next morning, as he and the "superfluous" officers had to investigate reports of British troops nearby.

The five escaping officers were now alone, only with their trusted batmen. They kept walking and at first light on March 1, Mount Popa was out of sight. After getting lost, they finally came across an Indian patrol and asked for directions to their HQ. The men refused, but agreed to carry a note there and soon a truck arrived to pick up Riaz and his four comrades.

"Ghaddaar" or Traitor Week

When their escape was discovered in the morning, a storm broke. Bose was away from Rangoon and was called back urgently. When he heard the news, he locked himself in his room for many days, and refused to meet anyone. He considered it a personal failure as he had been at Popa a few days ago. When he emerged, he issued an order authorizing all in the INA to shoot anyone even suspected of deserting. He also ordered a Traitors week to be held, where the men in camps were asked to burn effigies of the five officers, stab them with bayonets and stage plays attacking them. A competition was held, with judges deciding which was the best one. He was so upset that he told his commanders that if this happened again, he would shoot himself.[28]

The Last Stand at Popa

Back on Mount Popa, much was happening. When the escape of the officers was discovered on March 1, Sahgal was furious and sent out search parties hunting them down. This continued for many days. On March 5 Havildar Abdullah Khan, a tall 33-year-old Pathan from Mianwala formerly of the 1/13 Frontier Force Rifles, was leading one such patrol. At the outskirts of a village, they exchanged fire with a British jeep patrol. Cautiously approaching the first jeep, they found a dead soldier in it. Then they came across another soldier next to a second jeep. He was badly wounded in the abdomen and according to Khan begged him many times to finish him off. Khan shot him in the head. They found a third jeep that was stuck in mud and could not be retrieved. Khan took the two jeeps back to camp, along with the equipment in the third. Sahgal recommended him for the *Sher-i-Hiind* medal and took one of the jeeps for himself.[29]

Sarwar's Leaflets

Around this time, leaflets signed by Major Sarwar, one of the officers who had escaped, started appearing in Popa. The 715 men who deserted the 1st Division earlier may have seen the *Hamara Hindustan* leaflets, but the 2nd Division had not. They still believed they would be shot if they deserted or surrendered. These leaflets, signed by one who had just escaped, were proof that this was not true. It also had a map of an escape route. For many men, this was the catalyst that solved the same impossible dilemma faced by the men in the 1st Division, and they grabbed at the chance it gave them. Sahgal noted in his diary "There is no discipline left and morale is gone. They are also a source of nuisance to me as they wander about and give away my positions."[30]

On March 30, a joint Japanese-INA attack was planned at Legyi in the Popa area, but unfortunately the night before Sahgal, who was carrying the detailed orders, was ambushed in his jeep. He was able to escape but the plans were captured. Khan was sent looking for them but failed to do so. The orders needed to be changed at the last minute and the attack was postponed to April 3. Once again, they fought well but were outnumbered. This was the last stand at Popa.[31]

Around this time, Sahgal's regiment disintegrated as men began deserting to the Indian Army nearby after having held out under tough conditions for a month. On April 3, Havildar Khan joined them. When Sehgal heard, he cancelled his Sher-i-Hind recommendation. In his diary he said there was "great alarm and despondency". It was too late. On April 8, the Japanese ordered the division to withdraw and a wholesale rout began. Sahgal, Gurbaksh Dhillon and Shahnawaz Khan must have asked themselves, "when shall we three meet again?" They were not to know that they would, in just a few months, under the most dramatic manner imaginable.[32]

The End of the INA in Burma

Bose was in Rangoon and had been expecting the Japanese to hold off Slim's Fourteenth Army for the whole year. Even if that was optimistic, he was surprised when they told him as soon as April 21, 1945, that they were evacuating Burma. He left on April 24 with his key men to continue the movement from Bangkok. The INA in Rangoon was to surrender to the Indian Army when it arrived, and importantly maintain law and order until they did. During the Japanese invasion in 1942, there was a gap between when the British left and the Japanese came, during which there was much looting, especially of Indians. This time, peace had to be maintained in the city at all costs. An arrangement was worked out with the Burmese, and this was the last service of the INA. They surrendered when the British arrived on May 4, 1945. Shahnawaz Khan's 2nd Division gave up later that month.[33]

"Despite the INA's military failure....it hastened the process of India's independence" Sugata Bose

Poorly supplied by Japan, the INA did not stand a chance, thousands died of starvation and sickness. However, to avoid their sacrifice would have meant the INA not fighting at all. Bose was determined that they must, even if poorly equipped. He believed their sacrifice would resonate with Indians, and in this he was going to be right when the time came. Though the INA lost the battle, it won the hearts of the people of India after the war.[34]

Chapter 9

DESPERATION
BEFORE LIBERATION

"If the war did not end by 1945, there was definitely no hope of our survival."

Warrant Officer Clerk John Baptist Crasta[*]

As the INA faced its tryst with destiny in Burma in 1944, the Indian POWs in the Torture Islands of the South West Pacific Area were desperate. When they arrived in 1943 the situation had been bad enough. Then, the Americans started a blockade of the area. Their submarines attacked any ship with supplies and bombers pounded Japanese positions almost every day. But there was no large-scale attempt to recapture the islands as their focus turned north towards Japan. It left the POWs with much worse conditions. The diarist Captain Patel said that the men "crave and pray for the Americans coming but Americans seem nowhere near". Food became very scarce, and morale became so low that men stole from each other. From June 1944, Patel said there was no salt anymore, a necessity the men yearned for.[†]

Jemadar Chint Singh in New Guinea

In another part of New Guinea, was Jemadar Chint Singh of the 2/12 Frontier Force Rifles. His unit had been at Kotah Bahru in north Malaya when the Japanese had landed on December 8, 1941. He had later joined the INA and was one of the 4,500 who refused to remain after Mohan Singh was arrested. Shipped off to the Torture Islands, in a memoir written shortly after the war, he said "grass was our vegetable

---

[*] Crasta quotes and references in this chapter, from *Eaten by the Japanese: The Memoir of an Unknown Indian Prisoner of War*, The Invisible Man Press, New York, 2013, pg70.
[†] Patel diary quotes in this chapter, see INA225 where its diary starts on pg165.

and lizards, grasshoppers and mice were our vitamins".* They lived on this and sac sac, trees of which were found all over the island. In a long, gruelling process they extracted a white, tasteless sap from the trees. It was difficult to eat, but all they had. He cursed his fate and "abused all the gods we worship in India". There was a feeling of darkness all around and life felt like a burden. Singh wanted to commit suicide but was not strong enough to do it. The men talked constantly of food, what they used to enjoy earlier, the dishes they missed most at this time, and the feast they would have when they finally became free. The jolly Captain Gopal Dass, IMS, joked that he would invite them to his daughter's wedding back home and serve them lizard and sac sac.

The men somehow kept alive on hope, but many died with the words DESH† and AMERICA on their lips. Every day American planes flew overheard. To be given a peaceful end, they would be told the Americans would reach by the end of the month. Singh rued the treatment by the Japanese. He said, "we work tirelessly for 18 hours a day in the scorching heat of the tropics, worked like pack animals carrying loads over mountains 3,700 feet high, but they were never satisfied". He wondered if it was only towards Indians and regretted not being able to retaliate, as they were beaten if they talked back.

Warrant Officer Crasta in New Britain

Meanwhile in New Britain, Crasta said, "If the war did not end by 1945, there was definitely no hope of our survival. It would have been better to have died earlier like the rest, but having undergone such a long ordeal, it would be most tragic to die now". After having this gut-wrenching thought, he latched on to hope and said "No, no, we would see peace and better days. God would reward us! He had saved us from a thousand and one deaths. He would help us now too". He too added that salt was more valuable to them than gold.

The army had been a home for all these men, but that support system no longer existed. The identity of each soldier was linked strongly with their battalion. Even within it, men of specific castes and creeds were grouped together in companies as each had strict rules about food. That company was their family. After so many years of captivity when they were moved from one place to the other, very few men were together. Work parties of 200 may have men from 20 units, Sikhs,

---

* Chint Singh was one of the 4,500 POWs who left the INA when Mohan Simgh disbanded it (Chapter 7). For his quotes, see Pacific Manuscripts Bureau (PMB), Australian National University. PMB1249, A Brief Sketch of the Fate of 3,000 Indian POWs in New Guinea, henceforth Chint Singh.
† The Hindi word for country/home or India.

Muslims and Hindus, further split into a dozen castes and ethnic backgrounds. How they survived without the comradery of their family within the army cannot be imagined. Crasta was one such lone man, but he was not alone. Despite their own deprivations, he found humanity in Rup Lal and Lance-Naik Mohant Ram, both from another unit. At this time Crasta was desperately ill and Rup Lal shared his own food with him, while Mohant Ram washed and mended his clothes. He said "I did not belong to their unit, nor was of their place and caste". Yet they did what they could to make him comfortable.*

The Japanese worked the men like beasts and deprived them of food and medicines. They added to it with an onslaught of propaganda with news of astonishing Japanese victories, Subhas Bose's arrival in Singapore, grand INA parades and 1 million volunteers from Malaya. In April 1944 they were told Calcutta had been captured, Delhi bombed and the Japanese were marching towards it. They did not know what to believe. If it was true and Bose would soon unfurl the national flag at the Red Fort in Delhi, they feared for what mayhem the Japanese would have unleashed on their families and other Indians on the way.[1]

The Japanese say "I cannot go Japan, you cannot go India, we all die"

If all this was not enough, there was the fear of the end. In 1945 they knew the war had turned and the Japanese were losing, no matter what they said. They knew them well by now, and expected a fight to the death. The Indians would be taken down with them. Patel was told by a Japanese soldier "I cannot go Japan, you cannot go India, we all die". In New Britain where Crasta was, they had stockpiled weapons and used the POWs and civilian labourers to dig a vast network of 500 kilometres of tunnels, underground hospitals and bunkers to face the expected Allied invasion. General Imamura Hitoshi, the Japanese commander of the area, was based in Rabaul in New Britain. He said "owing to the establishment of the underground fortress, 70,000 of the Rabaul district's army were in firm belief of victory". They expected "heavy bombing and shooting", but eagerly awaited this "decisive battle" of their "holy war".†

In June 1945, Imamura ordered Indian POWs to fight the Allies along with the Japanese, and when they refused, their work hours were increased and meagre

---

*   Stanley and Crasta pg 70.
†   Patel Diary see above, Imamura, see *The Tenor of My Life* by Imamura Hitoshi, AWM MSS1089 pg243–248. Imamura had served as Japan's Military Attache in India in the 1930s and was an admirer of Buddha, Gandhi and Rabindranath Tagore.

food reduced even more. On August 2, they were asked again, given one month to decide, and warned that others who had refused had been executed. As things stood, Crasta himself believed that with the lack of food he would be dead by the end of 1945. Even if he miraculously saw the dawn of 1946, in the "decisive battle" the Japanese would die fighting, and he and all the other POWs with him would perish in the crossfire. Any way he looked at it, the situation was dire.[2]

The Americans Rampant, and the Japanese Desperate

The fate of Crasta, Patel, Chint Singh and other POWs in the Torture Islands was inextricably linked with the Pacific war, where American strength was rampant. After they cut off the Torture Islands, they turned north, to start the long journey, island by island to reach Japan. In between lay the occupied Philippines and many islands scattered in the Pacific with Japanese bases. Quite unknown earlier, these islands soon entered the lexicon of World War II. After a costly battle, Tarawa, halfway between New Guinea and Hawaii, was captured in November 1943, then used as a base to take the Marshall Islands in February 1944. Before they moved further north, the Americans engaged in fierce naval battles to cut off the Philippines.[3]

Next, the island of Saipan was invaded in July 1944. There were a small number of Japanese civilians present, and it was here that the Americans first saw a new and alarming aspect of the Japanese national character. So far they had seen their soldiers fight to the end. Now they saw how the military treated its own civilians, and how they in turn reacted. After the invasion, the civilians were herded onto the top of a cliff and asked to jump to their death. Without hesitation, the men and women grabbed their children in their arms and did just that. Only one family resisted, and were struck down by the army.[4]

After large parts of the Japanese navy were destroyed at Leyte Gulf, the Philippines was invaded in October 1944. American military might was immense. They always had had more men, warships and planes to deploy, as the Japanese ran out of their own. So as the bitter fighting in the Philippines continued, the Americans moved further north to the iconic battle of Iwo Jima. Halfway between Saipan and Japan, it was a vital staging post for the island hopping strategy. After a fierce battle, it was captured in February 1945.

The first part of Japan to be invaded was its southernmost island, Okinawa, the site of a gruesome battle. The civilians were asked to handover all their food to the military and commit suicide. They did so with razors, hatchets and sickles, while soldiers watched. A frightened child who cried out was taken from its mother's arms and strangled by one. An army that could be so brutal with its own people could not but be more atrocious with foreigners.

"The whole city of Hiroshima was destroyed instantly by a single bomb"[*]

At first, "geography had been on Tokyo's side."[†] There were no bases close enough from where American bombers could attack. However, once Saipan and the other Marianna Islands were captured in 1944, fire-bombing raids began using Boeing's B29 Superfortress, twice the size of the legendary British Lancaster bomber. Every day for months, Japan was bombed in preparation for America's invasion. Most cities were wiped out and hundreds of thousands of people died. In August 1945, the war was poised on a knife's edge and was expected to last another year of bitter hand to hand fighting in the streets with heavy casualties on both sides. This was what Crasta and the others feared would also happen to them in the Torture Islands. Only something unexpected could shorten the war. It was then that unexpectedly not one, but three such events occurred.

At 2.00am on August 6, 1945, Colonel Paul Tibbets taxied his B29 Superfortress Enola Gay down the runway at Tinian, an island near Saipan. In the belly of the plane was Little Boy, a huge new bomb. Over 10 feet long it weighed 5 tons. It flew northwest towards Japan, and soon after 8.00am it reached its target Hiroshima. Little Boy was dropped and exploded at 8.15am. "The whole city of Hiroshima was destroyed instantly by a single bomb".[‡] With the explosive power of 20,000 tons of TNT, it killed over 100,000 and wounded an equal number.[5] In a split second "this hitherto little-known Japanese city achieved a fame so terrible".[§]

In the race to make the first atom bomb, America had won and through this demonstration of its power, hoped the Japanese would be down on their knees. They were told more would come if they did not surrender. The Japanese did not believe it was an atom bomb and even if it was, that more could have been made. Besides, the death toll did not move them. There was no surrender.[6]

"The Luck of Kokura"[¶]

Then at 1.00am on August 9, the Soviet Union attacked the Japanese in Manchuria. It was this second unexpected event that made the Imperial Council of the six senior-most statesmen consider negotiations with the Allies. They argued for hours

---

[*] *Japan's Decision to Surrender* by Robert Butow, Stanford University Press, 1954 (reference courtesy Professor Peter Stanley), pg151.

[†] *Hitting Home – The Air Offensive Against Japan* by Daniel L. Hardman, Air Force History and Museums Program, 1999.

[‡] Butow pg151.

[§] Butow pg150.

[¶] https://www.atomicarchive.com Atomic Bombing of Nagasaki, The Missions accessed Nov 11, 2024.

and were deadlocked at three-three. While this heated debate was on, another B29 with a second atom bomb headed towards its target, the arsenal at Kokura. When it arrived, the city was obscured by clouds. The bomb could have been dropped, but the observation plane needed to view the impact, so they headed to the alternative target, Nagasaki. Thus, clouds overhead and the need of research data saved Kokura, but unfortunately meant the destruction of Nagasaki. The weather was clear, and after the bomb it became a "graveyard with not a tombstone standing".[*]

"We must bear the unbearable"[†]

While the council debated, they were told about this second bomb. Still, it was deadlocked, so there was no choice but to have an Imperial Conference. At ten minutes to midnight on August 9, Emperor Hirohito entered the bunker near his library to hear his leading statesmen and soldiers. They argued amongst themselves in his presence but could not agree on what to do. Finally, "Without the slightest hesitation but with visible emotion welling up within him, the Emperor arose from his chair at the head of the table. The others immediately snapped to attention and bowed in His Majesty's direction". He said, "the time has come when we must bear the unbearable…I swallow my own tears and give my sanction to accept the Allied proclamation on the basis outlined by the Foreign Minister".

Soon after noon on August 15, 1945, people in Japan heard the emperor's voice for the first time over radio, in fact for most it was the first they had ever heard him speak. He conveyed his decision to accept the provisions of the Allied joint declaration. The word surrender was not used, but that is what it was.[7]

The Japanese were shattered. Imamura had been unable to hear the emperor's speech and was given a transcript. The next morning, he sat before his men. "I started to read the Imperial speech. I choked on the way and sobbing here and there made me (it) more difficult to continue. After a while I could just manage to finish it". He too refused to call it a surrender, but an "Armistice".[‡]

"The happiest day of my life"[§]

A few hours after Imamura's emotional message to his men, Crasta noticed an unusual panic amongst the Japanese. Next morning, no work was assigned. The day after that, a rumour spread that peace had been declared, confirmed by a

---

[*] Butow pg154–9.
[†] Butow pg168–176 for this paragraph.
[‡] Imamura pg248.
[§] Crasta pg70.

Japanese nurse. Crasta refused to believe it. It was too good to be true. But on the 19th, the end of the war was announced at the morning roll call. It is impossible for us today to imagine what this meant for him and the others. Crasta said it was the happiest day of his life, as if a second birth had resurrected him from sure death. As the Japanese wept in despair, the Indians wept with relief.

"Do not celebrate this victory as my men may harm you"*

Captain Dr Sham Singh Sekhon, IMS, found out in a different way. Hundreds of miles away at a POW camp in Kuching, Borneo, he said that one day in the middle of August 1945 they heard the groaning sounds of American planes as they flew overhead, but for the first time no bombs. The next morning, they found leaflets in English and Japanese with the terms of surrender. Unusually, that morning here was no roll call. This camp had Indian, British and Australian POWs, and Sekhon was the seniormost Indian. Later that day, the camp commander, Lieutenant-Colonel Suga Tatsugi, called Sekhon and his British and Australian counterparts to his office. In another first, he offered them tea and chairs to sit on. He then formally announced that the war was over as "we could have fought man to man, tank to tank, and ship to ship, but we could not fight the atom bomb". When they returned to barracks, he advised "do not celebrate this victory as my men may harm you."

"May harm you" was an understatement. There was real fear. The war had ended, but the Allies were nowhere to be seen. They could be hundreds of miles away and may take days or weeks to reach. Meanwhile, the Japanese could kill them to destroy evidence of ill-treatment. Thinking of the dozens of instances of POWs shot, bayonetted or beheaded they had witnessed or heard of this was clearly possible. Fortunately for them, an order had been issued on August 19 by the Japanese Southern Army that controlled Southeast Asia and the Torture Islands. It said:

> From now on, all Army commanders will handle prisoners and internees as follows:
>
> 1. Work involving the use of prisoners will cease.
> 2. Food, clothing, sanitation, lodging etc will be same as for Japanese troops.[8]

There were hundreds of camps in this area and there were isolated cases where this order was not followed, but largely, it was.[9]

---

* In a discussion with Sekhon's son Jaideep Sekhon on November 14, 2023.

As the Allies were far away, it took time to take back control. The first surrender ceremony was on September 2, 1945 in Tokyo harbour, where 300 American and Allied warships had reached to visually display their might. On the aft deck of the battleship USS *Missouri*, General Douglas Macarthur, the American commander who had been defeated in of the Philippines in 1942, read out the instrument of surrender. It was first signed by Foreign Minister Shigemitsu and then others. Behind Macarthur stood Generals Arthur Percival and Jonathan Wainwright. They had surrendered to Japan in 1942 in Singapore and the Philippines, and now watched the Japanese surrender to them.[10]

"From this day, all my birthdays start"[*]

In the Torture Islands, the Australian Lieutenant-General Sturdee took the surrender from General Imamura on September 6, 1945 in Rabaul, New Britain. Then the search and recovery of POWs and internees began. Most of the Indian POWs were close by and 5,439 were found alive, the only survivors of 11,000 sent in 1943. An Australian soldier said of them "I was one of the troops who gave the Indians their first decent meal for two years. They were terribly emaciated, most of them being too weak to stand for any length of time. Never have I witnessed such joy and relief as these men expressed when escorted into an Australian camp. As they were departing for a base area an Indian expressed his relief with these words, "From this day, all my birthdays start".[11]

Thirteen at Dinner[†]

But what of Jemadar Chint Singh and the others in New Guinea? When the Australians landed, the Japanese told them 3,000 Indians had been shipped there, but none had been found. So far, Subedar-Major Baboo Ram, the diarist Captain Patel and others had led 185 out alive before the war ended. Where were the others? The Japanese had no answer, other than that it was a vast island and they were spread all over.[12]

The 3,000 men shipped to New Guinea had arrived in 6 groups. Chint Singh's originally had 545 men, but including him there were just 9 survivors. He recalled that suddenly in August 1945 their treatment at the hands of the Japanese became better. This made them uneasy, and when for almost a month they heard no news, the feeling grew. Then, on September 16, the nine survivors were told to go to Headquarters and they feared the worst. When they arrived the next morning, for the first time they were asked for their names and addresses in India. The possibility that the Japanese had surrendered tantalized them. Could it be true? Could it be that they had snatched life from the jaws of death? That night they tossed and turned. It

---

[*] *Smith's Weekly*, Sydney, October 13, 1945.
[†] Title from Agatha Christie.

was worse than the over 1,000 earlier nights they had spent on the Torture Islands. On each of those, they knew what to expect the next morning, another long, hungry, back-breaking and fearful day. That night was worse, as even though there was a faint hope that freedom maybe at hand, they were not sure.

The next morning one of the local inhabitants told them the war was over. It sounded like good news, but if it was true, they feared they would be killed before the Allies reached them. Then the Japanese said their emperor had stopped the fighting, so they would be taken to base and released to the Allies. The roller-coaster ride of emotions was almost too much to bear. The next day, September 18, the nine survivors paddled past the local villagers, many of whom had helped them at great risk to themselves. As he waved at them, Chint Singh saw the "ugly face" of a Japanese officer staring at him who could not touch them any more as their names had been sent to the Allies. Upon arrival, they found four Indian POWs there. Together these thirteen men had come here from Singapore twenty-eight months ago, and were the only survivors. At first they could not fathom the reality. Yes, they had seen a lot of starvation, sickness and death. But just thirteen survivors? Could it be that horrible? They were met by a Japanese officer who said the war had ended and that they were now friends. He urged them not to badmouth the Japanese when back in India. So far it was good news, but until they reached they reached the Allies, they were in fear of their lives.

On September 25 they moved to a new location. There they found a leaflet in the local pidgin* about the Japanese surrender. It made them feel a bit better, but they were not yet out of danger. It had been dropped by a plane and the Allies on the ground could be hundreds of miles and many days away. On the 29th, when the thirteen had dinner, they did not know it was the last time they all would be together.[13]

And then there were Eleven

The next morning, Sepoys Abraham and Jai Ram, who had been very sick, died. On his deathbed, Jai Ram told Chint Singh he felt free not being under the thumb of the Japanese like so many others had been. He died happy. They were now down to just eleven survivors.[14]

"Today we have been reborn"†

As they mourned their fellow soldiers, a Japanese boat arrived with a letter that gave the first concrete sign of their freedom. It was from an Australian officer,

---

* Pidgin is a simplified speech used for communication between people with different languages (Mirriam-Webster).
† Chint Sing PMB pg39.

Lieutenant F.O. Monk, in nearby Angoram, dated the previous day. Addressed to the Officer Commanding Indian troops, in it he said "I would like you to bring your Indian soldiers back to Angoram in the Japanese boat". It changed the whole course of the life of Chint Singh and his men. After a month of tension, they finally dared to believe they were free. It seems difficult to imagine, but he said they started to sing. They hardly had any possessions, so quickly saluted the graves of Abraham and Jai Ram, and stepped into the boat to freedom.[15]

When they reached, Chint Singh said "today we have been reborn". Monk greeted them and immediately offered everything at his disposal. They first asked for salt. They had not had any for 500 days. Then they had proper tea and biscuits, a hot bath and new clothes. They had been deprived of this for 1,500 days. For a period they just soaked in the freedom. After one and a half years of harsh captivity in Singapore, a horrible journey to New Guinea, and then two and a half years of absolute hell there, the men were ecstatic. Chint Singh learnt that besides his band of 11 survivors, another 185 had escaped before the war ended. He was happy for them, but it still meant that of the 3,000 sent to New Guinea, a staggering 2,800 men had died.[16]

On October 12, they were taken to a hospital in a bigger base. The Australians there too were very kind, and the men grew especially fond of Sergeant Ron Bader of the 2/15 Field Ambulance, who devoted himself to their care. Like a brother, he wrote letters on their behalf to their family back in India, and in the evenings took them out in ambulances to see movies. The bond between them grew daily.[17]

Abdul Latif, Munshi Ram, Dina Nath, Joginder Singh, Hamir Singh, Sher Singh, Gillu Ram, Shiv Singh, Bachan Singh and Chain Singh[*]

Besides such lively excursions, the eleven had an unpleasant but vital task, to hold the Japanese to account for the atrocities they and others had endured. For a month they gave evidence, and in mid-November it was decided to send them home. As Chint Singh had the best record of the atrocities, he was asked to stay behind. The ten others named here were to be flown to Rabaul in New Britain, to board a ship that was to take them back to India. The night before their departure, Bader arranged a farewell party. In gratitude, the ten wrote all of those who taken such good care of them, and specially Bader, a joint letter:

---

[*] Jemadar Abdul Latif 4/9 Jat, Havildar Major Munshi Ram 3/17 Dogra, Lance-Naik Dina Nath 3/17 Dogra, Sepoy Joginder Singh 1/14 Punjab, Havildar Hamir Singh 2/12 FFR, Lance-Naik Sher Singh 2/12 FFR (Frontier Force Rifles), Sepoy Gilu Ram 2/12 FFR, Sepoy Shiv Singh, 2/12 FFR, Sepoy Bachan Singh, 1/13 FFR, Sepoy Chain Singh 2/12 FFR, see AWM 54/1010/9/79 and Chint Singh PMB.

Gentlemen, we think this part, which we have passed in your company, is the most glorious of our lives. The affection and love shown by you is unforgettable in our life...We were in hell...Now we find this place (hospital) a heaven and we are firm that there is nothing after death, either hell or heaven. Officers and men of your division have done their utmost to help our men. Thank you for your fine conduct. Good luck and your safe return to your homes.[*]

On November 15, 1945 they excitedly boarded a Dakota at Jaquinot Bay. Bader and Chint were sad to see them go as they waved them off, but happy they were headed home. The next evening Chint Singh returned from the movies and found Sergeant Bader waiting. He looked shattered and took Singh to his tent and sat him down. Bader told him that soon after take-off, the plane had crashed into a mountain in bad weather and all twenty-eight people on board had died. Chint Singh said "It was a great shock to me and made me weep. It still sounded unbelievable so I went to the signals office and asked for confirmation". Unfortunately, it was true. It was a tragic end, but at least they had been happy and on their way home. One can only hope that the crash was sudden and their death quick.[18]

A few days later, Bader published this tribute.

> In memory of my sincere friends, 10 released Indian POW killed
> In aircraft accident New Britain Thursday, November 15, 1945.
> Inserted by one who will never forget. Sgt R. Bader. 2/15 Aust Field
> Ambulance. Wewak.
> They are not old as we that are left grow old
> Age cannot weary nor the years condemn
> At the going down of the sun
> And in the morning I will remember them.[†]

And then there was One

So, after all their trials and tribulations, besides the 185 men who escaped before the war ended, of the 3,000 sent to New Guinea, only one remained, Jemadar Chint Singh, 2/12 Frontier Force Rifles.

---

[*] Guinea Gold, Papua New Guinea, November 28, 1945.

[†] The West Australian, Perth, November 27, 1945 accessed November 11, 2024 (it says death on November 18, actually on November 15).

Chapter 10

JUSTICE FROM THE AUSTRALIANS

Lieutenant-Colonel Gurbaksh Singh DSO OBE, C/O of the Jind Infantry, who spent most of his captivity in Malaya, advised his men not to single out any Japanese for their ill-treatment during the war as he said doing so would haunt them for the rest of their life. He said this was war and people are often placed in situations where they do terrible things.[1]

This was a personal choice, but for crimes during World War II, the Allies had decided to pursue justice. The scale of the tragedy of the Indian POW experience in the Torture Islands was vast. After just 30 months, only 11 of the 3,000 men in New Guinea were liberated and half of the 11,000 in New Britain. It is perhaps unfair to compare death rates. Was their experience worse than the fifth of mainly British, Australian and Dutch POWs, the more than two-thirds of the Indian civilians who died building the Burma railway? Or of the 6 survivors out of 2,500 in Sandakan in Borneo, the 3.5 million Russians who died under the Germans, and the 1 million Germans under the Russians as POWs? The millions of Jewish, Russian, Ukrainian and other civilians killed by the Nazis? Everyone's experience was horrific in its own way.[2]

India's Debt to Australia

As the worst atrocities against Indian POWs were in New Guinea and New Britain, now Australian administered, it fell to them to take this up. And what a magnificent job they did! India and Indians have to be eternally grateful to Australia. Not only did they take care of our men, they made sure the Japanese who had treated them so badly were held to account.[3]

It was a sad fate for the thousands of Indians who faced the horrors of the weeks-long journey. Once they arrived, there was hard labour with little food and medical care. In late 1943 Allied bombing began adding another terror. In 1944 and 1945 they were dying of starvation. Bose had asked for them to be brought back to join the INA, but the Japanese refused and he left it at that. It was only the sudden end of the war that saved them.

Afterwards, there was little coverage of their plight in India and other than Chint Singh writing to the mother and brother of Captain Nirpal Chand who had been beheaded, the families of other victims may not even have been aware of the trials. Unlike the Australians, the British who had arrived in New Britain did not seem sympathetic. They did they not allow the Australians to give the Indians an allowance or let them use Japanese POWs to help build their recovery camps. Crasta, who experienced both, said "we love the Australians."[*]

Chint Singh and the ten other New Guinea survivors had a much better time of it. In a warm letter to the 6th Australian division he said they "worked as angels" to help the Indians and added that "The sympathy, love and affection showed by every individual of the Div[ision] will always be with us."[†]

The Trial of the Japanese who beheaded Captain Nirpal Chand, 2/17 Dogra Regiment

For those in New Guinea, the first steps on the long road to justice began in October 1945 when the eleven survivors arrived in the main port of Wewak. Many of their guards were now POWs, and had been identified to the Australians. Detailed statements were taken about specific incidents – what was the atrocity, when and where it happened, names of the victims, and the Japanese perpetrators.[‡]

Jemadar Chint Singh and one of the men who died in the air crash, Sepoy Shiv Singh, had been present when Captain Chand was beheaded on April 22, 1944 (Chapter 7). Their testimony taken before the crash identified the four Japanese involved, who were then interrogated. After a review of the evidence, they were charged with murder. As they pleaded not guilty, a trial had to be held.[§]

The Framework of the Trial

The Chand trial began on March 15, 1946 in Rabaul, New Britain. It was conducted by the Australian War Crimes Commission, and consisted of four court members who were serving army officers, a Prosecutor and a Defence, officers with legal

---

* Crasta pg77, Writing to Chand family Chint Singh PMB manuscript.
† Letter in AWM54 779-1-20.
‡ There was a dramatic re-enactment of this on November 9, 1945 to create a photo opportunity. On the process see trail documents below.
§ The quotations and account of the Chand trial AWM54/1010/6/100, interrogations in AWM 54 1010/3/108, Indian statements in AWM54/1010/3/118. Board of Inquiry before charges filed and Mitsuba interrogation in AWM54/1010/9/79 pg257.

qualifications, and a civilian Japanese interpreter. As the court members did not have legal experience, a Judge Advocate explained the nuances of the law. In a way, he acted as the Judge and the Court were in effect the jury. Unlike some other trials where the Japanese disputed the evidence, here they agreed to the facts – they had killed Chand. Their defence was that the Indians were not POWs but their allies, as they had been in the INA. As such Japanese military law applied, under which the execution had been legal.

The Defending Officer, Lieutenant D.G.E. Hill took his job seriously and put up the best defence possible. At the start he objected to unsigned interrogations of the accused being presented as evidence. This battle was lost when the Judge Advocate quoted a regulation that allowed this as it was signed by an interpreter. Hill would attempt to discredit the interpreter and the interrogation later.

"I firmly believed my actions were lawful in this instance. There was no other way out"

Captain Mistuba Hisaneo was in command of the Japanese soldiers and the Indian POWs when Chand was beheaded. He had been with them since they arrived from Singapore in May 1943 and painted a picture of harmony in the beginning. Things changed when the first American air raids began in August 1943. Then, he said, Chand, in charge of the Indian POWs, became more demanding. Mitsuba tried to portray him as a man of shifting loyalties and did the same with Jemadar Chint Singh, who had submitted evidence. He reported that Singh had said "the Indians would be on whatever side the wind blows".

Somehow, they managed to co-exist until April 1944 when the Americans landed in parts of New Guinea. To escape from them the whole group was to march to Hollandia, 300 kilometres away. Before they set off, Indians too sick to walk were left behind, given food for six months and medical orderlies for their care, said Mitsuba. At a halt mid-way in the journey on April 22, Chand refused to move further and instigated his men, armed with sticks, stones and machetes to threaten the Japanese. Mitsuba spoke to Chand many times to reason with him, but he refused and told him "If you want to kill me, you can kill me". As he had been ordered by his commanding officer Captain Izumi to take disciplinary action if there was trouble, he decided to behead Chand, and said "I carried out the execution of Nirpal Chand myself". As per the Japanese military code, when there was violence by a mob in the face of the enemy, mutineers could be executed without trial.

The defence crafted, probably by Lieutenant Hill, was good, even if the Japanese code seemed brutal. The American enemy was close, Chand had incited his men to mutiny, so action had to be taken immediately. Mitsuba's testimony and cross-examination was most important as he was the senior-most Japanese at the beheading, and with all the interpretation involved, it took the trial to its second day.

Lieutenant Murai Koichi, "I beheaded him"

Murai was next. He agreed with what Mitsuba said and added that though he did not see Chand give the order to mutiny, he saw the Indians armed with stones and machetes. Of his role in the act, he said "I beheaded him".

Lieutenant Imamura Kazuhiko said, "The first blow was delivered by Captain Mitsuba and Lieutenant Murai delivered the second blow"

Imamura also agreed with Mitsuba's testimony and added that he saw him trying to reason with Chand, who resisted with words and action. He assisted in the execution that he believed was lawful and was also ordered to do so by Mitsuba. His earlier interrogation report stated that Chand's hands were tied, and he had sat on his stomach, but he denied this now adding "no Japanese officer with a sword would do such a thing". On the stand he said Chand did not have his hands tied and was sitting down as "This was the customary position in Japan for such an execution". Then, "the first blow was delivered by Captain Mitsuba and Lieutenant Murai delivered the second blow." To Hill's question whether death by beheading was lawful and honourable in such a case, he said yes.

"Was it customary for an officer to carry out the execution?"

At this time the court asked Imamura this vital question. He replied that generally, the officer would be in charge, and a soldier would carry it out. The implication was that as the officers had executed Chand themselves, personal animosity may have been the motivation. As a good defence lawyer, Hill had highlighted through Murai's testimony that they had no personal hatred of Chand. This aspect, as to why the officers executed him themselves, was perhaps something he had not thought of. Having realized the implication immediately, he jumped in and asked Imamura if there had been any special reason why the officers carried out the execution themselves. He gave the perfect answer, with the Indians threatening them with machetes, the soldiers were at "action stations" and not available to do this.

The Case of Lance-Corporal Hibino Kazuo

The fourth and last accused was Kazuo. The most junior of them all, his evidence and cross-examination were probably the most interesting. The main goal of the defence was to ensure the accused were not convicted by claiming the execution was legal as per the Japanese code, but they probably knew this was a long shot. The second objective, perhaps asked for by the three officers, was to avoid Hibino being convicted, for which a totally different strategy was used.

On the stand Hibino insisted he had not been present, as confirmed by each of the 3 officers before him. What stood against him was his interrogation of November 1, 1945, which stated he had tied Chand's hands and while he was executed, watched out to ensure no Indians witnessed it. This is probably what did happen, but Hill tried to distance Hibino from it and was helped by the prosecution's own evidence – his unsigned interrogation. As he failed to have it excluded, Hill discredited it. When examined, Hibino said he did recall being questioned by an Australian but denied what was stated in the interrogation. He added that Chint Singh had been present. The unsaid implication was the whole confession was coerced and false. The interpreter, he said, was half Chinese and did not understand Japanese, so the interrogator could not know what exactly Hibino had said. In a last-ditch effort, the prosecution called an official of the translation service to give credibility to the interpreter.

However, Hibino inadvertently put a nail in the coffin for the case of the officers. Much had been said by all the four accused about the Indians being armed with stones and machetes. When the Prosecutor asked him what the Japanese had done when they saw them armed this way, Hibino said the weapons had been confiscated. The prosecutor did not comment on this further then but used this with devastating effect in his closing.

The defence called only one witness, Lieutenant-Colonel Tanaka Kengoro, who had a legal background. He said that normally a mutineer would be tried before execution, but in cases like Chand's of mob violence in the face of the enemy, no trial was needed, and it was the duty of the officer to act. This case had been reported, the action approved of and acknowledged by Lieutenant-General Adachi, commander in New Guinea. When cross-examined he added that the Indians had changed status from POW to allies when they joined the INA, and as such were under Japanese law. This had also been confirmed by the war minister.

Thus ended the second full day of the trial. The court was to reconvene on March 18 to hear closing arguments.

"This case bristles with doubt"

Lieutenant Hill of the defence was up first. He reminded the court that initially the Indians had been cooperative, but that changed after the American bombers

JUSTICE FROM THE AUSTRALIANS

arrived. He cast aspersions on Chand and Chint Singh when he said they were fair weather friends. As the Americans got closer, the group had to move to safer ground. He pointed out there was no doubt that Mitsuba left behind extra supplies for the sick, as this had not been questioned by the prosecution. Once the rest set off, midway, Chand incited his men to rise armed with stones and machetes and when Mitsuba reasoned with him said, "if you want to kill me, you can kill me". He dwelt on the many attempts to make Chand see reason, to demonstrate that his execution was not a murderous impulse or motivated by personal animosity.

"Their belief was a reasonable one considering the circumstances and their knowledge as junior officers"

Hill went on to say that whether the Indians were or were not in the INA, was irrelevant. Even as POWs, their treatment should be judged by Japanese law as they had not ratified the Geneva Convention. Under this law, Chand's mutiny meant death. Then he addressed the circumstances of the three officers. The accused were platoon commanders in the field who had been told Japanese law applied to the Indians. As per that code, Chand's mutiny was treasonous, and in the face of the enemy he could be executed without a trial, as any Japanese would have been. They followed the code and beheaded him. This had been reported to Headquarters and accepted as valid. Hill's last word was that "This case bristles with doubt".

"The Killing was wholly illegal even under Japanese Military Law"

It was now the prosecution's turn. Captain J.D. Steed of the Australian Army Legal Corps was equally passionate and sharp as Hill. After going through expected territory, he came to the kill, when he said what had been done was illegal even under Japanese law. Execution without a trial was permissible in "the face of the enemy", but he said the enemy were nowhere near. He also latched onto Hibino's statement that the machetes had been taken away from the Indians and the mutineers disarmed. So not only were the Americans far away, there was no imminent insurrection either.

Must be Guilty Beyond a Reasonable Doubt

The last word was from the Judge Advocate, Captain J.H. Watson of the Australian Army Legal Corps. His address to the court was similar to what American judges say to the jury before they deliberate when the law is summed up for them. He started with the onus of the prosecution to prove guilt beyond a reasonable doubt, which was not "a mere quibble, but doubt [that] materially influences you in the conduct of your personal affairs". The court had to decide if the beheading of Chand was murder. It must be unlawful, and not excusable or justifiable. It must be voluntary, not forced. Deliberate, not accidental. The motive must be malice. If there was any doubt, the accused must be acquitted. On which law was to be applied, the prosecution said international, while the defence said it should be Japanese. The court was advised that if they were considered POWs, the prosecution was right. Lastly Mitsuba said he had followed his commanders' orders, and the three other accused had followed Mitsuba's. The advice was that only legal orders could be followed. In taking all this into account, the court must disregard their own opinion and judge the evidence as per rules outlined.

The JAG and Prosecution pave the way for Hibino's Acquittal

In Hibino's defence, Hill had said earlier that though his earlier interrogation report stated he was present at the execution, in court he denied this. Despite it being technically admissible, the court should keep in mind it was not signed by him, and there was no evidence it was read to him as all such documents are. Against his sworn word in court, the document should fail and so he should be acquitted. By now the prosecutor Steed had decided not to press for Hibino's guilt and said he had probably lied in his interrogation and had not been present at the execution. After having fought for including Hibino's interrogation at the start, perhaps after hearing the defence and prosecutions closing, the Judge Advocate said that though the documents were admissible, the court must examine the circumstances under which they were made. He was basically saying without spelling it out to ignore Hibino's interrogation and only consider what he said in court. Hill's strategy had worked.

The Verdict and the Sentence

The court adjourned at 10.50am and the four members were back after twenty-eight minutes. Their verdict was – the three officers were guilty and Hibino not guilty. Before the court decided the sentence, Hill had a chance to request for mitigation. His Japanese co-counsel asked him to plead that the men "were quite frank and honest, admitted the killing, honestly believed they were justified and had legal authority". The court took twenty-three minutes to decide the sentence and returned with twenty years for Misuba and Murai who had done the beheading and five years for Imamuro who had assisted. All of them petitioned for their sentences not to be confirmed, but these pleas were rejected.

Mitsuba was charged with killing or ordering the death of more Indian POWs. He did so, he said, as some had stolen rice, others had quarrelled and disturbed work and finally shot some who were too sick to march. On March 21 he was sentenced to be hanged, again on another case on March 22, and a third time on April 4. On April 13, 1946, he committed suicide. He was brought to trial on a fifth case, but was already dead by then.[4]

The Command Trials to hold Generals to Account

Seeing the scale and extent of the atrocities, the Australians decided to hold the Generals who had commanded these men responsible as well. Such trials were not easy, as not only must the crimes be proven once more, but also that the General either knew and was hence complicit, or if he did not know was derelict in his duty. Five such "Command" trials were held, in four of which the atrocities against Indians was the main focus. This took many months to arrange. Evidence had to be gathered, senior lawyers arranged for both sides, the defence had to be given time to examine all the documents to be presented in court (what we know as "discovery"), strategy had to be decided, witnesses gathered and prepared.[5]

The trial of Lieutenant-General Adachi Hatazo, the commander of the Japanese Eighteenth Army in New Guinea, began on April 8, 1947. It was on that island that only 198 out of 3,000 Indians had survived the ill-treatment of his men. Adachi was then 70 years old, a career military man. Destined for the army from a young age, he joined a military school at 13 and went through the training and service that took him to three-star rank. After serving in China for many years, he took up his New Guinea post in November 1942 and remained there until Japan's surrender.[*]

Another Unsigned Interrogation

The prosecution's allegation was that Adachi's men had committed many "beastly" war crimes, he had known, and had done nothing to rein them in. Their case would have been easier had they not forgotten to get his interrogation signed. In a long session on December 17–18, 1945, he said that besides him, authority to execute offenders was only with divisional commanders of the rank of Major-General, and that too only for treasonous acts like contacting the Allies. Chand being beheaded

---

[*] Adachi Trial and quotations, see AWM54/1010/3/8.

by a Captain, for refusing to let his men too sick to take another step march another 100 kilometres, was clearly illegal by Adachi's own admission. Inexcusably, Adachi was not asked to sign this interrogation and it was never used.[6]

Adachi's "License to Kill"

When the trials began, one of the planks of the Japanese defence was that Adachi had issued an Emergency Order in October 1944 to control growing indiscipline in his army given the precarious military situation. In the face of the enemy, any offenders caught in the act or who confessed could be executed without trial by the local commander. No proof of this order and the reports that were to follow such an action were found as the Japanese said all the records had been destroyed due to enemy action. Indeed, a lot of papers would have gone up in flames because of Allied bombing, but Tokyo had also issued an order on August 16, 1945, the day after the surrender, to destroy all documents relating to POWs. Due to this, when the trials began there was little evidence of what the Japanese had actually done.[7]

The prosecution called this a "license to kill". Though it followed the Japanese military code, a specific order by Adachi reinforcing it made it easier for the Japanese to summarily execute Indians and others. They said "There is nothing so catching as liberty that degenerates into license. Once it becomes known that certain things of this kind can be done without any reprimand, then it becomes easy, and, in fact, almost inevitable that the persons will go further than perhaps…what was originally intended, and, if they do, the man behind the machine was liable".

This is exactly what happened. One Japanese officer said, "he had General Adachi's authority to execute Indians for any offence". Another said, "The senior officer of a locality regardless of rank could mete out any punishment to an Indian". Adachi denied this in this interrogation, but it is what his officers believed.

The Star Witness, Subedar Chint Singh

Given the status of the trial, both sides had pulled out all the stops. The court was presided over by a Major-General and five others officers. The prosecution was led by Mr L.C. Badham, KC (King's Counsel and a barrister-at-law) assisted by two officers with legal experience. The defence was headed by Mr Fujimoto Kafuji, assisted by a Japanese Lieutenant-Colonel and their own interpreter.

Before the trial the defence was given dozens of statements alleging crimes that were to be used as evidence. The operative law did not require the person who had made these allegations to be present, and the defence was denied the right to confront their accuser, making their job more difficult. This departure from international law was made as the accusers were POWs who had gone home or already died.

On the first day of the trial, the defence was surprised to be confronted by Chint Singh in person. Though his was one of the documents given by the prosecution, they did not expect to see him there as all the POWs had gone home. After providing detailed written testimony against Mitsuba and others, Singh had returned home in early 1946. Promoted to Subedar, he was called back to give evidence in person, the only Indian asked to do so in all the Australian trials. For a high profile case like this, the prosecution wanted to add credibility to their evidence. As most of the atrocities under Adachi were on Indians in New Guinea, Singh was asked to be present to back this up in person. Arrayed against him were the accused, a Lieutenant-General, supported by four senior defence witnesses including a full General and a Lieutenant-General. In addition, a Captain and a Lieutenant came to testify on conditions for junior officers in the field.

Singh's role was vital and his testimony and cross-examination took as much time as Adachi's. He had been present when many of the atrocities had occurred, even if he had not witnessed the executions. His job was to bring a face to the names of all the Indians who had suffered. Articulate, fluent in English and by now well versed in legal nuances, he was almost a perfect witness. In such a long testimony he often talked about Singapore and the prosecutor Mr Badham had to tell him to "Get your mind on what happened after Wewak". Once, he said, after a day's labour, "we came back home" which made it sound like a happy environment and not captivity. Badham jumped at it and said you mean back to the camp? There were also instances of him "leading the witness" to ensure that Singh clearly specified things he had left unsaid. The defence tried to discredit him by saying he had shifting loyalties as had been alleged in the Chand case and by highlighting a factual inaccuracy in his testimony. Singh took it all in his stride and handled the cross well.

The second star witness was Captain Nirpal Chand who spoke from his grave, as it was his beheading which was discussed the most.

The General's Defence

The defence claimed that the Indians had joined the INA and were as such allies of Japan and under their military law. The executions had been valid as per this code as stated in the Chand case. Ironically both the sides quoted Adachi's Emergency Order to prove their case about his role as a commander. The prosecution said it was a "license to kill" and the defence said it showed he had taken action, even including cannibalism as a crime when it was not yet in the Japanese code. They added that seventy Japanese had been executed under its ambit, so it was fairly applied.

Another irony came up in the discussion of their status when the prosecutor said it was beyond belief that the Indians had joined the Japanese in Singapore. This would have been treason and they would have lost any safeguards. In fact, the Indians in New Guinea had joined Mohan Singh's INA and left it when he was arrested. It seems neither the Australians nor the Japanese in Rabaul knew what had really happened in Singapore in 1942.

The trial took two weeks and ended on April 23. The court took one hour and fifty-nine minutes to deliberate and found Adachi guilty. He did not wish to ask for mitigation and after ten more minutes, he was sentenced to life in prison. Lieutenant-General Adachi Hatazo committed suicide on the night of September 8, 1947.

Including the command cases, the Australians held 100 trials for atrocities against Indian POWs. In sixty-four cases, all or some of the Japanese accused were found guilty. Thirty-six men were sentenced to death by hanging and others were given jail terms from six months to life in prison.[8]

We saw here the brutality of war and what it made the Japanese do, the same people who today are renowned for their grace and kindness. Despite having lived through hell under them, many Indian POWs admired those Japanese traits that were honourable and recalled fondly some of the guards who were kind. And so now we turn to the story of what happened to the Indians when they returned home.

Chapter 11

BACK HOME – A SUDDEN RETURN OR A DEAFENING SILENCE

A Telegram from Colombo

On October 25, 1945, Baltikalanda Uthaiah Thangamma was in her husband's home in Coorg when suddenly her brother rushed in, breathless. He had run 5 kilometres from her father's home with a telegram in his hands. It was from her husband, Jemadar Baltikalanda Medappa Uthaiah, 1st Mysore Infantry. She had last seen him six years ago when the then 27 year old, rising rapidly up the ranks of the Mysore State Forces, had left for a prestigious training course. While he was there, World War II broke out and he was ordered to join his battalion that was getting prepared to serve. He was unable to go home to visit his young pregnant wife, who heard about his new orders in a letter from him. She waited for weeks and months hoping he would be back for the birth of their first child, but he was not allowed. A baby girl was born but Thangamma was depressed and the child was looked after by her sisters. A year later, Uthaiah's unit was shipped to Malaya, dashing hope of a reunion. After the war began a few months later in December 1941, all she knew was that many men had died and she had no news of her husband. Again she waited and prayed, there was no news. After a year he was presumed dead and the young, beautiful Thangamma was encouraged by her father and mother-in-law to remarry, a common practice. She refused and wanted to see her husband's dead body first.[1]

Visits to temples and prayer gave her strength to resist the pressure and coaxing of her family. Years went on with Thangamma moving between her father's and husband's homes to avoid their pleas. She remained steadfast. Then, on that fateful day in October 1945, out of the blue her father received the telegram from Colombo from his son-in-law saying that he was arriving shortly in Bangalore. This was the first communication from him since he had left. Thangamma was elated, her husband was alive. For six years she had waited and waited, hoping for the impossible, and it had finally happened.

Mariammal's Wait

Thangamma's dearest wish was met and her husband had returned. Her trauma and her wait was shared by thousands of Indian wives. One of them was Mariammal, who kept on waiting. Her husband, Sapper Marimuthu of the 13 Field Company Madras Sappers never came home. After he sailed from Bombay to Singapore on December 21, 1941 she did not hear anything from or about him. With four young children, including an infant, she somehow endured. Four years later when the war ended, POWs who survived came back, but there was still no news of him, just a deafening silence. Then in 1946, a fellow soldier from a neighbouring village who had been in Singapore, told the Sapper's brother he had died there in 1942. From that day she wore the Hindu widow's white saree. What had exactly happened to him could not be ascertained as most records of Indian POWs were destroyed by the Japanese. Mariammal died on August 3, 1995 without knowing more.[2]

The Green Channel – On the MV Highland Brigade Home

This was the story of over 60,000[*] families in India. After hearing almost nothing about their husband, father or brother for five years, when the war ended, they waited patiently. Though the war had ended abruptly, the British had arranged what they called a Green Service akin to what we know as the Green Channel to get POWs back home as fast as possible. In Crasta's Torture Islands most of the survivors were in New Britain, from where repatriation ships were arranged. Crasta boarded the fourth such shipment on the MV Highland Brigade that left on November 13, 1945. After two months recuperating, his journey home was peaceful. When they stopped at Singapore, he found that the war had sucked out the gay atmosphere, there was nothing in the shops that had been so full of bustle earlier. From there they sailed to Bombay and when they arrived on December 2 he found it to be much livelier than expected. When he eventually reached home, he found his mother in a black saree, worn by Christian women in mourning. She had not heard from him in five years and thought he was dead. One can only imagine the emotions as the two met, echoed in thousands of such joyous reunions across India.[3]

Jemadar Chint Singh had been declared missing during the war. The family feared the worst but kept on hoping, with his elder brother writing to his battalion's home base for news of him. Soon after he was liberated, Chint Singh wrote to his wife and brother. Describing what they had been through was very difficult. He had

---

[*] There were 67,000 Indian troops in Britain's Malaya Command, that covered Singapore, Malaya and Borneo.

been through war with men next to them having their brains blown out. Then he spent years in humiliating captivity followed by the horrific conditions under the Japanese. He had even contemplated suicide. It was a struggle, as he did not know how and what to write. Even when he came home in 1946 after providing detailed evidence for the trials held by Australia, it was difficult to describe what he had gone through.[4]

The Only Indian in Changi

Meanwhile in Singapore, after the sudden end of the war, the 5th Indian Division made a cautious occupation on September 4, 1945. Besides the Indian POWs in their own camps, at Changi where all the Britons were, they were surprised to find an Indian. He was Lieutenant Baleshwar Prasad Singh, 1/7 Rajput. A forest officer from Benares before the war, he joined the army and was captured in Burma in 1943. In a POW camp there, he was so staunchly anti-Japanese that they wanted to segregate him from the others, so he was taken far away to Changi. The Japanese strictly segregated everyone by nationality, but they did not want him anywhere near other Indians, so he was kept with the British in Changi. He spent the rest of the war smuggling news to Indian camps across Singapore.[5]

The Three Musketeers

In one of those camps were two of The Three Musketeers, officers of the 2/10 Baluch Regiment, Captain Mohammed Anwar Khan Durrani and Lieutenant Ismail Khan. The third musketeer was Lieutenant Abrar Hussain who had been sent to the Torture Islands of New Britain in December 1942. Before the three split up, they earned the sobriquet The Three Musketeers as they were close friends and spent all their time together. Ismail was the mischievous one and would inveigle Durrani into mixing up the fastidious Hussain's carefully arranged shoes. Choice expletives were exchanged when this happened, but this was of course par for the course between close friends serving together. Hussain was one of the lucky few who survived almost four years in New Britain, and married Ismail Khan's sister after the war.[6]

Charan Singh's Camera

Lance-Naik Charan Singh arrived in Singapore in September 1945 with the other Indian troops. In the Service Corps, his job was to feed them and he reached out to local merchants to source supply. He also had a camera and took photographs of the Japanese and of the city, a rare record from an Indian soldier. He was not present at the impressive surrender ceremony held at the Padang before the city hall on September 12, 1945. This was arranged by Vice-Admiral Louis Mountbatten, related to the British royal family and soon to be the last viceroy of India. The Indian Army was represented by Brigadier K.S. Thimaya, later to be chief of Army Staff in independent India.[7]

The Repentant British at Changi

Besides the Indian soldiers of Indian Army, there were their former British commanding officers who had been kept separately at Changi since their surrender to Japan over three years ago. During the war, means were devised to maintain contact and they were aware that their men had felt let down and abandoned. Lieutenant-Colonel L.V. Fitzpatrick, Mohan Singh's battalion commander, and other British officers were aware of this and wanted to stay with their men after liberation. Fitzpatrick accompanied his men back to India where he spent two months before returning to the UK in November 1945.[8]

The Second Controversial INA Plane Crash[*]

On August 16, the day after Japan surrendered, Bose left Singapore for the last time. He flew to Bangkok, Saigon and from there was headed to Manchuria to seek Russian help. He was convinced that India needed help to achieve independence. After seeking Hitler, then Tojo's help, he now sought out Stalin.

On August 21, the Japanese announced to the world that he had died in an air crash. No one believed it. With his dramatic escape from Calcutta in 1941, his stealthy submarine journey from Germany to Asia in 1943, Bose had disappeared earlier to come back to life. Besides, he had been thought dead in an earlier air crash on March 24, 1942 – the one that had claimed the lives of Giani Pritam Singh and others. Besides this past history, he was so much larger than life, it was impossible to believe he was dead. But he was. The plane he was in had taken off from Taipei around 2.00pm on August 18, 1945, crashed a few minutes later and, fatally burnt, he died later that day at 11.00pm.

---

[*] Bose's Death on this date had been doubted, however the Chairman of the Netaji Research Bureau and his grand-nephew Sugata Bose agrees in his book His Majesty's Opponent that he did die on August 18,1945.

But his story does not end here as he and his INA continued to haunt the British as we will soon see.

Auchinleck's Dilemma – how could one Demand Loyalty without Punishing Disloyalty?

When the war ended, London told Delhi that they would leave it to them to decide how to handle the INA. The ball was now in the court of General Claude Auchinleck, the Commander-in-Chief of the Indian Army. First, he sent a mission to investigate the mysterious death of Bose, and when they determined that he had indeed died, he took several momentous decisions.

Though India became independent exactly two years to the day after the war ended, at that time it seemed many years away. It was expected that as it had for decades, Britain would continue to rely heavily on the Indian Army throughout its empire. At that very time, Lance-Naik Charan Singh was feeding the Indian soldiers liberating Britain's colony Singapore. Auchinleck's dilemma was that he believed that the men who joined the INA did so in good faith, and that Indians should not be judged by the same yardstick as Britons for loyalty to the king. This meant the INA soldiers were not guilty. However, he also needed a loyal army. He believed there had to be some repercussion for the soldiers casting aside their oath to the king. After all, how could one demand loyalty without punishing disloyalty? So, he decided on a compromise. Technically anyone who had volunteered for the INA was guilty of treason for which the punishment was death or transportation for life. During the war, the INA men had been interrogated and categorized. Whites, whose loyalty to Britain was not in question, returned to their units. Greys were those who had been affected by the talks of India's freedom but not considered fundamentally disloyal. They were to be sent to reconditioning camps and then back to their units. Blacks were those fundamentally disloyal to Britain. Of course, thousands of soldiers could not be hanged, so he decided to try the "blacked of the black", those who had committed atrocities again fellow Indian soldiers.[9]

JIFs and BIFs

The Auk (as he was known) lifted the wartime censorship on the INA, so when they returned to India, found a media frenzy extolling their spirit. At railway stations they were mobbed by crowds and when fraternizing with their Indian Army guards converted them into saying Jai Hind and singing the national anthem. Hundreds refused to be interrogated as they did not consider themselves answerable to the Indian Army. Those who did agree hit back in their own way, calling any of their interrogators who were Indian, BIFs, or British Influenced Forces. This was in response to the British term for them, Japanese Influenced Forces which had degenerated into the pejorative JIF and accusations of "Jiffery".*

The INA itself was split

Some wanted to just go back without a fuss to what they loved most, being a soldier, but it was not that easy. There was a rift between those in Mohan Singh's 1st INA who had left as they did not trust the Japanese, and those in Bose's 2nd INA who considered them traitors for doing so. The British considered both INAs traitorous. This was further complicated by the role of the Congress Party. After speaking out during the war against the INA seeking Japanese help for independence, Gandhi and Nehru saw the public support for them and considering it politically useful, took up the cause of those in the 2nd INA being tried by The Auk.[10] The Congress was expected to do well in the upcoming elections and so those in the 1st INA were worried about their future as neither the British nor the Congress had their back.

Finally, there was the conflict between the POWs brutalized by the INA and those who had done this– when the victims came home their families were aghast and wanted justice. They were seething that the Congress was defending them. In some cases, the brutalizer could not return home as his victim was from the same village and he feared for his life. The POWs who had not volunteered were also resentful that despite the hardships they faced, the INA was getting all the glory. In fact, some even posed as INA members so they could get help from the Congress.[11]

The Politization of the Indian Army – British Josh and Congress Propaganda

Before the war, the British had kept the men of the Indian Army away from politics Once the war started, the British knew that in the upcoming clash in Burma, the Indian Army would be exposed to INA propaganda. To counter this in advance, a program called Josh was started, so the men were aware how badly the Japanese treated POWs and civilians. However, this turned out to be a double-edged sword. Though it did achieve the goal of making them aware of the reality of any Japanese

---

* Jiffery INA255, Kevin Noles, *Waging War Against the King*, fraternization, see Daily Intelligence Summaries HOME_POLITICAL_I_1945_NA_F-21-6_KW-1 in NAI henceforth Intelligence Summaries.

occupation of India, it also encouraged the men to consider themselves a citizen as well as a soldier. Once this had happened, there was no going back. After the war, the Congress swooped in with messaging that was "extremely strong stuff and cleverly put across". As an example, in December 1945, the 9/16 Punjab Regiment reported that the Congress propaganda reaching through men returning from leave had resulted in a majority of the men not wanting any trials.

Across units, some officers and NCOs were concerned when they heard the Congress announce that the INA would form the nucleus of the army of independent India. What then would happen to them? Would they lose seniority, be marginalized? Comments from some of the men in November 1945 show the differing emotions swirling about the Congress and the INA.

A 35-year-old Havildar with five years' service said, "INA had 2 sorts of men – one who worked for India and the other for himself...Congress will be the means of securing freedom for India...there be no change in the Army when the Indians take over...those members of the INA who shot their fellow countrymen should be shot themselves".

A 28-year-old Naik with four years' service said "I think those members of the INA who were forced into the INA should not be punished but the others should. Any officer of the INA who shot his own countrymen of the INA is guilty of murder".

A 23-year-old Lance Naik with four years' service said, "I know nothing about the INA. I know of the Congress and Leader Mahatma Gandhi, and they are working for the freedom of India".

In Sialkot, the men fully sympathized with the INA as they would have been badly treated by the Japanese if they had not joined, and their action was at best an indiscretion. It was said that they "took an unlaudable but commonsense way out of a difficult situation".

Most of the men in the 6th battalion of Kumaon Regiment had no knowledge of the INA. When told, they said "they are probably guilty, but we have won the war and should be merciful". Many had kinsmen in the INA and did not want them punished.

The British had not yet lost control of the army, but it was rapidly slipping through their fingers.

The Second Famous Red Fort Trial in Delhi

The first INA trial began on November 5, 1945, at this historic site chosen by The Auk. The press pointed out that the Red Fort was a symbol of India's past greatness and the site where the British had deliberately held the first famous trial, of the last Mughal Emperor Bahadur Shah Zafar in 1858 after the "mutiny". It was also the stated goal of the INA to unfurl the national flag on its ramparts and to hold the trials there was a deliberate slap in the face.[12]

A Public Relations disaster for the British

Auchinleck also decided not to hold the trial in the media, so to speak, by refusing to publish details of the atrocities by INA men on fellow Indian soldiers, believing that it would all come out in the trials and the people would agree that holding the accused to account was the right thing to have done. The trial originally to be held first, one of an INA officer beating an Indian soldier to death, would not have got much sympathy from the people. But due to a technicality, it was delayed. The first trial instead was of treason, of having joined the INA and fought against the British and Indian armies. In a country primed for independence, there would have been no public support for this. Most of all, the three young, presentable and well-spoken accused were Major-General Shah Nawaz Khan and Colonels Prem Kumar Sahgal and Gurbaksh Singh Dhillon, respectively a Muslim, a Hindu and a Sikh. In one fell swoop the British had laid down their cudgels against the three largest communities in India. It was a public relations disaster beyond belief.[13]

The men on trial and their family

The INA finally achieved its destiny and the propaganda lion roared. The British noted with characteristic understatement, that "The measure of sympathy (of the public for the INA) is substantial, and is not confined to towns or to any particular community"*. There had been no counterpropaganda by Auchinleck to show that out of 22,000 INA men from the Indian Army, only 30 were being tried, that too for atrocities. And now it was too late.[14]

The trial was a time of great strain for the family of the three men. They knew their sons could be hanged. Khan's younger brother, who had fought against the Japanese in Burma, Dhillon's wife and Sahgal's parents and siblings were there every day. Of the three accused, Dhillon's elder brother Jemadar Gurdial Singh wrote to a friend "My younger brother is in excellent health and in dashing spirit, and his fellow officers are the same. I see them off and on in the court. They do not care a damn for what may come in the trial".†

---

* Intelligence Summaries.
† Ibid.

The Prosecution's Case

This was headed by the seniormost government lawyer, the Attorney General of India Sir Naushirwan Engineer. His case was that the INA was a rebel group and all its members had betrayed their oath to the king. On the additional charge of murder, he said the shooting of deserters, even if after a court-martial, was illegal as the INA itself was illegal. He spent a lot of time reading out documents and questioning witnesses that proved that the three men were in the INA. They had never denied this, and it did not need to be proven. In fact, the vastness of the evidence showed that the INA was a real army.

The Defence by the Congress

Some of the biggest legal luminaries defended the men, including Bhulabai Desai, Nehru and Asaf Ali, though Desai led the charge. In a careful cross examination of some of the prosecution witnesses, he demonstrated they had joined the INA willingly. This was meant to taint the allegations of atrocities alleged by other witnesses. If men joined willingly, there was no need for coercion, so the atrocities must be false. Though beatings and killings had happened, legally they were irrelevant as none of the three had been charged with them, stressed by Desai in his closing. The prosecution had showcased them to air the atrocities before the people of India. It did not work. The press and the people were fully on the side of the INA.[15]

The Auk had already decided to remit the sentences arising from a presumed guilty verdict. This was too little too late.[16] When the verdict and his decision to remit and free the men was announced on January 3, 1946, it was seen as a victory for the people. Britain had lost India.

The INA Lion Devours the British Lion

"The British lost their Indian Empire because of the war, despite their having won it".*

Perhaps Britain had lost India long before this. After absorbing the news of Mohan Singh's INA, a note by the War Office in London in December 1942 said "it is plain that we have now come to a parting of ways". The British themselves had "bred a new class of officer who may be loyal to India and perhaps to Congress,

---

* MZKiani pg199.

but is not necessarily loyal to us". The note went on to say that "For the first time since the mutiny, this issue is making a major impact on the loyalty of the Indian army".* The INA fostered by Fujiwara and Giani Pritam Singh, and formed by Mohan Singh, had succeeded without firing a shot.

Bose took it to the next level and when the Japanese decided to invade India in early 1944, the INA got its chance. It did not matter that only the INA propaganda units were at the front and the Japanese kept the fighting units away. What mattered was that they had taken up arms and were ready to fight, and did fight in minor engagements whenever they got the chance. This symbolism was the legacy of Bose. He had got it right.

Bose had one goal – to reach Delhi, even if Hitler, Tojo or Stalin were in tow. Once he got there, he believed he would handle them somehow. To achieve this, he was fearless and often courted danger by exposing himself to Allied air attack, knowing that his death would encourage the movement.[17] He was also willing to sacrifice thousands of Indian lives. With little arms, food and medicines, he committed INA men to the slow death of starvation and sickness in Burma. He needed the INA to take up arms even if it was a token fight. For those Indians who were not part of his movement, like Chand, Crasta, Chint Singh and thousands more in the Torture Islands, and even more civilians who died in labour camps in Burma after his arrival,[18] he did little to alleviate their suffering. If he had fought with the Japanese to stop this as Mohan Singh did, there would have been no INA in Burma, no postwar trial and independence perhaps delayed by five to ten years. Both wanted independence, but there was a key difference. As a soldier, Singh chose to protect his men, even if doing so meant independence was delayed. As a politician, Bose was willing to sacrifice them to meet the broader goal. The price paid in Indian lives and the risks taken of asking the most fascist leaders in history for help was not evident in 1946. What captured the minds of Indians was that the INA had taken up arms, and this was a victory for Bose. It was also a victory for Mohan Singh who started the INA without which Bose would not have been called by the Japanese and end up fulfilling his destiny.

Then the way Auchinleck held the trials, wrapped it all up in a neat bow. In 1946, when British MPs and ministers came to India, they saw that the country was rife with discontent. The Royal Indian Navy had mutinied, the Indian Army would not fight its own people, and of course using the British Army to enforce control was impossible. So the decision was taken to leave India sooner rather than later. Eventually, India became independent on August 15, 1947.[19]

---

* British Library IOR/L/WS/1/1711 henceforth BL1711.

Of the men and women in the INA

Some joined to fight for India and never surrendered. Among them was Major Misra who had got the Gwalior Lancers across in February 1944, and was last seen on April 28, 1945 leaving Rangoon, probably on some last ditch mission, and killed in an Allied air raid.[20] Of the others, the few who got a chance to fight did so well against heavy odds. When they were desperate and starving in 1944 some understandably surrendered. In 1945 when the war seemed hopeless, many more did. Perhaps the best description is what an Indian soldier said of them, that they took a "commonsense way out of a difficult situation."[*]

The Victims in the Red Fort Trial: Hari Singh, Duli Chand, Daryao Rao, Dharam Singh, Khazan Shah, Aya Singh and Mohammad Hussain

Lastly, like many trials, this one too became more famous by the names of the accused. Besides treason against the king, between them Khan, Sahgal and Dhillon had also been charged with murder and abetment of murder of these seven men whose names few mention. In March 1945, they had deserted the INA, were caught, court martialled and shot. It is tragic this happened as just a month later Bose ordered the INA in Rangoon to surrender.[21]

After Independence in 1947

The POWs who had not volunteered for the INA and most of those categorised white went back to their units, as did those rescued from the Torture Islands. But it was not plain sailing.

After Jemadar Uttiah returned home in November 1945, he went on leave and then rejoined his battalion. Then he found that due to a cloud over the nature of his involvement with the INA, his promotion was blocked. He consulted his commanding officer, who told him if that he was in this position, he would resign. So he took early retirement and became a teacher. He did not hold any grudges and encouraged his son to join the services, who scaled great heights and retired as Air Marshal Balatikalandra Uthaiah Chengappa.[22]

The other INA men who had been discharged were not allowed to rejoin the army, where many were apprehensive. The INA had a full General (Mohan Singh)

---

[*] Intelligence Summaries.

and four Major-Generals, most of whom were captains four years ago but now would become the seniormost officers if they rejoined the army. In 1948 Nehru announced, "They would not be...reinstated...since there had been a long break in their service and...it would psychologically affect the present Army at a time when the latter had been exposed to considerable strain".[*]

Recognition of the POWs

The British did not forget the POWs and awarded many honours in recognition for fortitude during captivity. The over twenty-two MBEs included the musketeer Lieutenant Abrar Hussain and the only Indian in Changi, Lieutenant B.P. Singh. Notably, Lieutenant-Colonel Gurbaksh Singh, who had kept the Jind Infantry away from the INA, was recommended by Auchinleck for the CBE, two grades higher than the MBE. When Bose personally asked him to join, he told him "if I could betray one master, I could betray another".[†] The two parted civilly. In London his CBE was downgraded to an OBE, still the only one granted to an Indian POW from Singapore in World War II.

General Sahib and his Brothers in Arms

When General Mohan Singh had been arrested in December 1942, he spent the rest of the war in captivity. Two of his closest companions, Captain Rattan Singh and Rifleman Chitra Bahadur Gurung, 2/2 Gurkha Rifles were with him throughout. In the last stretch in Sumatra from January 1944 to August 1945, it was just the three of them. They made a pledge that if India gained independence, they would live together as brothers. After surrendering to the British on September 12, 1945, Mohan Singh was taken to Pearl Hill jail in Singapore, then to the Red Fort in Delhi where he was the only one kept in solitary confinement, and finally to a camp in the Kabul Lines in Delhi Cantonment. He was released on May 4, 1946. After the partition of India he moved from his home Sialkot, now in Pakistan, to Jugiana near Ludhiana. The three were already together and lived as brothers in Singh's house for the rest of their lives. To redeem his pledge of brotherhood in full measure, Singh divided his property equally with his brothers-in-arms during his life. Rattan Singh married his wife's sister, and Chitra Bahadur another Sikh lady. In keeping

---

[*] Ghosh pg275–6.
[†] Gurbaksh OBE WO-378/87/332, many other awards *London Gazette* September 25, 1947.

with the traditions, the elder sons and all the daughters were brought up as Sikhs. It was an incredible extended family. The children had in effect three fathers and three mothers and at times were closer to their "other" mother than their biological one. This continues down to the third generation today.[23]

The Astounding Case of Brigadier Mahabir Singh Dhillon

After Major Dhillon escaped to India on October 26, 1942 carrying with him a vast haul of documents on Mohan Singh's INA (Chapter 3), the British eventually decided to award him the MBE in March 1943. He returned to the army and on April 17, 1943 married Urmila Khanna. On November 14, 1955, then Brigadier Dhillon and his wife were shot dead, allegedly by his nephew, over a property dispute. His mother-in-law filed a petition asking the court to determine who died first. Though there were split seconds between the shots, the sequence had critical legal implications. If Dhillon died first, his property would pass to his wife and her descendants. If Urmila died first, her property would pass to him and his combined property to his descendant, his brother, the father of the alleged killer. The court agreed with his mother-in-law that Dhillon had died first, and so his property passed to his wife's next of kin. Despite having lived an adventurous life, nothing could trump this climax.[24]

A Letter in the Mail

On March 26, 1977, General Mohan Singh received a letter connecting him to his interrogator in Singapore thirty-two years previously, Colonel Hugh Toye. They had both retired now and It was an incredible exchange, very rare for two former protagonists. Toye's admiration of Singh shows in his interrogation. At over 200 pages, it was the longest. It started with an image of Singh's defiant posture making a speech, refers to his piercing eyes and his great oratory. On a personal level, during the interrogation, Toye gave him vitamin pills, smuggled in Singh's close friend K.P.K. Menon disguised as his own assistance, and kept on his bodyguard Rifleman Chitra Bahadur 2/2 Gurkha Rifles on his staff while in Singapore. In perhaps a unique case, he allowed Singh to read the report about himself and make any changes. His handwritten comments, largely cosmetic, were incorporated. Given the mood in Indian Army HQ, Toye had to tone down the sympathy he had for Singh in his report, lest it be dismissed as too liberal.[25] This admiration is quite evident in the decade long exchange that ensued.

The letters are incredible to read as each say more about events and people than they do in their memoirs. They exchange reviews of related books, how history had focused only on Bose and not what Singh did earlier. Toye confesses that he is partly responsible as the first significant history of the INA, Bose by a western author was his book, *The Springing Tiger*. that focused on the Bose era. Toye tried to correct this by publishing an article on Mohan Singh's first INA, but it was not enough. Over the years, he discussed plans for a revised edition to fix the imbalance, but it eventually did not happen. The correspondence lasted ten years, almost until Singh's death in 1989.[26]

Gradually, one by one, the veterans died. Their memories did not die with them, left behind in a handful of books and stories told to their family. Most relatives start by saying they have nothing to add, but they do. Every word their POW father uttered, every nightmare they experienced remained in their son or daughter's mind, and it is to this personal commemoration that we end this story with.

COMMEMORATION

Sapper Marimuthu – Column 160 of the Kranji War Cemetery

The Commonwealth War Graves Commission does a laudable job of honouring those who served. Its cemetery at Kranji in Singapore has the names of 24,000 war dead without graves. It was in its very peaceful yet emotional setting that the search by Sapper Marimuthu's family to find out what happened to him finally came to fruition. For decades they kept looking and in January 2024 found his records here. On April 11, 2024, his youngest daughter and many family members stood before column 160 at Kranji and had the pleasure of seeing his name carved in stone in recognition of his service in the war. He had died on August 10, 1942 in Singapore. It was a very poignant moment and well worth the decades long search. Their quest for more about how he was injured and finally died continues.[1]

Twenty-Five Years Later at Wewak

Major Chint Singh, then serving with the 2 Dogra Rifles, returned to Wewak in New Guinea in 1970 to commemorate twenty-five years of the end of the war, where he was able to reconnect with his Australian comrades. In 1971 plaques commemorating Indian POWs were placed in New Guinea, carved on stone sent from Chint Singh's village. His younger son Narindar became a teacher in Australia and one day in 2002 in an ABC radio broadcast spoke about his father's friendship with the Australian soldiers who had rescued and cared for him, and opened up their home to him. He got an immediate response and was able to connect with the descendants of his father's friends. In 2016 he published a book, *Chint Singh The Man Who Should Have Died*, using his father's typed manuscript about his time in New Guinea. It is named after the look Captain Mitsuba gave him when he was giving evidence against him – it seemed to say "we should have killed him when we had a chance". There is another reason for the name – Chint Singh could very well have been on the plane in which ten of his fellow soldiers crashed to their death in November 1945 on their way home (Chapter 9).[2]

Crasta's Guard, his Daughter and his Book

Soon after Warrant Officer John Baptist Crasta reached home, in January 1946, on sheets of papers from his brother's shop, Mayor Footwear Co. Kinnigoli, he wrote his own story. It is perhaps the most complete book on a Singapore POW's experience, starting with being shipped from India and ending with his return home, with the horrors of all else that happened in between. In it he talks fondly of his Japanese guard Mecna who was very kind to him. Later in life he named his favourite child, his daughter, Meena after him. Crasta showed the manuscript to his officers who dismissed it as not written well. His son Richard thought so too and wanted to burn it. Fortunately he did not and later in life realized how moving and evocative it was. As a 50th wedding anniversary present he had it published in 1997.

The title "*Eaten by the Japanese*" refers to cannibalism and was not chosen by Crasta, but by Richard. This is an example of how the suffering POW was able to forgive his tormentors, but his family was not. Richard says he does not hold grudges against the Japanese, but an apology would be good.[3] Unlike Germany which has apologized as a nation for the suffering it inflicted, Japan has not. This remains contentious to this day, especially with China and Korea.

Brigadier Pillai's Quest

Lieutenant Pillai, who had escaped in May 1942 and retired a Brigadier, wrote a manuscript on his escape. His story was well-known and whenever he entered a club or an officers' mess, people would point him out as a Great Escaper. His eldest son, Rear-Admiral Sampath Pillai, Indian Navy recalls that the family kept on urging him to publish it but he refused. As it had happened so long ago, he wanted to verify his memory with the report he had submitted in August 1942 to Army HQ. However as it was classified, he was not allowed access, and died in 1989 without having set eyes on it again. Eleven years later while visiting Singapore, his next son Dr Krishna Pillai went to the archives searching for material on the year of his escape, 1942. On a whim he looked up Pillai, and found the report. After all these years it had finally been declassified and now in the public domain.

Dr Pillai discovered something else. One day in Delhi in 2002, Mr Natarajan, a business acquaintance, asked him if he was Pillai's son. He then told him that decades ago when he was Lieutenant S. Natarajan, also an engineer in the Indian Army, he had been asked to watch over Pillai, in effect be his minder. Despite having awarded Pillai a medal, in every case of a person who had returned to India after spending time under the Japanese, the British could not be perfectly sure of his allegiance. Pillai possibly knew Natarajan was watching him, but in any case his role was ended after a year. This was an extraordinary revelation for the family, and added to the drama of Pillai's life in the war.

The family continued its quest to know about Pillai's escape and in June 2007, Brigadier Pillai's third son, Colonel Ravi Pillai, 63 Cavalry Indian Army, came to Singapore with his mother, Professor Jaya Kothai Pillai, to visit the sites where Lieutenant Pillai had been. Professor Pillai was the driving force behind the publishing of *Three Thousand Miles to Freedom*, her husband's manuscript, brought out in 2009 by Colonel Pillai.[4]

Khan Zada's Daughter

When Captain Pritam Singh had escaped three days before Pillai in 1942, with him were captains Balbir Singh and Gangaram Parab, 4/19 Hyderabad Regiment. All of them made it and in 1987 then retired Colonel Balbir Singh came to Singapore to retrace his steps all the way back to India. Near the Thai-Burmese border he went to the village where decades ago the fiery Pathan Khan Zada had helped him so much. He was no more, but he met his daughter, then a little girl and now a grown woman. She remembered the three escapers and the Japanese who had come looking for them. The colonel died in 2006 and in 2010 his son, the noted military historian Colonel Jasbir Singh, published his story, *Escape From Singapore*.[5]

The POW Community – Courage in Adversity[*]

To recognize their courage in adversity, there is a vibrant community of descendants of Far East POWs (FEPOWs). Besides websites, Facebook pages and research, they hold a conference in Liverpool every two years that brings together historians, authors, doctors and most importantly, family members, and I was fortunate to attend the first one after Covid in June 2023. During a break I came across a lady quietly crying in one corner, thinking of the horrors her father faced when he died racked with disease in an ill-equipped hospital in a forced labour camp of the Thailand-Burma railway. However, she comes every time as it's cathartic. One was upset for another reason. Her father was lucky to remain in Singapore and did not go to the death camps, but he felt guilty all his life for having survived.

---

[*] Term taken from Prof Peter Stanley, *"Great in adversity" Indian prisoners of war in New Guinea*, Journal of the Australian War Memorial, Issue 37, October 2002.

Another spoke of her returning POW grandfather who headed straight for a pub in Liverpool. When exchanging stories with other soldiers, he was told he had it easy as he had not been fighting. He never spoke about his POW experience ever again.

Nightmares, Forty Years Later

The keynote address was on psychology. I had wondered why it was on the agenda at all, but it turned out to be the most interesting talk of all. Today PTSD is well known, but in 1945 it wasn't. The science shows that almost all who go to war have it and POWs get it worse than combatants who did not get captured. They also get a more severe version that lasts longer, and affects their health decades later. All this was shocking to hear and to many POW descendants present, explained a lot.[6]

PTSD also affected sleep. Both Pillai and Crasta had nightmares about air raids decades later. Major-General Kiani of the INA said "for many years after the war, I never dreamt without being attacked from the air."* It also resulted in phobias and compulsions. After having mainly (very little) rice for so many years in Asian POW camps, some hated it so much they could not stand the sight of it. Others could not have a meal without it.[7]

The British FEPOW community have only one grouse – not enough focus on the war in Asia. That's perhaps because the war in Europe was closer to home. It is similar in India – we focus on post-Independence wars and not on the bravery of Indian soldiers before it. The British do commemorate the colonial Indian Army, but even they miss things out. On the way back from the Liverpool conference, I stopped at the National Memorial Arboretum near Lichfield which has a wonderful FEPOW pavilion, but no reference to Indian POWs. In the garden outside there is a square block that on its four sides lists twenty Hell ships carrying FEPOWs sunk by Allied attack. It mentions Ikoma Maru sunk on January 21, 1944 with a loss of 418 lives. These men were all Indian. It does not mention *Buyo Maru*, the ship in which Captain Sen and 497 Indian POWs were travelling and which was sunk on January 27, 1943 with the loss of 195 lives. It is also missing Ryusei Maru sunk on February 25, 1944 in which 4,968 Allied POWs died including over 2,000 Indians.

So far I have focused on researching this book and now hope to bring together POW families, and to get the *Buyo* and *Ryusei Maru* added to the plaque at the Arboretum.

---

* Kiani book pg102.

Sat Sri Aakaal Dadaji[*]

To end the end of the book, I have to mention September 7, 2024. It was on that day that Lance-Naik Charan Singh turned 100. Dadaji, as I have the privilege of calling him, was the soldier who came to Singapore in late 1945 after its liberation, and his job was to feed the others He retired in 1958 and lives in the same house he was born in a 100 years ago, near Ropar, Punjab, where I have had the great honour of meeting him. With the help of Lieutenant-General Harsha Gupta[†] and many others (names unknown to me), the army and his family arranged a grand celebration to commemorate his centenary. The look of pride and happiness on his face was priceless. *Sat Sri Akal DADAJI.*

---

[*]   *Sat Sri Aakall* is Sikh greeting, *Dadaji* means grandfather.
[†]   Who retired as Adjutant-General of the Indian Army in 2022.

ACKNOWLEDGEMENTS

It all began in the summer of 2022 when I acquired a manuscript made in Singapore's Changi Prison during World War II. It was then that I started reading more about the city that had been my home for over twenty years. Romen Bose's book on Singapore at war was fascinating and when I wrote to him, he was a great help. He introduced me to Jeya Ayadurai MBE, now my friend and mentor. Jeya has given me opportunities to speak at the museum he runs and also taught me how to, and is the first godfather of this book. For it was on October 7, 2022, when he told me something I had not known, that in World War II the Japanese sent Indian Prisoners from Singapore to labour in islands in the Pacific. That phone call was the start of this journey and this book.

I was intrigued, but it was early the following year before I did anything about it – the first book I read about this was *Eaten by the Japanese* by John Baptist Crasta and then I reached out to his son Richard who has told me so much about his father's war and, most vitally, the family reaction to it that has been invaluable.

The second godfather is Major-General Syed Ali Hamid who has guided me with sources, reviewed my chapter outline, sharpened the title and most of all held my hand through the writing. He also introduced me to (then) Lieutenant Abrar Hussain's son Abid, who in turn connected me with (then) Captain Ismail Khan's daughter Laila, and (then) Captain MAK Durrani's (all of 2/10 Baluch) son Akbar.

The third godfather is the Gurkha soldier and military historian, Major-General Ian Cardozo. I can't believe I was taught by Ma'am and studied with his youngest son Vikram and didn't know about him. He set me straight right in the beginning of my writing, patiently listened to me fret and introduced me to the fourth godfather (there are eight in all!), Squadron Leader Rana Chhina, MBE, Director of the Centre for Military History and Conflict Studies, New Delhi. Squadron Leader Chhina has introduced me to numerous key people, most of all Lieutenant-General Harsha Gupta (the fifth godfather), who has been of immense help tracing family members of veterans without whom the story could not have been told.

The one godmother of the book is Dr Bernice Archer. The manuscript I had bought in mid-2022 was written by civilian internees and I read Dr Archer's bible on the topic. When I emailed her, she was very kind and introduced me to the vibrant FEPOW (Far East POW) community at their biannual conference in 2023, where I also met one of my publishers, Pen & Sword. I made many friends there, notably Rosemary Fell, Elizabeth (Liz) Moggie and Colin Hygate. On the way back I met Jonathan Moffat, a walking WWII archive and always ready to help.

The conference organizer, Emily, introduced me to Kevin Noles, the sixth godfather. Kevin is also a former banker and has enviably found a space in researching history. His articles are incredible and he pointed me to the treasure trove of CSDIC (I) records on the Indian Army in the National Archives India, one of my main sources.

The seventh godfather is Thomas Abraham, the CEO of Hachette India and my brother's friend from college. His starting contribution was on how to write a book proposal. Despite being a banker for decades, this was new to me. It was only his guidance on how to present it that got my publishers interested. Since then, he has held my hand through every step of the way. On writing book proposals, I must also thank P.K. Basu, the author of *Asia Reborn: A Continent Rises from the Ravages of Colonialism and War to New Dynamism*, another friend of my brother from college.

Googling took me to the escape of Lieutenant M.M. Pillai and to his incredible family. He has four sons, a Rear-Admiral, a Colonel in the cavalry, a senior multi-national official and a Harvard professor. Colonel and Mrs Pillai have hosted me several times at their home in Gurgaon. The MNC official Krishna Pillai added a lot of detail to his fathers postwar history. The first Pillai I spoke to however was the Admiral, whose number Squadron Leader Chhina got me. Besides telling me about his father, he mentioned a book on the Indian Army in Dunkirk, *The Indian Contingent* by Ghee Bowman. I read the book and emailed Ghee and he kindly pointed me to sources in the UK, shared with me his own book proposal, introduced me to film makers and finally to the eighth (and last) godfather, Mandeep Singh Bajwa. Alas Ghee passed away on May 10, 2025, a great loss to those interested in World War II and anyone who new him.

Mr Bajwa jokingly told me that everyone calls him colonel due to his knowledge of the army, and though he comes from a distinguished military family, is not an army man himself. Over a sumptuous lunch at his Chandigarh home, he regaled me with stories about the men in the book. He also introduced me to Jaideep Sekhon, the son of Captain Dr Sham Singh Sekhon, a POW in Borneo.

During lunch at Mr Bajwa's, arrived the grandson-in-law of General Mohan Singh, the founder of the INA. Harbir Singh Dhillon is the quintessential gentleman, like a brother to me now. The epitome of Punjabi hospitality, I realized he is a chip off the old block when I met his father, Harbinderjit Singh Dhillon. Uncle is the most endearing person I know and welcomes me to his home like a son each time I visit. Aunty is the most graceful lady imaginable. Harbir's wife Noor is the grand-daughter of General Mohan Singh (G.M.S. as we refer to him with great respect and fondness). Like many, I had never heard of him and find his achievements astonishing, and even more so the creation of his extended family after the war with Captain Rattan Singh and Chitra Bahadur, his companions in exile. His son Harrmohanjit and daughters Manjeet and Sarabhjeet freely shared the incredible family archive of letters and memories and welcomed me to their homes, as did his daughter-in-law (Noor's mother) Darshanjit Kaur.

Harbir is tenacious. While driving from Mr Bajwa's home in Chandigarh to his in Jalandar, I saw a signboard on the highway saying we were approaching Ropar. I told him there was a 99-year-old veteran who lived nearby and the next time I come we should try looking for him. He parked his car on the highway off-ramp and said no next time, tell me what you know about where he lives. In ninety minutes we had arrived. It was a typical Indian village scene with the car getting stuck in the mud and Harbir walking a mile to find a tractor to drag us out, but we got there. Meeting Lance-Naik Charan Singh has been the most rewarding experience of all.

One day after meeting Chinna Sir in Delhi, I was having lunch at the superb canteen serving typical army mess food. Sitting at a table next to me was an officer and we got talking. He introduced me to another military historian, Andrew Kerr, who in turn connected me with various British families with Indian Army connections, and to Stuart Leasor of Chiselbury Publishing, whose father John has written numerous books on Singapore at war. Stuart came with the subtitle of my book and introduced me to people who could help me in researching UK archives, one of them was Caroline Lees. I wrote to her with my requirements including a list of officers whose family I needed to trace. Top of the list was GMS's C/O, Lieutenant-Colonel LV Fitzpatrick (LVF). She replied explaining that the timing was not right, but hang on – her husband, Alan Macdonald, was LVFs grandson. I fell off my chair when I read that email – since then Caroline and Alan have kindly shared their family archive, that has added so much to the telling of the story.

A similar roundabout journey starting with clues from Jonathan Moffat, led me to Mrs Joan Clough, the daughter-in-law of Lieutenant-Colonel George Clough, who commanded the 4/19 Hyderabad Regiment. Joan kindly shared a similar treasure trove.

The Chinna connection also led me to Narinder Singh Parmar, the son of (then) Jemadar Chint Singh who plays such a prominent role in the story. His neighbour (relatively speaking) in Australia is Professor Peter Stanley whose articles on the Papua New Guinea chapter of Indian POWs are pathbreaking. Besides this, he has also guided me on aspects of why Japan ended the war.

Another link Squadron Leader Chhina made for me was with the Coorgi community through Major-Geneal Arjun Muthana, related to the Thimaya's, and who linked me with Jemadar Uthaiah's son, Air-Marshal Chengappa.

Other family members of veterans who helped me out include Ashali Varma, Nikhil Benegal, Dinesh Katoch, Mani Chinnaswamy, Colonel Dharampal Singh, Harmala Gupta, Surya Vaz, Sajid Hussain, Ahmad Iqbal Chaudhary and S.M. Habeebulllah.

ACKNOWLEDGEMENTS

More googling led me to Maddy's Ramblings, in fact those of Manmadhan Ullathi. He introduced me to Ananda Sivaram, the son of M. Sivaram, an Ian official of the Indian Indepedence League who published a superb memoir in the 1960s. Ananda introduced me to Subhashini Ali, the bluest of INA royalty, her parents being Colonel P.K. Sahgal of INA trial fame and Major Dr Lakhsmi Swaminathan, the first commander of the all-female Rani of Jhansi Regiment. Subhashini has always been open and very helpful. Amongst her many introductions were to Adnan and Imran, the sons of Colonel Mehboob Ahmad of Patna, India, both of whom were in turn very informative.

On the POWs who joined the INA, Mr Bajwa introduced me to Major-General Shah Nawaz Khan's grandson. I visited him one evening after a very late lunch, but could not resist the pakora (spicy Indian fritters) spread he had provided. And then General Cardozo connected me with Shubham Sharma. This young man with high ambitions is the most knowledgeable and enthusiastic INA man I have met. His network is incredible and he works hard to commemorate them, though it still remains an uphill struggle.

One of the biggest gaps in my research is on my home, Singapore. Through a roundabout route, some of that gap has been filled. Lieutenant-General Gupta introduced me to Tejpal Rehmill and through him I met the vibrant Sikh community in the UK. I attended his tour of the Indian soldiers in Hampton Court Palace, and the evening before I left London on that trip in summer 2024, he invited me to the superb Punjab Restaurant in Covent Garden. There I met Amrit Maan OBE FRSA and his father. They told me about their Indian Army relative Havildar Darshan Singh and later Amrit introduced me to Dr Opinderjit Kaur MBE, then a visiting Professor of Sikh Studies at the NUS, Singapore. I attended Opinderjit's talks at the Silat Road Gurdwara, and there met the Sikh's of Singapore. Simranjeet Singh and Arunajeet Kaur have provided great help in my journey.

Amongst historians of an earlier era, my favourite is Dr Tilak Raj Sareen. I was fortunate to have met him in January 2024, a few weeks before he died on March 8, 2024. He is a rare one who shared his source documents in reams of books published over the decades, instead of hoarding them only for his own use by which helps researchers a great deal by seeing some of the complete archives documents in the flesh.

I also had the privilege of getting to know Raghu Karnad, Dr Diya Gupta, Mukund Padmanaban, Alan Jeffreys, K S Nair, Brian Farrell, Rajesh Rai, Ashis Ray, Ashok Nath, Jon Cooper and Radhika Sangha along the way.

For my research, I must thank Dr Asha Joshi, at the Member of the Managing Board, Indian Archaeological Society and Editor of its journal Purapravah, who made introductions to the National Archives of India. There, Mr. Syed Farid Ahmed, Mr Naoroibam Raju Singh, Dr Vandana, Mr Bal Kishan, Salma, Mr Mohummed Tayyub and Mr Bishnu Das, Dr Amlesh Kumar Mishra and Dr Narendra Yadav at the India MOD Historical Section, at the AWM Dr Karl Peters and Gabrielle Young, at the National Army Museum London Chelsea Taylor, Roshin Dadlani for her work on the INA statistics, Peter Cundall and Lynette Silver for their assistance on Japanese shipping details, and, Eriko Ogihara-Schuck, Yayoi Tsutsui of Japan.

In Pen & Sword, I must thank Tara Moran who I met in Liverpool in June 2023 and who patiently took me through the book from start to finish, Harriet Fielding who has edited and produced it, tolerating my novice questions and idiosyncrasies. Margaret Moran's editing was a master class in English, Jon Wilkinson designed a brilliant cover and Matthew Potts / Charlie Simpson ran an awesome marketing campaign. The maps were made by SJmagic DESIGN SERVICES India. I cannot thank my publicist Rachna Kalra enough. She drove the whole marketing campaign along with Sohela Singh of Penguin, Riishi Mazumdar of Indian History Collective and Ayushi Srivastava of Digital Growth.

The cover concept is courtesy Angie Mui in Singapore. The actual art and sketches inside the book for both editions are by Giorgio Albertini. I cannot thank him enough for his brilliant work.

I was introduced to my publishers in India, Penguin, by Sumant Bharat Ram. Gappu, as he is more well known, is an incredible friend and did more for me than I, knowingly, did not for him. He knows what I'm referring to. He connected me with Gaurav Shrinagesh, CEO of Penguin India, SEA and MENA, who is also the grandson of General SM Shrinagesh, Chief of Army Staff of India in the 1950s. My editor, Gurveen Chaddha, and producer Nikita Dahiya made this book possible. Manali Das did a careful copy edit that made it all much cleaner. The cover design is by Sparsh Raj Singh. Sohela Singh ran the marketing campaign. A very special thinks to my publicist Rachna Kalra who taught me a lot and got the right things done.

Other friends played a major role too. Kamalini and Sanjay Jain, and Parul and Kushagra Khanna let me stay at their homes in London while I did my research, Ben and Rana Behl, Pradip Kishen and D.P. Singh made valuable introductions, Dhruv Shrikent read my first chapter and gave me a lot of food for thought, and latterly on the title. As did TS Anil. Pallavi, Aditya, Inakshi, Tashwinder, Premika, Naresh, Chandrima, Ashish Goyal, thank yoA special thank you to my friend and mentor Ratnesh Mathur who is like a brother to me. He has pushed me for years to do this, as has his wife Sangeeta. Ratnesh also gave me great advice when I had "data-block" while writing – he said "Hazy, you know the story, just write a chapter in one go, correct the details later". This was of immense help, much more than he will know. Finally, he introduced me to Naresh Fernandes to whom I am very grateful for publishing my articles in https://www.scroll.in. Liz Coward, though a published author is more of a friend. We met in early 2023 and since then she has guided on me how to go about my own journey. Krishna Srinivas advised me on how to navigate social media, Devjyoti Barooah read my posts with a toothcomb, and Sriram Balakrishnan held my hand all along. Most of all, I must thank the

Titus family. Alpana's mother very kindly introduced me to Lieutenant-General "Tindi" Sharma, Engineer-in-Chief of the Indian Army and besides the privilege of knowing him, his grandson Shagat Shawnik pointed me towards the (now) centenarian Lance-Naik Charan Singh. Most gratitude goes to Ajoy Titus – he read every chapter and took me though the whole progression, thanks Titus.

To Dr Robert Lyman, MBE FRHistS, a big thank you for agreeing to write the foreword of the Pen & Sword edition. And to Srinath Raghavan, for the Penguin India edition. From the day I wrote to them out of the blue, they have been incredibly helpful. It is such an honour to have them associated with my work. Robert also introduced me to the indomitable Phil Craig, who in turn led me to Damien Lewis, Paul Woodward of WW2TV and KS Nair., all of whom I have to thank. Special thanks to Vijay Balan who gave invaluable inputs that made the manuscript much better. Vijay was quick, incisive and made sure I kept my focus on the forgotten soldiers I was writing on. And to Caroline and Mihir Bose for welcoming me to their home and to Mihir for correcting my manuscript.

Last but not least is family. Midway through my writing both Ma and Deuta (my parents) passed away. My sister, Gayatri, told me that as I had promised them, I would write the book, I should lock myself in the front room, and write, write, write, while she took care of family matters. Thank you forever, Miana.

I must mention my wife, Hena. Most authors thank their partners. I am too, but in my case it really would not have been possible without her letting me pursue my dream while she worked. Thank you sweet.

Finally, I must mention my parents. Ma encouraged us to read and though we were not wealthy, there was always money for books, and I recall hours spent in Teksons South Ex in New Delhi browsing. In later life, my father kept bemoaning the continuous haul of books I would return with each time I went to Bahrisons, Midland or The Bookshop. He told me, 'You love this so much, why don't you write something?' Whenever he came across an interesting book, he would tell me about it. He suggested writing styles, such possibly historical fiction. Though there are eight godfathers and one godmother of this book, my father is the father of this book. Thank you, Deuta.

NOTES ON PRIMARY SOURCES

1. The INA Papers in the National Archives of India (NAI)

These have largely been created/collected by the Combined Services Detailed Interrogation Centre (India) or CSDIC (I) of the Indian army. The C/O most other officers were British. Staring from the fourth quarter of 1942, over 20,000 men returning from Japanese occupied territory during the war and captured later were interrogated at the front in Assam at Forward Interrogations Centres/Units to determine if they were spies and assess their loyalty to Britain. In 1944 over 400 Indian POWs escaped in the Papua New Guinea area, interrogated by CSDIC (I) A section based in Australia. After screening, over 1,500 interesting cases from all of these were sent to CSDIC (I) in Red Fort, Delhi. In addition, there were over 2,000 CSDIC (I) interrogations in Singapore and Southeast Asia of soldiers in the INA and civilians in the Indian independence movement.

These are not transcripts of the interrogation, but a report written by the interrogator of what they thought was noteworthy. As pointed out by Kevin Noles (*Waging War Against the King*, published by The British Empire at War Research Group, Research Papers, No. 6 (2014), pg8), we hear "a variety of voices…an officer seeking to excuse his joining of the INA, a defiant volunteer still dedicated to the cause, or the judgmental conclusions of the interrogator himself". Though in most cases the interrogators name is not noted, interestingly, many were Indian. When assessing what is said, any praise, derogatory comments, reference to controversial events by the subject has been included only if verified by other sources.

In addition, CSDIC (I) prepared many Chronologies/Histories/Reports on various topics including INA numbers, incredible research done at that time in 1945–1946. These have been made after analyzing the thousands of interrogations, so have been taken at face value. In the one case where I disagree with the assessment, have specified that it is because they had not yet seen evidence that came out later.

Besides these, the CSDIC (I) collected copies of INA records that survived the order of Mohan Singh and Subhas Chandra Bose to destroy them. These tell us how the INA was organized and administered. Interrogations of key Japanese involved such as Fujiwara, translations of Japanese reports and orders portray their view of events and people. They also contain reports made by British officers of the Indian Army about their men. Finally, they have propaganda leaflets, newspapers, speeches and diaries of Indian soldiers in various languages.

Taken together they provide a comprehensive picture of thousands of Indian soldiers – their family, life in army and experience in captivity, told from their viewpoint, that of the Japanese and what the British thought of it all. They also provide a physical description of the subject, very useful in the telling of the story. As they figure often, the referencing has been abbreviated, hence, e.g. INA 499 refers to the INA Papers File 499.

2. Other Indian Archive Documents

The NAI Home Political section includes Intelligence Summaries made by the Indian Army with assessments of the INA during the war and Indian Army after it ended. These include opinions of Indian soldiers of the INA and politics in India. India MOD Historical Section in New Delhi 601 series have rich details of World War II.

3. AWM – Australian War Memorial/National Archives Australia

The AWM has hundreds of liberation questionnaires, affidavits and Courts of Inquiries on Japanese atrocities. These were reviewed and eventually 100 war crimes for atrocities against Indian POWs were held by Australia and I have only considered these. The trial transcripts include Indian evidence, Japanese statements and how the prosecution and defence conducted the trials. Additional details are in the UN War Crimes site https://www.legal-tools.org. The trial records are catalogued by defendant, so searches need to be done accordingly. The AWM has numerous photographs of Indian POWs.

4. British Archives

The richly thumbed India Office Records in the British Library have of course been accessed. The National Archives (UK) at Kew have transcripts of trials run by the British, records of Indian civilians from Malaya who perished building the Thailand-Burma railway, as well as medal citations for Indian POWs. The National Army Museum London has narratives of Indian Army units by their British officers.

5. Other Public Records

US National Archives have patrol records of US submarines that sank Japanese ships carrying Indian POWs. Japanese shipping records have been accessed through http://www.combinedfleet.com maintained by English speakers with access to them. The Commonwealth War Graves Commission has death records, Singapore Liberation Questionnaire (first page only) are in https://lq-cofepow.org. Then https://www.findmypast.com for family records of British officers in Indian Army, rolls of those in Changi Singapore. Finally Australian newspapers are in https://trove.nla.gov.au.

6. Family Archives and Memories

These have been a rich source, especially those of Mohan Singh, the great escaper Pillai, the man who got justice for his comrades Chint Singh, and the incredible chronicler of his time in the Torture Islands Crasta. And Asad Shiraz's fathers account of the first air raid in Singapore. Then there were the poignant stories of the waiting wives Thangamma and Mariammal. From the British side, Mohan Singh's C/O Fitzpatrick and Clough of 4/19 Hyderabad Regiment, provided detail.

SELECT BIBLIOGRAPHY OF SECONDARY SOURCES

Aiyer, S.A., *Unto Him A Witness—The Story of Netaji Subhash Chandra Bose in East Asia*, Thacker & Co, Bombay 1951

Barkawi, Tarek, 'Culture and Combat in the Colonies: The Indian Army in the Second World War', *Journal of Contemporary History* Vol. 41, No. 2 (April 2006)

Barkawi, Tarek, *Soldiers of Empire*, Cambridge University Press 2017

Bose, Mihir, *The Lost Hero—A Biography of Subhash Bose*, Revised and enlarged edition, Vikas Publishing House, 2014

Bose, Mihir, *The Indian Spy, The True Story Of The Most Remarkable Secret Agent Of World War II,* Aleph, 2017

Bose, Sugata, *His Majesty's Opponent*, Belknap Press, 2011

Bose, Romen, *A Will for Freedom*, VJ Times Singapore 1993

Butow, Robert, *Japan's Decision to Surrender*, Stanford University Press, 1954

Chatterji, Major-General A.C., *India's Struggle for Freedom*, Chuckervertty Chatterjee and Co, Calcutta 1947

Corr, Gerald, *The War of the Springing Tigers*, Osprey Publishing, 1975.

Crasta, John Baptist, *Eaten by The Japanese: The Memoir of an Unknown Indian Prisoner of War*, The Invisible Man Press, New York, 2013

Das, S.A., and Subbaiah, K.B., *Chalo Delhi – An Historical Account of Indian Independence Movement in East Asia*, The Economy Printers Kuala Lumpur, 1946

Dhillon, Gurbaksh Singh, *From My Bones*, Aryan International Press 1998

Durrani, Mahmood Khan, *The Sixth Column*, Cassell London 1955

Evans, Humphrey, *Thimayya – a Soldier's Life*, New York Harcourt, Brace and Company, 1960

Farrell, Brian, *The Defence and Fall of Singapore* Monsoon Books, 2005

Fay, Peter Ward, *The Forgotten Army: India's Armed Struggle for Independence 1942–45*, The University of Michigan Press, 1991.

Fujiwara Iwaichi, *F Kikan—Japanese Intelligence Operations in Southeast Asia During World War II*, written 1947–8, published 1969, English translation published Kuala Lumpur Heinemann, 1983.

Ghosh, K.K., *The Indian National Army—Second Front of the Indian Independence Movement*, Meenakshi Prakashan, Meerut 2022 edition

Giani, Kesar Singh, *Indian Independence Movement in East Asia*, Lahore, 1947.

Gill Colonel Naranjan Singh, *Story of the I.N.A.*, Publications Division, Ministry of Information & Broadcasting, Govt of India, First Edition, December 1985, Reprint 2001

Gordon, Leonard, *Brothers Against the Raj*, Viking, 1964, Reprint 1990

Hardman, Daniel L., 'Hitting Home—The Air Offensive Against Japan', Air Force History and Museums Program, 1999.

Harper, Tim, *Underground Asia – Global Revolutionaries and the Assault on Empire*, Allen Lane, 2020

Hauner, Milan, *India in Axis Strategy*, German Historical Institute London 1981

Hillgruber, Andreas, 'England's Place in Hitler's Plans for World Domination', *Journal of Contemporary History* Vol 9/ No. 1 (January 1974)

Ienaga, Saburo, *The Pacific War 1931–1945*, Pantheon Books, New York, 1978

Khan, Major-General Shahnawaz, *My Memories of I.N.A. & its Netaji*, The Other Press Malysia, 2019

Kiani, Major-General Mohammad Zaman, *India's Freedom Struggle and the Great INA*, Reliance Publishing House, 1982

Kirby, Major General S Woodburn, ed, *The War Against Japan Volume 1-5 History of the Second World War United Kingdom Military Series*), Her Majesty's Stationery Office, 1957-69

Lebra, Joyce, *The Indian National Army and Japan*, ISEAS edition 2008. This is a reissue of *The Jungle Alliance*, published in 1971.

Lyman, Robert, *A War of Empires – Japan,India, Burma and Britain 1941-45*, Osprey 2021.

McQuade, Joseph, *Fugitive of Empire*, Vintage Books 2023

Nair, AM, *An Indian Freedom Fighter in Japan*, Orient Longman, published in 1982.

Michino, Gregory F., *Death on the Hellships – Prisoners at Sea in the Pacific War*, Naval Institute Press, Maryland, 2001

Noles, Kevin, Waging War Against the King, published by The British Empire at War Research Group, Research Papers, No 6 (2014)

Noles, Kevin, 'Renegades in Malaya: Indian Volunteers of the Japanese F Kikan', *British Journal for Military History* Volume 2, Issue 2, February 2017.

Noles, Kevin, 'Divided Loyalties in The People's War', eds. Wilson & Fennell, McGill University Press 2022

O'Kane, Rear-Admiral Richard H., *Wahoo: The Patrols of America's Most Famous World War II Submarine*, Random House 2009

Palta, K.R., *My Adventures With the INA*, Lion Press, Lahore 1946

Pamar, Narinder Singh Parmar, *Chint Singh: The Man Who Should Have Died*, Shawline Publishing, Australia, 2021.

Pigot, G., *Sherdil-ki-Paltan, History of the 1ˢᵗ Battalion 14ᵗʰ Punjab Regiment*, Naval & Military Press and Imperial War Museum London, 2013

Pillai, Brigadier M.M., MC, *Three Thousand Miles to Freedom*, Lancer Publishers (India), 2009.

Rai, Rajesh, *Indians in Singapore 1819–1945*, Oxford 2014

Roy, Kaushik, *Battle for Malaya – The Indian Army in Defeat 1941-1942*, Indiana University Press, 2019

Sahgal, Lakshmi, *A Revolutionary Life: Memoirs of a Political Activist*, Kali for Women 1997

Sareen, T.R., *Japan and the Indian National Army*, Agam Prakashan, Delhi 1986

Sareen, T.R, *The Indian National Army: A Documentary Study* Vol 1-5, Gyan Publishing House, 2004.

Singh, Gajendra, *The Testimonies of Indian Soldiers and the Two World Wars*, Bloombury Academic, 2015.

Singh, Major-General Gurbaksh, *Indelible Reminiscences*, Lancer Publications 2013

Singh, Lt Gen Harbaksh Singh, *In the Line of Duty*, Lancer Publications 2000/ reprint 2022

Singh, Col Jasbir Singh, *Escape from Singapore*, Lancer Publications, 2010.

Singh, General Mohan, *Leaves from Diary*, Free World Publications, Lahore, 1946

Singh, General Mohan, Soldiers Contribution to Indian Independence', *Army Education Service*, 1974 3rd edition

Sissons, D.C.S., The Australian War Crimes Trials and Investigations 1942–51, Bridging Australia and Japan, The Writings of David Sissons, historian and political scientist Volume2, edited by Keiko Tamura and Arthru Stockwin, published 2020 by ANU Press, The Australian National University, Canberra, Australia

Sivaram, M, *The Road to Delhi*, Charles Tuttle & Co, 1967.

Stanley, Prof Peter, *Remembering the War in New Guinea, Where most of them perished: Indian POWs in New Guinea,* Australia Japan Research Project article in AWM

Stanley, Prof Peter, *"Great in adversity" Indian prisoners of war in New Guinea*, Journal of the Australian War Memorial, Issue 37, October 2002

Sturma, Michael, 'Japanese Treatment of Allied Prisoners During the Second World War: Evaluating the Death

Toll', Murdoch University Australia, *Journal of Contemporary History* 2020 Vo 55 (3).

Sundaram, Chandar S., 'A Paper Tiger in Battle: The Indian National Army 1944–45', *War & Society*, Volume 13, 1995, Issue 1

Sundaram, Chandar, 'Seditious Letters and Steel Helmets: Disaffection among Indian Troops in Singapore and Hong Kong 1940-41 and the formation of the Indian National Army', in *War and Society in Colonial India* edited by Kaushik Roy, 2006.

Sundaram, Chandar, 'The Indian National Army: Towards a Balanced and Critical Appraisal', *Economic & Political Weekly*, 25 July 2015)

Raghavan, Srinath, *India's Wars*, Penguin 2016

Ram, Moti, *Two Historic Trails in Red Fort*, Roxy Printing Press, New Delhi, 1946

Toye, Hugh, *The Springing Tiger – A Study of Subhas Chandra Bose*, Cassell, London 1959.

Toye, Hugh, 'The First Indian National Army', *Journal of Southeast Asian Studies*, Vol. 15, No. 2 (September 1984),

Tsuji, Colonel Masanobu, *Singapore The Japanese Version*, Ure Smith Sydney, 1960

Warren, Alan, The Indian Army and the Fall of Singapore, in *Sixty Years On - The Fall of Singapore*, ed Brian Farrell & Sandy Hunter, Marshall Cavendsh 2002

ENDNOTES

Prologue

1. Mercenary – reference conversation with Lieutenant VN "Tindi" Sharma November 3, 2023, Mihir Bose's Lost Hero pg418.
2. 67,000 Indians – War Against Japan, HMSO Vol. 1 pg473.
3. *The Defence and Fall of Singapore*, Brian Farrell.
4. Farrell.
5. Salooni Reports 612/665 (INA499 part3). 5/2 Punjab had some of the most prominent INA men – Kiani, the adjutant Captain Ehsan Qadir, Captain Rodrigues, the MO Captain Raju, Jemadar Udhe Singh, Havildar Shiv Singh and others. Despite his actions in January 1942, Salooni however did not later join the INA.
6. *Official History, War Against Japan,* Volume 1, pp. 274–81.

Chapter 1: The Spectacle at Farrer Park

1. Biggest defeat Churchill statement *The Telegraph*, London, February 16, 1942.
2. Captain Mohammad Akram had over twenty years' service, and was the 1/14 Punjab's Subedar-Major, the senior most Indian below officer rank. He was commissioned in 1941, joined Singh early on and was in effect his deputy until his untimely death in March 1942. See Report 1442, INA 379 part 85.
3. Subedar Allah Ditta, 7/22 Mountain Artillery was another early recruit and played a prominent role in the campaign. See INA File, 380 part 2, Report 833, henceforth Allah Ditta.
4. Singh speech see IWO Abdul Hayat Khan Report 80/ INA499, henceforth Abdul Khan.
5. Proud and erect see MS-Toye introduction.
6. Downcast eyes of officers Soldiers Contribution to Indian Independence, published by Army Education Service 1974 third edition by General Mohan Singh, pg109 henceforth Singh, MS-Toye para 67, Fujiwara said they all cheered when he spoke (F. Kikan – *Japanese Intelligence Operations in*

Southeast Asia During World War II by Fujiwara Iwaichi, written 1947–1948, published 1969, English translation published Kuala Lumpur Heinemann 1983, pg185 henceforth Fujiwara).

7. Singh Biographical details MS-Toye and Singh Chapter 1.

8. Racism/Discrimination mentioned in almost every Indian memoir, and by Singh's C/O Lieutenant-Colonel L.V. Fitzpatrick (letter to his wife in family archive with his grandson Alan Macdonald).

9. Difference between discontent and rebelling, see Kevin Noles – *Waging War Against the King*, published by The British Empire at War Research Group, Research Papers, No. 6 (2014), pg14, henceforth Noles War.

10. Bangkok being an espionage centre see Fujiwara pg24.

11. Japan's plans on India see Fujiwara pg8, Subhas Chandra Bose The Springing Tiger by Hugh Toye 1959, Jaico 1991 edition pg6, henceforth Toye, Number of Indians in Southeast Asia – INA File 495 File 4, pg293.

12. Giani Pritam Singh biography, see *Indian Independence Movement in East Asia* by Kesar Singh Giani, published Lahore Jan 1947 with a Foreword by SC Bose's brother Sarat Chandra Bose, pg16 Kesar Giani was the Civil Administrator of the Provisional Government of India launched by SC Bose on October 21, 1943. Besides personal knowledge, he had access to all the official and many secret documents based on which he wrote this book, henceforth Kesar Giani. He says the INA did not suddenly appear, the stage had been set by revolutionaries like Rash Behari Bose, Swami Nityanand Puri and Pritam Singh (pg20).

13. Fujiwara biography INA File 254 on Fujiwara Kikan, pg6–10 henceforth FK. He said he had no prior India experience, though this is unlikely:
    - Southeast Asia visit May 1941 see The Indian National Army by K.K. Ghosh, 1969, Meenakshi Prakashan Meerut 2022 edition pg41, henceforth Ghosh.
    - Sivaram said he had laid out his plan months in advance (M Sivaram, an Indian journalist who was a Propaganda officer with the Indian Independence League Bangkok, INA File 715, CSDIC (I) V Detachment Interrogation Report 309 + his memoir The Road to Delhi, Charles Tuttle & Co., 1967, henceforth Sivaram).
    - His fellow intelligence officer Colonel Kodamatsu added he had seen Fujiwara meet Rash Behari Bose many times in Tokyo Army HQ before the war (Hikari Kikan INA 974 pg6). It is to be noted that Kadomatsu himself denied any pre-war involvement with India, though (this time) Fujiwara pg8 says he had, having visited Bangkok in July 1941 to assess the situation.
    - Lebra also mentions R.B. Bose visits to Army HQ but does not specify who he met (The Indian National Army and Japan, by Joyce Lebra, ISEAS

edition 2008, pg50 henceforth Lebra. This is a reissue of the Jungle Alliance published 1971.

14. Parentage metaphors – *The War of the Springing Tigers* by Gerald Corr, Osprey Publishing 1975, pg125, henceforth Corr), Indian National Army A Documentary Study Vol. 1, published by Gyan 2004, pg72 henceforth Sareen.

15. Fujiwara meeting Giani Pritam Singh: Fujiwara pg27 onwards, SEATIC INA427 pg18 henceforth SEATIC.

16. Fujiwara focus on looking at goal of Indians – Lebra pg2.
    • No copy of pre-war Fujiwara-Giani agreement exists. Details are from SEATIC pg19. Fujiwara also says there that idea of getting Indian soldiers to join was the Giani's.

      On Fujiwara exceeding instructions see Kevin Noles – *Renegades in Malaya: Indian Volunteers of the Japanese*, F. Kikan in British Journal for Military History Vol. 2, Issue 2, February 2017, pg103 henceforth Noles FK. Tokyo decided to see what happened on the ground (*The War of the Spring Tigers* by Gerald Corr, Osprey 1975 pg65, henceforth Corr).

17. Giani Pritam Singh pre-war Indian Army contact:
    • An early British assessment (August 1945, FK pg100) says they were aware of Japanese sponsored contact with anti-British elements.
    • On his approach to soldiers (if not to officers) CSDIC V Detachments Information Report 1 (FK pg26) says Colonel Tamura the Japanese Military Attache in Bangkok helped him to send men to Malaya/Burma to subvert troops.
    • The same report says two Ghadarites from Shanghai were sent by him to Malaya in November 1941 as fifth columnists (also in Kesar Giani pg18).
    • Fujiwara pg32 describes Pritam Singh's contact in the Malaya border areas with Indian troops.
    • Lebra pg5 refers to him distributing leaflets to Indian soldiers there.

18. See Chapter 3 that describes Gill's mission in more detail.

19. On Singh's pre-war contact.
    • Rumours see FK pg99, INA History pg239.
    • His leave coincided with Gill's visit (MS-Toye para 16/19).
    • His explanation of 30/11/42 statement on fighting the British see Singh pg52–4, Lebra pg16 and Corr pg67.
    • Akram (Singh's early INA deputy) is said to have met the Giani in 1941 before war began (Report A10, INA File 500).
    • Singh denied any pre-war contact (Ghosh pg49 note 41 and in his post-war letters to Toye in Singh family archives), Backed up by his ADC Rattan Singh (MS-Toye para 201).

20. Fifth column, see Officers' Chronology INA File 109, pgs 14 (Lieutenant Das) and 21 (Captain Munro), Aziz Report 993, Noles FK pg108 and many other sources.

21. The Giani, Fujiwara and team reach Thailand/Malaysia border on December 10, 1941 (SEATIC pg20, Kesar Giani pg26), details of Giani's team, see FK pg29, Loudspeakers see Sivaram, feeding well see Report 19/INA 499.

22. Singh's surrender has many versions. My assessment is based on:
    - His meeting the Japanese before surrender, see Balbir Singh Report 16, *Khan* and *A Daring Journey to Freedom – Escape from a Japanese Prisoner-of-War Camp: Memoirs of Colonel Gangaram S. Parab, MC*, published 2014. In his Reminiscences in Fujiwara's book, an earlier negotiation is implicit as he said he joined the Japanese on the day of his surrender before he had any talks.
    - On him meeting Sugita, see Dhillon Report 1034/INA 499. Sugita was in the area (Fujiwara pg64), and they could have met on/after December 11 (Baboo Ram had said Singh had disappeared that day).
    - In his 18/2/64 statement to the Indian parliament, he said "War in the Far East broke out on the 8th Dec[ember] 1941. Having negotiated with the Japanese, I finally joined them on the 15th December". Very diplomatically, this covers this and the many other versions that exist, see https://www.rsdebate.nic.in.
    - An August 1945 (FK pg99) British report concluded there was no earlier collusion with the Japanese, however this was decades before Singh's 1964 Parliament speech.
    - The version Singh wanted history to remember him by is in Chapter 4 of his book, where he said that on December 11 after witnessing the brutality of war and realizing the real worth of life, he decided to fight for India's freedom. Seeing Japanese propaganda leaflets, he decided to approach them and arranged the surrender.

23. Lieutenant-Colonel Fitzpatrick's full name – https://www.findmypast.com.

24. Actions taken as soon as war broke out:
    - Leaflets see Singh article in *Bombay Chronicle*, December 8, 1946 (INA File 470), Report 1041/INA499 and Khan. Singh said in first days of war Army HQ had asked for Indian officers to translate leaflets (MS-Toye para 25).
    - F. Kikan in Khaki, see Fujiwara pg48 (their attire made them look like the Indian Army, very helpful given their role in trying to reach out to those same soldiers).
    - F band being white, see Baboo Ram INA File 495 part 4, pg90. On the letter F being red, see *In the Line of Duty* by Lt Gen Harbaksh Singh, Lancer Publications 2000/reprint 2022 pg105. Henceforth Harbaksh S.

- F band meaning Fujiwara, Friendship, Freedom FK pg13, F Kikan organization, see FK pg16.

25. Singh in Alor Star on December 15, see Singh's Reminiscences in Fujiwara's book. Restoring order, see Fujiwara who names Akram pg79, twenty men stated in FK pg92.

26. Whisky fuelled all night talks – MS-Toye para 31, Pritam Singh during these see Corr pg91.

27. Yamashita meeting: different dates – MS-Toye and Corr says 16th, SEATIC/Toye 17th, FK 18th·

28. Start of Singh's involvement MS-Toye para 34 onwards, 250 Fujiwara Volunteers see FK pg185–194, Fujiwara happy corralling troops (FK pg15).

29. Jan1, 1942 Taiping letter INA File 75 pg9; this says its first use of term Indian National Army. Corr pg91, Ghosh pg37 also say Singh used the term first, though Toye (pg3) says it was Fujiwara. For INA fighting Indian Army in Malaya referred to in the letter, see INA History INA 403 pg19 and Report 1028/INA499.

30. Fujiwara and Singh skating over ally status, Corr pg90. On this, after the war Singh said "Whether I believed the Japanese to be sincere at that time it was very difficult for me to decide. Even if chances of sincerity were 1 to 10, I wanted to test it. It was worth it. In any way it was going to bring out the truth. If they were trying to use us as it suited them, we were also trying to use them as it suited us. I was prepared for both eventualities" (MS-Toye Appendix B).

31. Jan leaflets: SEATIC pg26, Pritam Singh's diary in Kesar pg27, Corr pg93–4, GSD pg91 says leaflets signed by Singh, Pritam Singh's speech in Khan.

32. Singh joining late night missions see Pritam Singh diary in Kesar Giani pg28.

33. Singh instruction on air defence see Shingara Trial INA File 482 part 1, p73.

34. Number of Indian POWs in Malaysia from Kesar Giani pg31, Singh's parliament speech.

35. Kuala Lumpur Camp-Subedar Onkar Singh 5/14 Punjab became Commandant over the dozen officers present (see Singh and Report 959/INA 499.

36. Fujiwara Kikan in campaign: For an excellent article on this see Noles FK.
    - See FK, SEATIC, Fujiwara, Singh and Reports 699, 729, 765, 770, 938, 947, 979 (flag raisers), 987, 991, 1049 in INA 499.
    - Allah Ditta not denying rumours, see FK pg15.

37. Indian unit surrenders:
    - See INA File 415 part 5 (Prosecution Memos) on Captain Burhan-ul-Mulk 2/10 Baluch, Captain Tehl Singh 1/8 Punjab. For Burhan's own account, see Report 958/INA 499 which also mentions Captain PK Sahgal 2/10 Baluch (for more on the latter see Sahgals Report 940/INA499 and The Forgotten Army, India's Armed Struggle for Independence 1942–45, Peter

Ward Fay, The University of Michigan Press, 1991. A large part of it is based on interviews with Swaminathan, the Commander of the INAs all female Rani Jhansi Regiment, and Captain PK Sahgal, 2/10 Baluch who also joined the INA. They married after the war. Henceforth Fay.

- Lt Bakhtawar Singh 3 FdCoy Bengal Sappers, see Aziz Report 993, Info Report 2 (INA 874).

38. Captain Tehl Singh meeting Allah Ditta at Kranji, see Report 989/ INA 499.

39. Mohan Singh reaching Singapore: MS-Toye para 64, Report 976 and 699/INA 499 on bungalow guards.

40. Preparation for Farrer Park (FP) on February 16, 1942 – Hunt (INA History P29/ INA 403, henceforth Hunt). In his book pg108 Singh says he met Gill on 16th (in his OWN book Gill does not mention this and in pg25 says he first heard about the INA at FP on February 17 – *Story of the I.N.A.*, Colonel Naranjan Singh Gill, Publications Division, Ministry of Information & Broadcasting, Govt of India, First Edition, December 1985, Reprint 2001, henceforth Gill).

41. Loudspeakers (Report 1076/INA 499), food, see Hunt and Khan.

42. See Khan, Report 80/INA 499.

43. FP video IWM Catalogue No. JYY 60/National Archives Singapore Accession No. 2011005477l.

44. public humiliation of British, see Noles War pg17, on details see Hunt where he does not mention obeying Japanese orders but being administered by them. Many Indian officers refer to this handover as feeling they were treated as cattle, and it absolved them of their earlier oath to the British King none of the soldiers refer to it all. The INA JAG Lt Nag also said he was not asked during the war if this handover meant their oath need not be considered binding, It may have been a well thought out defense decided by some officers to absolve them of their oath, used effectively in the post-war INA trials.

45. Fujiwara speech, see Khan.

46. Fujiwara speech translation – Many references to Gill translating for Fujiwara. In his book (pg26) Gill said Hunt spoke in English and he translated for him, though no one else mentions this and its quite sure Hunt spoke in Hindustani. Perhaps Gill misremembered after forty years or did not want to admit he had translated for Fujiwara.

47. MS speech, see Khan.

48. Giani Pritam Singh speech, see Khan, slogans see Khan & Bains Report 983/ band Report 1017 INA 499.

49. Officers at pavilion.

- 100+ officers' Report 993, Fujiwara saying Rangoon will fall in a month Report 954, Balbir drinks Report 16, all in INA 499.

- Jind drinks: pg91 LtCol Gurbaksh Singh – Indelible Reminiscences, Lancer Publications 2013, henceforth Jind.
50. Soldiers reaction after speeches, see Khan.

Chapter 2: The Rise and Fall of Captain Mohan Singh's First INA

1. POWs settling down: Overnight stay e.g. Report 876, Food/meds Reports 955/956 and Lt Col Chatterji NAI's INA File 387, Bulls sent for milk, see Fay pg93.
2. Made to clear rubble-Khan and other reports.
3. Changi Guards – MS-Toye para 77, Santa Singh, see *From My Bones* by Gurbaksh Singh Dhillon, Aryan International Press 1998, pg103 and Chapter 7 henceforth GSD. Fracas with British POW, see FIC Interrogation in INA File 270 (his book has a different story, pg130).
4. Next Changi commander Rana, see Report 941 for him using a revolver, see Report 592. See Nag's Report 950 to compare GSD and Rana.
5. Gunners – CSDIC (I) Information reports 16/17 see INA File 379 part 7/8, INA Chronology Memo 10. For debriefs, see Reports 1379/1396, and for soldiers in Andamans Report 26a, 314,428, 956, 1227.
6. Singh start of propaganda the day after Farrer Park, see Report A89 INA File 500 and many others.
7. Propaganda plan: Key officers, see INA Chronology pg11 – Lt Col Chatterjee, Major Khosla and MZ Kiani, Captains Jahangir, Shahnawaz Khan and Patnaik.
8. Preferential treatment – Meds (INA 218, pg278), restaurants allowed and streets out of bounds (INA 218, pg81), wine/women (Jind, MS-Toye para 192).
9. Propaganda – Radio (see KPK Menon's CSDIC (I) S Section Report 500 in INA File 272, and personal account in INA History pg57 both together henceforth KPK), *Syonan Times* was the renamed *Straits Times of Singapore* run by the Japanese from 1942, army commands (Singh pg120 and Report 592).
10. Plays Bhandari Report 1236 and Subedar Mohd Abdul Latif Report 951.
11. Singapore politics – see Goho Report INA File 385 part 3 and Indians in Singapore 1819-1945 (Oxford 2014) that includes many oral histories.
12. Tokyo invite March 1 – see SEATIC pg28.
13. On Rash Behari Bose, see *Lebra, The First INA* by Hugh Toye, Journal of Southeast Asian Studies, Vol. 15, No. 2 (September 1984), henceforth Toye 1, and for a sympathetic account of him, *Imperial Fugitive* by Joseph McQuade, published by Vintage Books, 2023. Also RBBs associate AM Nair's memoir, *An Indian Freedom Fighter in Japan*, published by Orient Longman, 1982.

14. Goodwill mission see MS/Toye, FK, SEATIC, KPK, Singh, Fujiwara, Kesar Giani.
15. Otagura translator, see SEATIC pg18 Bangkok, MS-Toye para 27 Alor Star.
16. Tokyo air crash see MS-Toye para 80–3, Singh gives more details in a 1946 interrogation at Red Fort, see INA File 379 part 85, pg19. In his 1974 book, Singh does not delve into suspicions about the crash.
Fujiwara gives a different account from Singh, saying they left Singapore together and split up in Saigon (SEATIC and Fujiwara). On Fujiwara's search of Giani's house, see Report 950.
17. Opinion on Rash Behari Bose, see Singh/KPK and Fugitive of Empire that give the opposing views.
18. Tokyo resolutions, see Kesar Giani pg46–51.
19. Tojo meet Tokyo, see Toye's *First INA* pg372, and Goho (also for sightseeing in Japan). However, Fujiwara pg239 says they did not meet Tojo.
20. 25k volunteers by Jun 1942, see INA Chronology pg6 (INA 415).
21. Sook Ching Massacre of Chinese men Pillai pg33, JAPANIZATION?
22. Japanization of Singapore, Singh pg121.
23. Motives. This section has been written after consulting the INA papers, memoirs and these works:
    • Kevin Noles, *Divided Loyalties in The People's War*, ed. Wilson and Fennell published by McGill University Press, 2022, + Noles War and Noles FK.
    • Srinath Raghavan's Chapter 12 Indian National Armies in his book *India's Wars*, Penguin, 2016.
    • Tarek Barkawi, *Soldiers of Empire*, Cambridge University Press, 2017 and *Culture and Combat in the Colonies: The Indian Army in the Second World War*, Journal of Contemporary History Vol. 41, No. 2 (April 2006), pg325–355.
    • Gajendra Singh, *The Testimony of Indian Soldiers and the Two World Wars*, Bloombury Academic, 2015.
    • Chandar Sundaram, *The Indian National Army: Towards a Balanced and Critical Appraisal* (July 25, 2015 in *Economic & Political Weekly*) and Seditious Letters. Am grateful to the author for sending me these articles. Plus Toye, Singh, Ghosh, Lebra, Gill.
24. Bangkok see Kesar Giani, Singh, MS-Toye, KPK, Goho, Gill, Report 953 (Lt Col Loganathan).
25. LEBRA p216, INA403 pg240 – Berlin announce MS, MS eloquence, MS bkk speech long emotional and deeply affect the audience. He spoke in Hindustani and as many present did not understand it, it was translated into English by Major Prakash Chand (Report 953).
26. MS oath full text (INA History pg237/244), why Singh did this see MS-Toye and Report 993.

"It has been decided to raise the Indian National Army under the command of General Mohan Singh of an independent status entirely composed of and commanded by Indians. Its object is to obtain complete independence for India free of any foreign domination and to take any steps towards the fullfilment of this objective. Are you prepared to join unconditionally this National Army?"

27. Deputy Military Provosts note on Concentration Camp, see Report 957. Singh denied there was such a camp (MS-Toye 178–187). Toye visited the location after the war and said some of the accounts were exaggerated such as isolation cells (see Report A25 in INA File 500), however it was beyond doubt that beatings and ill-treatment happened, 600–1,000 yards away was B1 Bidadari camp, so they would have seen. The threat would have been enough (MS-Toye Para 190–4). Singh's battalion mate Captain Shahnawaz Khan (quoted in GSDs Report 1034) and Subedar Allah Ditta (see Allah Ditta para 40) said the camps were started by Singh.

28. For convincing VCOs, see Report 79 in INA File 500.

29. Separation camp Dhalgarkar see INA File 495 part 4 pg 82, Singh's reasons for doing this see Aziz's Report 993 and Singh's book (where he says he took them out one night for a treat and everyone thanked him). Numerous reports list those present at a particular time, eg INA History/Das p212.

30. 40k Volunteers see INA Chronology pg14.

31. Pandya CSDIC (I) A Section Report A10 (INA File 500).

32. Gill pg33, Pandya CSDIC (I) A Section Report A10 (INA File 500).

33. Kapurthala Report 993, Jind/CBE recommendation UK NA WO-373-87-332 (he was given an OBE), on oath, see Singh pg111.

34. Unit-wise details see INA Chronology pg14, and Gurkha/Baluch pg16, for medical, see Officers' Report where overall only 37% joined while all the seniors did.

35. Half of officers joined see INA File 379 part 9, Report on 416 Indian officers POW in Singapore, henceforth Officers' Report. Aziz, see Report 993, Opportunists Report 955/960.

36. Interrogations see Noles DL and Gajendra Singh.

37. On Sawyer/British officers in Changi see Toye's 1st INA, expected more to volunteer see Deakin in INA History/INA 403.

38. Order 1 and September 9, 1942, INA File 218, henceforth Singh Orders.

39. Mohan Singh made fun of how the British created a hierarchy of Indian officers referring to it as "KCO, ICO, ECO, VCO, XCO, YCO, ZCO". The first four were actually terms and the last three were his sarcasm. See Report 634/ INA 499.

40. Thimaya on VCO, see his Report 954 and Lt Ahmad Report 960. Earlier, Singh planned a three-tier promotion for VCOs, with Subedar Majors becoming

Captains, Subedar-Lieutenants and Jemadars Second Lieutenants (INA Chronology pg17). More details on Medical VCOs see Rai's Report 955.

41. Singh's letter to Toye August 24, 77 where he said 60% of officers including VCOs joined INA under him. Colonel Sawyer (IWM) said 25% VCO joined. From Singh Orders we find 380 VCOs were gazetted, and the total number is approximately 1,157 (NAI File HOME_POLITICAL_I_1945_NA_F-21-5, pg51), so works out to 33% 16,700 in INA Division, see INA 224 p115, named after leaders Gill/pg34, Inspection September 10, 1942 see INA Chronology pg7. Organization, arms only for 6,000, constituent units, see Red Fort Trial INA File 495 part 5, pg114.

42. Communal issues – INA Chronology Memo 17, Burhan Report 958, guilty verdict scc BL IOR/L/WS/1/1577.

43. Statistics derived from Officers' Report, Sikh Raj see Burhan Report 958.

44. Toye pg10–12, The Council of Action minutes were fabricated to present a different picture Toye states in Singh's interrogation report para 130.

45. Issues with Japan, see Kesar Giani, Singh, Lebra, Toye1 pg375 onwards.

46. Gill arrest see Mohan Singh pg188, Gill pg1 and pg45, Lebra pg86, Raghavan CSDIC (I) S Section Report 1144 INA 385 part IV.

47. Council resignations see Kesar Giani, Singh, Raghavan, Lebra, Toye. On dispute between Indian leaders, see MS-Toye para 118. Singh meet with officers 15 Dec 42 – Ehsan Qadir/ Vichy France see Report 993, those present Report 953, earlier meet 7 Dec see Report 586.

48. See Gilani (MS-Toye para 161), Goho Report 1310/INA 385 part IV and Mufti INA164.

49. Singh arrest see Singh, MS-Toye, Reports 953/956/958.

50. Khan statement in Trial INA 495 File 5, Lakshmi in Fay pg108.

51. Toye views of Singh from letters in Singh family archives (Toye to Singh July 4 and November 1, 1977, and October 13, 1982).

Chapter 3: A Double Cross or a Triple Cross?

1. On his arrest see Gill book pg1–6, Mohan Singh reaction MS-Toye para 153.

2. Thimayya of India, A Soldiers Life, by Humphrey Evans, Harcourt, Bruce and Company, New York 1960 pg117, Gill refers to the same meeting in his book pg13.

3. On Gill's early life, see Gill.

4. On British knowledge of infiltrators, see INA File 715 Report 409, Gill's interrogation INA File 379 Part XXXXIX Report 1096 (henceforth Gill Report).

5. Gills spy mission: besides Lebra pg85, Sareen pg99 see.

- CSDIC (I) memo – he reports that in Bangkok most Indians were involved in business and not politics except Pritam Singh – FK pg10. It is quite possible they met then. Gill returned on December 1 (Gill pg20).
- His political experience – he was part of team led by General Barstow that reviewed a Sikh mutiny in India in 1940. Both were in Malaya in 1941, Barstow commanded the 9th division adjacent to the 11th where Gill was a staff officer. He may have recommended Gill for this mission. On Barstow mission see A Survey of Sikh Situation, sent to me courtesy Chandar Sundaram. The mission includes unnamed Sikh officers, Gill says in his book he was one.
- Trip details see Gill, Gill Report, CSDIC report INA File 254 pg10, Dr Jagdish Singh INA File 715 Report 336 (henceforth Jagdish Singh) and MS-Toye para 103.
- Fujiwara in bungalow near station see his Book pg29, his denial of being in the next room in Gill's hotel see INA File 254/pg19.
- On Gill being sighted – by Giani Pritam Singh see INA File 499 Report 978 (Ehsan Qadir), by the Japanese see Singh pg189.
- Gill visit rumours see Natarajan Report 876/INA 499.
6. Chanda Singh see INA254, Post-war Gill contacted by IIL during campaign from Khan.
7. Gill and Mohan Singh relationship – Gill Book, Singh's book, MS report para 92.
8. Second Bkk trip.
   - Hotel register see MS para 71, Goho INA 385 part 3, Gill Report.
   - On Terauchi, see Hussain (INA File 499 Report 934, he was Gill's Personal Secretary February–July 1942), Plus, on February 25, 1942 Mohan Singh told officers that Gill had gone to Tokyo for negotiations (likely instead this Saigon visit) see Indelible Reminiscences Lt Col Gurbaksh Singh, 1 Jind Infantry pg…, Lt Col Chatterji said in third week of February 1942 Gill had gone to Saigon to meet high Japanese military officials (India's Struggle for Freedom, Major-General A.C. Chatterji, Chuckervertty, Chatterjee & Co., Calcutta 1947, pg10).
   - Gill does not mention the Saigon trip in his memoir probably as he wanted to play down his support of the Japanese. Neither does Singh, as he wanted to play down the key role Gill played at this stage. Fujiwara doesn't mention it either, though he certainly went with Gill as mentioned by many witnesses.
   - On meeting Terauchi on December 15, 1941, see Kesar Giani pg26, Mohan Singh pg78 (meeting a Japanese general on the same day). May seem surprising that Japanese Generals were in the front line, but they were, e.g. Yamashita met Mohan Singh on December 16 in Alor Star (Chapter 1).
   - On Mohan Singh needing Gill more at the start, see Corr pg131.

9. Captain Hussain Report 934/INA 499, henceforth Hussain. It is quite likely that Gill was shunted out to Bangkok due to his rivalry with Mohan Singh.

10. Dhillon – trusted friend, see Gill Report, being Mil Secy, see Harbaksh Singh pg105.

    Gill's Personal Secretary was Captain S.M. Hussain 4/19 Hyderabad gives an account of Dhillon and Gill in Singapore and then Bangkok – he was there with them until July 15. On Indian meals see Jagdish Singh. Dhillon's account is in Report R/14 in British Library IOR/L/WS/1/1711 (henceforth Dhilllon).

11. Bangkok conference – rivalry, see Chopra Report 435, Gill mood/Iwakuro solution see Hussain, Gill Report, Gill book, MS para 108–110.

    On the mission, the sources are the interrogations of those in Gill's team in INA File 499. Grewal (Report 620), Tehl (989), Shiv Singh 1010 give detailed overall accounts. A good soldier's perspective is Sumer Singh (Report 95). Those by the civilians Musafir (62) and Sardar Sher Singh (94) are the best reads.

    After wading through them all, CSDIC (I) made 5 reports that are in INA 250, dated November 11, 1942 (pg39), March 31, 1943 (pg34), June 12, 1943 (pg35) and January 21, 1943 (INA 822/pg134).

12. Recruitment see Grewal, Shiv Singh, Sumer Singh.

13. Civilian recruitment See Musafir Report 62 and Constable Pritam Singh 96.

14. Journey to Bangkok, see Bakhtawar, Gurdip Singh 31, Musafir, rest to Grewal, Shiv Singh, Charan Singh 24, Europe Hotel, see Musafir, Gill message, see Sarma Report 37 (and similar Mookerjee 36 and Gurdip 31).

15. Test, see Musafir 62 and Sumer Singh 95.

16. Training see Grewal, Sher, Sumer and Pritam Singh.

17. Back to Singapore see Bakhtawar, Musafir and Pritam Singh. Recruitment, see Pardesi 1020 Narandar 1022 and Jagdish Singh. Suzuki Hospital is mentioned in many reports and its old name by Lee 952.

18. Civilian volunteers, see Sher Singh 94, Baroda Seal (INA 250/pg17 henceforth Seal).

19. Plan of three routes and coded signals, see Dhillon, Grewal, Tehl Singh.

20. Gulab and Chameli Instructions, see Musafir, Mookerjee, Charan Singh.

21. Ram Sarup group, see Udhe Singh (Report 1087) and Grewal (620).

22. Captain Pritam Singh, see Report 19, on his shaving, see Lee 952 and Dalbir Singh 106.

23. Dhillon's escape, see Dhillon, Bakhtawar, Gurbachan 22, Gurdip 31, Dalip 159, Dutta 177 and team Gulab Kulkarni 23, Roy 21, Sarma 37 and Musafir 62.

24. Fate of other groups.

    Chameli – Sumer 95, Jendramuni 97, Pritams 96.

Corop Charan24, 25 Biswas, Mook 36, Chuhar 47, Chakravarty 366, Seal + Chuhar Singh 47 and a report dated August 10, 1943 on him where CSDIC seems to have got his identify wrong (INA 250/pg32).

fourth unnamed group, see Mazumdar 263, Chowdhury 377.

25. Letters Udhe 1087, Das 447, Grewal 620, Bakhtawar 20.
26. Letter discovery Puran 677, Grewal, Tehl Singh and Chopra 435.
27. Gill's defence statement to Japanese, including what he thought of Dhillon, see INA75.
28. Lebra pg86, Raghavan CSDIC (I) S Section Report 1144 INA 385 part IV.
29. Team arrest is covered by each in their reports and by Dr Lee Report 952.
30. Other interrogations, see Dhillon.
31. Dhillon Deceptions, see Reports 159/177, Sher Singh Report 94/ Kesar pg26, hunt for Dalbir Singh CP Orders FK/INA254.
32. Awards, see UK National Archives WO 373/62.

Chapter 4: The Great Escape From Singapore

1. This section is taken from the following sources.
   - The report by Pillai and Radhakrishnan dated September 7, 1942 after they reached Delhi. Source AWM 54 779-10-4. This has however been largely written by Radhakrishnan as can be seen by the commentary and author's discussion with Pillai's eldest son Rear Admiral (Retd) Sampath Pillai, Indian Navy. Additional details including telexes between GHQ Delhi and London, correspondence with Buckingham Palace on seeking The King's approval for the MCs, are in WO-373-61-980.
   - Natarajan's account is from his interrogation dated April 8, 1945. He had stayed behind in Burma and when the Allies had recaptured parts of Burma, he was brought to Delhi for this. See CSDIC (I) No. 2 Section Report 877 in NAI's INA Papers File 495 part 5.
   - Pillai's account is taken from his book *Three Thousand Miles to Freedom*, Brigadier MM Pillai MC, Lancer Publishers (India) 2009. After the war, Pillai had written a narrative that he presented at Staff College Quetta in Oct 1945. The comment by the Commandant was "a good story, well told, I would have found it more interesting if you had shortened account of preparation & told us more about actual journey". It's likely Pillai took this advice to heart as the book does focus more on the journey.
   - These three accounts, recorded separately, decades apart and each with a different lens, are amazingly quite alike on the broad strokes:
     o Pillai's book is the longest account, so most of the atmosphere and detail comes from him.

- On dates, some are clear – left Singapore on May 7, reached Penang May 9, crossed into Thailand on May 14 and Burma on May 23. From then to when they reached an Indian patrol on August 2, dates are unclear. I have constructed a timeline based on distances and when one/ more of them mention how many days various sections took.
- The authors have also spent more time on specific incidents that their partners may have stressed on less. In this case, if it is mentioned by two of them, I have included it.
- The third difference is that Radhakrishnan does not mention his trouble with crossing water bodies, while Pillai provides great detail. On this I have taken Pillai's account as I do believe it happened.
- The last difference is on the conflict between Natarajan and Radhakrishnan where each provides their side of the story. I have largely stayed away from this as it is difficult to tell who was right. Radhakrishnan basically said that Natarajan spoke too openly about their escape. Natarajan complained that the other was too harsh and lacked sympathy for his injured foot. Pillai was silent – his son Colonel Pillai said he did not bad mouth people and may have left out criticisms.

Besides information on the escape, Pillai and Radhakrishnan's September 1942 report brought the first news of conditions in Singapore, Malaya, Thailand and Burma to India HQ. It covers:

- Changi civilians, Australians at Seletar, Indians at Bidadari, Nee Soon, Tengah, Tyersall, Buller.
- Shipment of 9,000 Indian POWs for labour away from Singapore.
- Other escapes.
- Assessment of chance of escape for British/Australia (nil), Indians, good.
- Suggestions on propaganda in Southeast Asia and India.
- Names of those who helped them along the way, outlining a support system for an escape route.
- Attitude of locals before, during the war and after surrender, assessment of loyalty.

2. Discussion with his son Colonel Ravi Pillai, 63 Cavalry, Indian Army.
3. 323 unit, see Report 897/INA 499.

Chapter 5: The Rash Behari Bose Era

1. For the Japanese invasions starting in December 1941, see the official history – The War Against Japan by Major General S. Woodbury-Kirby, Volume 1 HMSO, 1957.

2. On what Japan wanted from the countries it invaded, they had a detailed plan – by year, territory and resource how much they wanted for their war effort (India MOD 601/ 9725/ H).

3. On reaction and atmosphere after Mohan Singh arrest, see Chopra CSDIC (I) No 2 Section Report 435 in INA File 499 part 2, India's Struggle for Freedom, Major-General A.C. Chatterji, Chuckervertty, Chatterjee & Co., Calcutta. 1947 pg50 (henceforth Chatterji), *From My Bones Memoirs* by Colonel Gurbaksh Singh Dhillon of the Indian National Army, Arya Books International 1998 pg198 (henceforth Dhillon), *India's Freedom Struggle and the Great INA* by Major-General Mohammad Zaman Kiani, Reliance Publishing House, 1982 pg70–1 (henceforth Kiani).

4. Administration Committee appointed by RB Bose on December 31, 1942 consisted of Majors Bhonsle, Kiani, Prakash Chand, Captain Ehsan Qadir and Lt. Col. Loganathan, see INA File 224. Chand stayed away from this, there were other officers who worked to rebuild the INA.

5. Discussions after Mohan Singh's arrest, see CSDIC () No. 2 Section Report 551 Subedar Shingara Singh, 5/11 Sikh Regiment INA File 499 part 2, Report 953 Lt. Colonel Arcot Doraiswamy Loganathan, IMS, INA File 499 part 6 (henceforth Loganathan), *The Springing Tiger*, Hugh Toye Cassell 1959 pg13 (henceforth Toye) and *The First Indian National Army*, Hugh Toye, Journal of Southeast Asian Studies, Vol. 15, No. 2 September 1984 pg380 (henceforth Toye 1st INA).

6. Iwakuro further statements, see Loganathan, and in the same file, Report 993 on Major Aziz Ahmed, Kapurthala Infantry and Ghosh pg151. On being treated worse than POWs see Jemadar Chint Singh 2/12 Frontier Rifles in AWM 54/1010/3/108.

7. Text of RB Bose's *Our Struggle*, see INA311, distributed in January 1943, see CSDIC (I) No. 2 Section Report 1135 in INA File 499 part 9. According to Mohan Singh this was written by Captain Jahangir, 1st Bahawalpur Infantry (see *Leaves from Diary General Mohan Singh*, Free World Publications Lahore 1946), pg21. On joining if SCB was to come, see *The Indian National Army – Second Front of the Indian Independence Movement*, K.K. Ghosh Meenakshi Prakashan, 1969 pg152 (henceforth Ghosh), *Japan and Indian National Army*, Dr T.R. Sareen, Agam Prakashan Delhi, 1986, pg106 (henceforth Sareen), Toye 1st INA pg380 and *His Majesty's Opponent* by Sugata Bose, Belknap Press, 2011 pg243 (henceforth Sugata).On other aspects Ghosh pg146–156, Chatteji pg51, Dhillon pg199 and *The Indian National Army and Japan*, Joyce Lebra, 2009, reprint of *Jungle Alliance*, 1971 pg98 (henceforth Lebra).

8. On the community, see CSDIC (I) No. 2 Section Report 978 on Captain Ehsan Qadir 5/2 Punjab in INA File 499 part 6, Report 711 in INA File 499 part 4, Major Sangha's Report 1198 in INA File 499 part 9 on Sikhs,

on Garhwali's see Reports 1216 on Lt Rathuri 5/18 Garhwal and Subedar Man Singh Bhandari 2/18 Garhwal in INA File 499 part 10. On Dogra's see Subedar-Major Baboo Ram 1/14 Punjab Report 876 in INA File 499 part 5 (henceforth Ram). On Gurkha's see XXX. On an overall unit-wise analysis of about 80% of those in the First INA and how many rejoined the second INA, see INA File 414.

9. RB Bose Questionnaire, see Chatterji pg51, Ghosh pg151, Ram, INA File 499 part 6 Report 945 on Lt Tajammal Hussian 6/14 Punjab, Report 950 on Lt Nag 3 MRC and Report 955 on Major Kulwant Rai.

10. On officers holding out from rejoining Second INA, see Report 1125 (INA 499 part 9), Loganathan, on the form to be signed when re-volunteering, see INA 431 pg36.

11. Bhonsle and Kiani announcement see INA 232.

12. On conditions at the Seletar Camp, see Report 711 INA File 499 part 4, Reports 1218, 1219 and 1223 in INA File 499 part 10, and Ram. On taking back possessions from the ex-volunteers, for a differing account stating that they refused to give them up, see Captain Jahangir 1st Bahawalpur Report 1001 and Captain Gurbaksh Singh Dhillon 1/14 Punjab Report 1034 (INA File 499 part 7). On numbers, see Report 711, Information Report 13 INA File 379 Part V, Toye pg14, Ghosh p154.

13. Filling the gap – 8k in Malaya see INA430 pg57, on Gujjars/Ahirs in March 1943, see Red Fort Trials by Moti Ram, 1946 Exhibit QQ pg320 (henceforth Moti Ram), on the experience of one such recruit, an Oriya coolie in the Pioneers, see Report 857 (INA 499 part 5). On letter to Malaya, see INA 431 pg31, Shah Nawaz Khan Report 1002 (INA 499 part 7) on outcome of trip, on instructions on questions see AIS Dara Report 1188 (INA 499 part 9), on being 2,000 short end-May 1943, see Moti Ram Exhibit SS pg321.

14. On the conference in April 1943 to cement RB Bose's role, see Loganathan, Mufti, Chatterji pg63, Ghosh pg155–6, Raghavan's Report 1144 in INA File 385 part 3, INA Diary in INA file 161 pg28.

Chapter 6: The Symbolism of Subhas Chandra Bose

1. *The Indian Spy - The True Story of the Most Remarkable Secret Agent of World War II* by Mihor Bose, Aleph 2017. The Great Escape by Sisir Kumar Bose, Netaji Research Bureau 1975. In a letter dated November 1, 1977 from Colonel Hugh Toye to Mohan Singh (Singh family archives) Toye mentions Bhagat's role and Britain's decision to not try to arrest Bose in Kabul.

2. Mein Kampf – Mihir pg314.

3. Indian Legion, see *The Indian National Army and Japan*, Joyce Lebra, 2009, reprint of *Jungle Alliance* 1971 pg109–110 (henceforth Lebra), on 3,000 who joined see INA 420 part 2, *The Springing Tiger* by Hugh Toye, Cassell 1959 pg69 (henceforth Toye).

4. England's Place in Hitler's plans for world domination by Andreas Hillgruber, Journal of Contemporary History Vol. 9/ No. 1 (January 1974), Of options most likely is Theory two on pg2, see sympathy towards Britain pg15–16.

5. On SC Bose in Berlin/Europe 1941–1944, see Toye pg 68–78, Lebra p110, *The Indian National Army – Second Front of the Indian Independence Movement* by K.K. Ghosh Meenakshi Prakashan, 1969, pg126–7 (Henceforth Ghosh), *The War of The Springing Tigers* by Gerald Corr, Osprey 1975, pg142–3 (henceforth Corr), His Majesty's Opponent by Sugata Bose, Belknap Press, 2011 pg219–221 (henceforth Sugata), *Brothers Against the Raj* by Leonard Gordon, Viking 1964 Reprint 1990 pg482–8 (henceforth Gordon), *The Lost Hero – A Biography of Subhash Bose* by Mihir Bose, Revised and Enlarged edition, Vikas Publishing House, 2014 pg283–314 (henceforth Mihir), Abid Hasan in INA File 471 part 2 (henceforth Hasan).

6. On the Japanese asking Germany to send Bose to Asia in Jan 1943 see Mihir pg344, Corr pg144, *Japan and Indian National Army*, Dr T.R.Sareen, Agam Prakashan Delhi, 1986 pg112 (henceforth Sareen), *The First Indian National Army*, Hugh Toye, Journal of Southeast Asian Studies, Vol. 15, No. 2 September 1984, pg380 (henceforth Toye 1st INA), Mufti memoir INA164 (henceforth Mufti), Boses phone call Jan 1942 see Hasan CSDIC (I) S Section Report 1410 in INA 471 part 2 (henceforth Hasan).

7. On the submarine trip see I-29 in www.combinedfleet.com, Corr pg144–6, Gordon pg487–90, Mihir pg370–1, Sugata pg232–6, *From My Bones – Memoirs by Colonel Gurbaksh Singh Dhillon of the Indian National Army*, Arya Books International, 1998, pg203 (henceforth Dhillon).

8. Bose preparations in submarine, see Toye pg80. Role play Gordon pg469.

9. British view of Bose, Sareen pg119.

10. *On Bose in Tokyo* – see Lebra pg114–6, Ghosh pg165–6, Corr pg146–7, Sareen pg115, Gordon pg492–3, Mihir pg374, Sugata pg240, F Kikan by Lt.Gen Fujiwara Iwaichi, Heinemann, 1983 pg248.

11. First INA enabled Second INA, see Dhillon pg199 and various references to RB Bose's efforts above. And Toye letter to Singh Nov 9 1983 (Singh family archives).

12. Bose arrival in Singapore, most accounts indicate he landed at Kallang, for the real story see *A Revolutionary Life Memoirs of a Political Activist* by Lakshmi Sehgal (henceforth Sehgal), Hasan and Kiani.

13. On term Netaji, see Gordon pg460, Mihir pg308, Sugata pg208–11, Ghosh pg122. On July 4, see Mufti, Sehgal, INA Diary (INA File 161). Cathay

capacity see https://biblioasia.nlb.gov.sg/history-cathay-cinema-2022/. The Japanese were concerned about the title Netaji as they felt it meant Fuehrer. There was no other prominent Asians in Singapore and Malaya and they did not like him being hailed as a great leader wherever he went as if he was the ruler of Southeast Asia and not them. See *An Indian Freedom Fighter in Japan – Memoirs of AM Nair*, Orient Longman 1982, pg236 (henceforth Nair) and *Unto Him A Witness* by – *The Story of Netaji Subhash Chandra Bose in East Asia* by SA Aiyer, Thacker & Co. Bombay pg157 (henceforth Aiyer).

14. Sugata pg245.

15. On Bose at the Padang July 5 see – Mufti, Sehgal, INA Diary, Sugata pg245, Mihir p378, Ghosh p170. On Caesar see Dhillon pg205, India's freedom struggle and the great INA by Major-General Mohammad Zaman Kiani, Reliance Publishing House 1982 pg75 (henceforth Kiani).

16. On PGFI stance of Japan see Toye pg93, Lebra pg129, Ghosh p178, Sareen pg118, Gordon pg501–2. On achieving legal status see Nag Report 950 in INA 499 part 6, on Japanese alarm, see Nair and Aiyer, on oath see Indian Independence Movement East Asia 1947 – Kesar Singh Giani Part II pg68, declaring war on US see Sugata pg258 and Dhillon pg210.

17. Dr Lakshmi Bai, various reports INA 499.

18. On Ran's see Sehgal and *My Adventures with the INA* by KR Palta, Lion Press Lahore 1946, pg91 (henceforth Palta).

19. Indian POWs numbers when Bose arrived = 15,000 INA (see note on Filling the gap) + 20,700 non INA in Singapore (INA224 pg274) + 6,500 in Malaya (8,300 in Nov 1942 see INA430 pg57 less 1,800 who joined INA, see Khan Report 1002 INA 499S).

20. On Timor see Report 1362 on Cap I R Rao, IMS in INA File 499 part 12.

21. On Bose attempts at recruiting POWs, see Report 961 on Cap S. P Jain, IMS (INA File 499 part 6) and Report 1115 Major Mehtab Singh RIASC in INA File 499 part 9.

22. Ghosh pg176 says 2,000 joined Bose as does Kiani Report, Lieutenant-Colonel Deakin 5/2 Punjab in INA 403 says 1,500.

23. Sareen pg124 mentions the mental surrender of INA soldiers to Bose. Also that earlier Mohan Singh created similar loyalty but some officers and civilians resented him. During the RBB era there was no loyalty.

24. Bose asking for them back from SWPA see Ghosh pg175–6.

25. Report 13, INA 379 Part V.

26. Civilians recruits allowed by Japan see Sareen pg121. On civilian recruits in Singh era INA 218 pg296–7, INA431 pg44–7.

27. Wahab Khan Report 372/INA715.

28. Indian civilians motives, Indian in Singapore, Rajesh Rai, OUP 2014 pg250.

29. Terauchi and Bose talks see Toye pg86, Ghosh pg172, Lebra pg123, Sareen pg125, Gordon pg498. Poorly equipped, Ghosh pg122 and Khan pg97. Quote to Rani's Ghosh pg180–1.
30. On Bose and Mohan Singh, Report 993 on Major Aziz, Report 956 on Major Raju (INA 499 part 6), Chatterji pg81, Nair pg222, Mufti, Fujiwara pg 251, Palta pg71, Deb Nath Das Report in INA286, Kiani Report. On correspondence b/w them, see Lebra pg124 and Corr pg149.
31. Andamans, see Toye pg100, Ghosh pg187–8, Lebra pg132–4, Sareen pg121–3, Gordon pg503, Sugata pg264. The Chief Commissioner Bose was allowed to announce was to cooperate fully with the Japanese military authorities, see Exhibit EEEEE Moti Ram pg375.
32. Mohan Singh/ Bose on Indian soldiers joining INA when they invaded Lebra pg124–5, similar view by others Gordon pg498. On Wavell speech, see CSDIC (I) Section Report 528 on Jemader Bela Gumba Gowd, 1st Mysore Infantry INA 826.

Chapter 7: In Hell Ships to Torture Islands

The best starting point for Indian POWs in Papua New Guinea is *Remembering the war in New Guinea – Where most of them perished: Indian POWs in New Guinea, and 'Great in Adversity' Indian Prisoners of war in New Guinea, Professor Peter Stanley (Australian War Memorial).*

1. Buyo Maru, see Sen AWM 54 1010/4/170 pg47, Jiwan Singh AWM 54 1010/4/164 pg96, Morton Report, US National Archives, NAID 74859023 pg48 onwards and his Narrative NAID 278490254 pg6 onwards, Wahoo: *The Patrols of America's Most Famous World War II Submarine* by Rear-Admiral Richard H. O'Kane, Random House 2009, Chapter on Third Patrol, US Naval Institute, July 2003, Proceedings, Vol. 129/7/1,205, US Naval History and Heritage Command, H-Gram 22 – Loss of the USS *Wahoo*, http://www.combinedfleet. com (Buyo Maru, Pacific Maru), Border Morning Mail (Albury, NSW), January 15, 1947 – Japanese Left Indian POWs to Drown. For other significant Hell Ship sinkings with Indian POWs, see authors article in https://www.scroll.in.
2. 3,000 men, see INA 224 pg274, Gunners and Changi Guards, see Chapter 2, Borneo engineers Report 698 INA 499.
3. Iwakuro takeover of POWs, see Chapter 2, shipping to SWPA, see Report 13 INA 397 part V, Captain to General refers to Mohan Singh, Major Sardana reduced to Sepoy, see Report 897 in INA 499 and Patel's diary INA 225 pg165 onwards, departure, see Sen.
4. Last Minute Reprieve Report 1125 and Fejoo Ram Report 711 (INA 499).

5. 17k to SWPA see Report 13 (INA 397). Plus the over 2000 who died on the way in the sinking of Ryusei Maru (www.combinedfleet.com) Survivors see Chapter 10 on Liberation.

6. Voyage, see Crasta, ship/dates, see Captain Charmarette 1st Hyderabad (AWM 54 1010/4/ 170 pg91) and Report A73/75 INA 500.

7. Torture Islands, see Crasta, Patel Diary, Chint Singh Pacific Manuscripts Bureau Australia National University PMB 1249, henceforth Chint Singh.

8. Dire medical situation, Pillay AWM54 779-3-118.

9. The camps of 275 and 58 men totalled 333. There were 42 survivors, so 291 died.

10. Died October 31, 1944, see https://www.cwgc.com.

11. But Massacre, see Report 804/1361 in INA 499.

12. Admiralty Islands Reports A1/2/8/19 INA500, Reports 551/618/698/711/742 INA 499, *Yank* magazine June 9, 1944, First rescue, see Report A27 INA500.

13. Baboo Ram rescue, see Report A122 (INA 714) and Report 876 (INA 499), *Free After Years of Waiting – The Cairns Post* Oct 31, *1944* by Roy Macartney, on him being an early INA supporter, see Report 1462 (INA742).

14. Patel and beheading – Reports 108/112/ 147/177 (INA 714), Report 40 (AWM 54-423/11/51 – Part 3), Report 850 INA 499, Rattan Singh Military Medal citation WO-373-64-100.

15. Pillay Reports 35 (AWM 54-423/11/51 – part 2), Reports 110/105 (INA 714), AWM54 779-3-118, and Report 850 in INA 499. For Papuans who helped, also see Report 41 (AWM 54-423/11/51 – part 3). Ikeba trial, see ICWC File 21446 (https://www.legal-tools.org).

Chapter 8: The Indian National Army in Burma

1. Indian civilians retreat from Burma + Hump to Chiang.

2. Burma railway deaths, see Hugh Toye quoted in Mihir pg428–9.

3. Misra INA218, Gwalior Lancers, see Reports 494, 526, 570,615, 770, 1004, 1015 in INA499.

4. Misra award, see Reports 633, 622, 1004 INA 499.

5. Misra, see Report 1442 INA 385, Reports 460, 463, 496, 722, 770, 942, 1008, 1019 in INA 499, Latif and Ram Lakshman see Reports 984, and 463, 507, 637 in INA 499.

6. Leaflets distributed – INA 225 and Reports 463, 625, 942 in INA 499.

7. Loudspeakers INA 225 and Reports 634/722 INA 499.

8. Lt Col Chatterji Report INA 387.

9. Japanese right wing plans, see Milan Hauner, staying fifteen to twenty years, see Singh pg307 on KPK Menons Trial in 1944. Note that Menon sent Singh a

long review of his book with many comments but did not wish to amend the account of his trial (letter in Singh family archives).

10. Preparation for occupation see Ehsan Qadir Report 989/INA 499, Hikari Kikan/ diary INA 225 diary, Japanese plan Toye's Springing Tiger pg106 and Reports 987/1023 INA 499, future hope Report 2/INA 854. Motives joining INA, see Chapter 2. 4,000 INA = 3,000 Subhas Regt + 1,000 Bahadur, 87,000 Japanese Gordon pg512.

11. Euphoria fizzles out – Kohima flag Report 633/INA 499 and Sugata pg276, Bahadurs' Imphal flag, see Sugata pg275, diary entries INA 225, Naga chiefs, see Sugata pg276.

12. Indian Army joining INA in 1944, besides Lancers, see Manning incident Report 1002/INA 499.

13. Japanese commander Mutaguchi threw away Japanese lives without any military justification, see *The Pacific War 1931–1945,* Saburo Ienaga, Pantheon Books, New York, pg182, henceforth Ienaga.

14. Bose return Rangoon Gordon pg516.

15. Negotiations with Japan 1943, see Chapter 6, in Jan 1944, see Shahnawaz Report 1002/INA 499 (henceforth Khan Report) and Sugata pg267, Japan plan Paper Tiger/Sundaram pg41.

16. Arakan battalion Khan Report, Arakan Mowdok Ghosh pg199, Lebra pg178.

17. Khan's two battalions see Khan Report and Sugata pg276.

18. IJ Kiani, see INA 383, 1st Division leave behind heavy equip Sugata pg277, only fifty bullets Ghosh pg210, line roads for Bose Toye pg105.

19. Palel attack, see Toye Appendix III, and INA 854.

20. Palel after attack, see INA 854 and Reports 608/610/612/623/634 in INA 499.

21. *Hamara Hindustan,* see Report 714 and fear of Red Fort Report 633 in INA 499.

22. 1st Div survivors, see Reports 929/1002 in INA 499, Toye pg126 and I.J. Kiani.

23. Tamil Mutiny Reports 770/888 in INA 499 and Paper Tiger pg53.

24. Murgi and Hands-Up, see Hikari Kikan INA 255.

25. Bose birthday, see Sugata pg287, Reports 956/978/996/1001/1004 in INA 499, Toye pg138, MZK.

26. Bose being sorry Report 894/INA499.

27. Irrawaddy – boat with flag Toye pg137 + overall, see Dhillon Chapter 13 and Report 888/INA 499.

28. Dhillon at Popa Report 894/INA 499, escape of officers Sugata pg290, Reports 897/894 INA 499, Bose reaction Toye pg142 and Reports 953/955/960/964/93/985/987/1002 in INA 499 and MZK.

29. Jeep patrol Report 988/INA 499.

30. Leaflets after escape Reports 894/933/938/940/963 in INA 499. Sahgal diary in Toye pg144.

31. Legyi jeep and Coy under Naik Kanwal Singh a graduate of the Officer Training School Neesoon fought well see Shanawaz Report 1002/INA 499, Abdullah Khan Report 988/INA 499, April 3 and Sahgal diary, see Toye pg144, Sundaram in Paper Tiger pg53 also says they fought well.
32. Havildar Khan medal rescind, see Report 988/INA 499, April 8, retreat order/ disintegration Shahnawaz Report 1002/INA 499, April 12 start withdrawing see Dhillon pg322 and Toye pg144.
33. Rangoon end, see Chatterji INA 387 and Reports 945/948/953/954 in INA 499, 2nd Division, see Shahnawaz Khan Report 1002/INA 499 and Dhillon Ch17.
34. INA sacrificed in battle, letter dated April 11, 1986 from Toye to historian T.R. Sareen where he says Bose had no idea what supplies were needed. This letter was forwarded to Mohan Singh by Sareen and now in Singh family archives.

Chapter 9: Desperation Before Liberation

1. Propaganda in Torture Islands, Reports 670, 711, 804 INA499.
2. Japan demand Indians fight with them, see James in AWM 54/1010/4/152.
3. American's Rampant SOURCE.
4. Saipan and Okinawa – *The Pacific War 1931–1945,* Saburo Ienaga, Pantheon Books, New York, pg185.
5. https://www.atomicarchive.com Atomic Bombing of Hiroshima, Enola Gay, see Delivering Little Boy, impact, see The Bomb Explodes, accessed Nov 11, 2024.
6. *No surrender After Hiroshima,* Butow pg151–3.
7. Hirohito speech August 15, 1945, http://www.ahf.nuclearmuseum.org, see Jewel Voice Broadcast, accessed Nov 8, 2024.
8. Post-surrender Japanese POW order, see MAGIC decrypt, *Researching Japanese War Crimes*, Published by The National Archives and Records Administration for the Nazi War Crimes and Japanese Imperial Government Records Interagency Working Group, 2006, pg133.
9. Cases of POWs being killed, Naurang Khan and Chint Singh SOURCE.
10. https://www.nationalww2museum.org/war/articles/japanese-surrender-tokyo-bay-september-2- accessed Nov 11, 2024.
11. Rabaul surrender AWM C42257, Guinea Gold, Papua New Guinea, Sep 13, 1945, and *Smith's Weekly*, Sydney, Oct 13, 1945, https://www.trove.nla.gov.au accessed November 11, 2024.
12. POWs in New Guinea – Japanese said 2,800 had been sent, actual number was 3,000 SOURCE, Japanese spread all over Guinea Gold, Papua New Guinea, Sep 3, 1945, https://www.trove.nla.gov.au accessed Nov 11, 2024.

13. Chint Singh PMB pg30–37.
14. Chint Singh PMB pg38.
15. Chint Singh PMB pg38.
16. Chint Singh PMB pg39. 3,000 to New Guinea SOURCE.
17. Chint Singh PMB pg47–51.
18. Chint Singh hearing of air crash, see *Chint Singh The Man Who Should Have Died* by Narinder Singh Parmar, Shawline Publishing Australia, 2021.

Chapter 10: Justice From the Australians

1. Talk with his niece Harmala Gupta, November 7, 2024.
2. Indian POW deaths see Chapter 9, Indian civilians killed Burma Railway see Mihir Bose p428-9, for the others, see *Japanese Treatment of Allied Prisoners During the Second World War: Evaluating the Death Toll* by Michael Sturma, Mudoch University Australia, Journal of Contemporary History, 2020 Vol. 55 (3).
3. Legal framework, see *The Australian War Crimes Trials and Investigations 1942–51*, D.C.S. henceforth Sissons.
4. Mitsuba see AWM54/1010/3/34, www.legal-tools.org Mitsuba/Hirooka and Mitsuba/ Otsuki.
5. Command trials, see Sissons.
6. Adachi interrogation in AWM54/1010/3/8, it was not submitted as evidence in his trial.
7. Japanese order to destroy documents, MAGIC decrypt in Researching Japanese War Crimes, Published by the National Archives and Records Administration for the Nazi War Crimes and Japanese Imperial Government Records Interagency Working Group, 2006, pg135.
8. Trial statistics, Sissons.

Chapter 11: Back Home – A Sudden Return or a Deafening Silence

1. Adapted from an email from Air Marshall Chengappa, Nov 25, 2024.
2. From Sapper Muttiah's granddaughter Mani Chinnaswamy.
3. Green Service INA167, Crasta's book and conversation with Richard.
4. Chint Singh's family in war from discussions with his son Narindar. On his letters, see Chint Singh Manuscript in PMB.
5. Reoccupation of Singapore MISC/1568/H in NAI, B.P. Singh WO-373-104-140 and questionnaire, http://www.cofepow.

6. The Three Musketeers, courtesy Akbar Jahanzeb Durrani.
7. Charan Singh visit to his home November 2023, Thimaya at surrender, see MISC/1568/H in NAI.
8. Fitpatrick post-war memo and letters from his family archives (his grandson Alan Macdonald).
9. Auk Dilemma and Trial politics, see Ghosh pg237–78, Gordon 547–555, Mihir 455–460, White Grey, see British Library IOR/L/WS/1/1711.
10. Congress and INA Ghosh pg292.
11. INA brutalizers see Intelligence Summaries.
12. Trial venue Ghosh pg238.
13. Pre-trial Mason introduction in Toye's Springing Tiger.
14. All INA trials list, see INA420, 22,000 army men in INA 415.
15. Trial Ghosh pg238 on venue, Moti Ram trial transcript.
16. Auk's decision – British Library IOR/L/WS/1/1577.
17. Bose courting danger Mihir pg422-3, Sugata pg289, Gordon pg612+ Khan pg172 and Kiani pg146.
18. Civilian deaths in Burma, Mihir pg428-9, WO-325-56.
19. Morrison and Cabinet Mission Mihir pg462, Sugata pg322, Ashis Ray's recent book *The Trial That Shook Britain – How a Court Martial Hastened Acceptance of India's Independence*, Routledge India 2024, Gordon pg556 says INA trial impact was only one reason for Britain deciding to leave.
20. Misra April 1945 see INA 379 part 85.
21. 7 victims of Red Fort – see charge sheet in Moti Ram.
22. Discussion with his son Air Marshal Chengappa.
23. Mohan Singh jail dates, see Leaves from *My Diary, Brothers in Arms* – discussions with his son Harmohanjit Singh and daughters Sarabhjeet Kaur and Manjeet Kaur Sidhu. Solitary confinement see Dhillon's book.
24. Dhillon case see Mahabir Singh vs Pirthi Singh Dhillon, Punjab and Haryana High Court, July 26, 1962.
25. Toye views of Singh from letters in Singh family archives (Toye to Singh July, 4 and Nov 1, 1977, and Oct 13, 1982).
26. Mohan Singh Toye Letters.

Commemoration

1. Sappers family discussions with his grand-daughter Mani Chinnaawamy in 2024.
2. Chint Singh book.

3. Crasta book and talk with his son Richard.

4. Discussions with Rear-Admiral Sampath Pillai, Dr Krishna Pillai and Colonel Ravi Pillai.

5. Escape from Singapore Col Jasbir Singh, Lancer Publications 2010. Parab's daughter and son-in-law published his own manuscript *A Daring Journey to Freedom – Escape from a Japanese Prisoner-of-War Camp: Memoirs of Colonel Gangaram S. Parab, MC* in 2014. The original is now in the Kumaon Regimental Centre archives.

6. Liverpool FEPOW Conference 2023.

7. Nightmares discussion with Richard Crasta and Admiral Pillai, rice phobia heard at Liverpool.

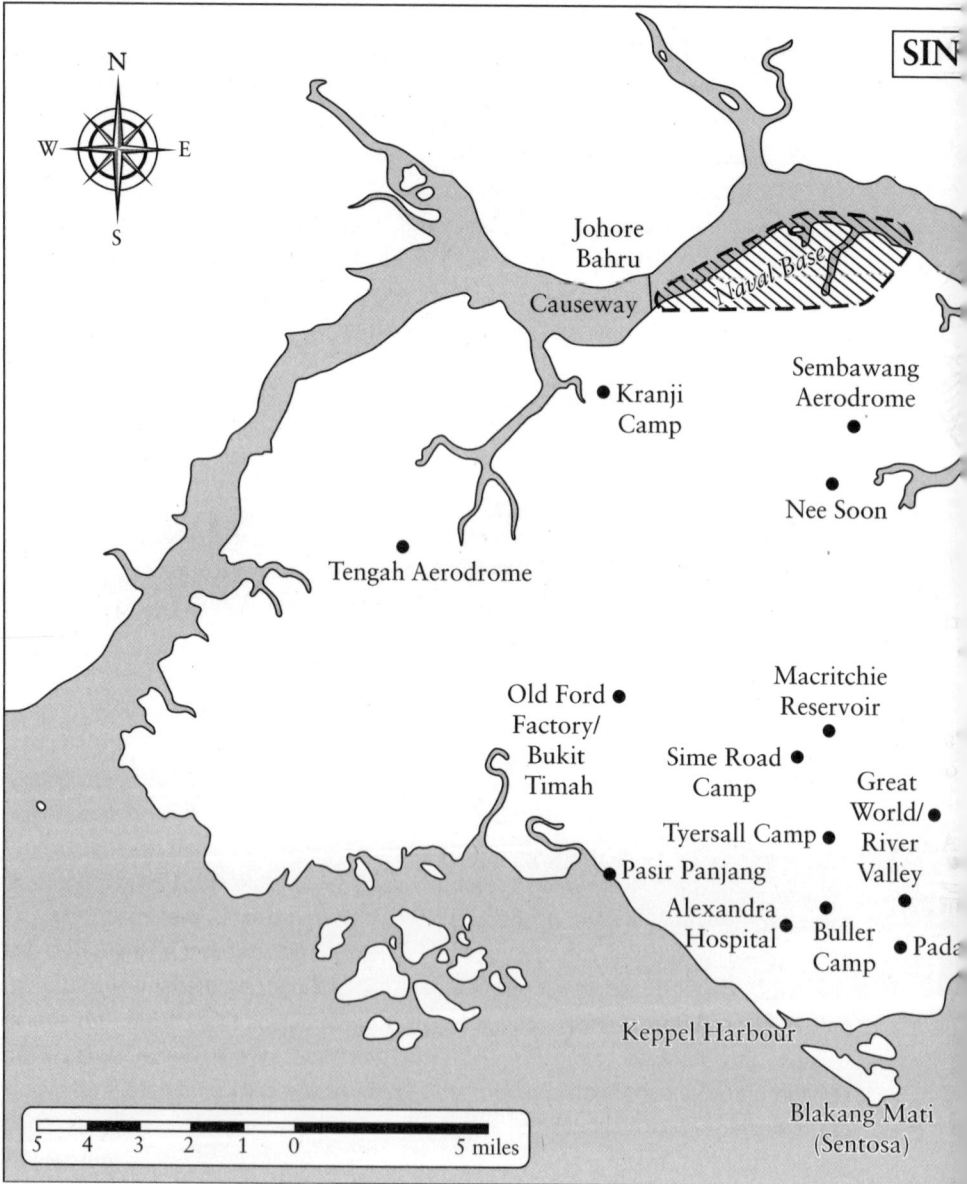

N
W E
S

SIN

Johore
Bahru

Causeway

Naval Base

Kranji
Camp

Sembawang
Aerodrome

Nee Soon

Tengah Aerodrome

Old Ford
Factory/
Bukit
Timah

Macritchie
Reservoir

Sime Road
Camp

Great
World/
River
Valley

Tyersall Camp

Pasir Panjang

Alexandra
Hospital

Buller
Camp

Pada

Keppel Harbour

Blakang Mati
(Sentosa)

5 4 3 2 1 0   5 miles

(SJmagic DESIGN SERVICES, India)

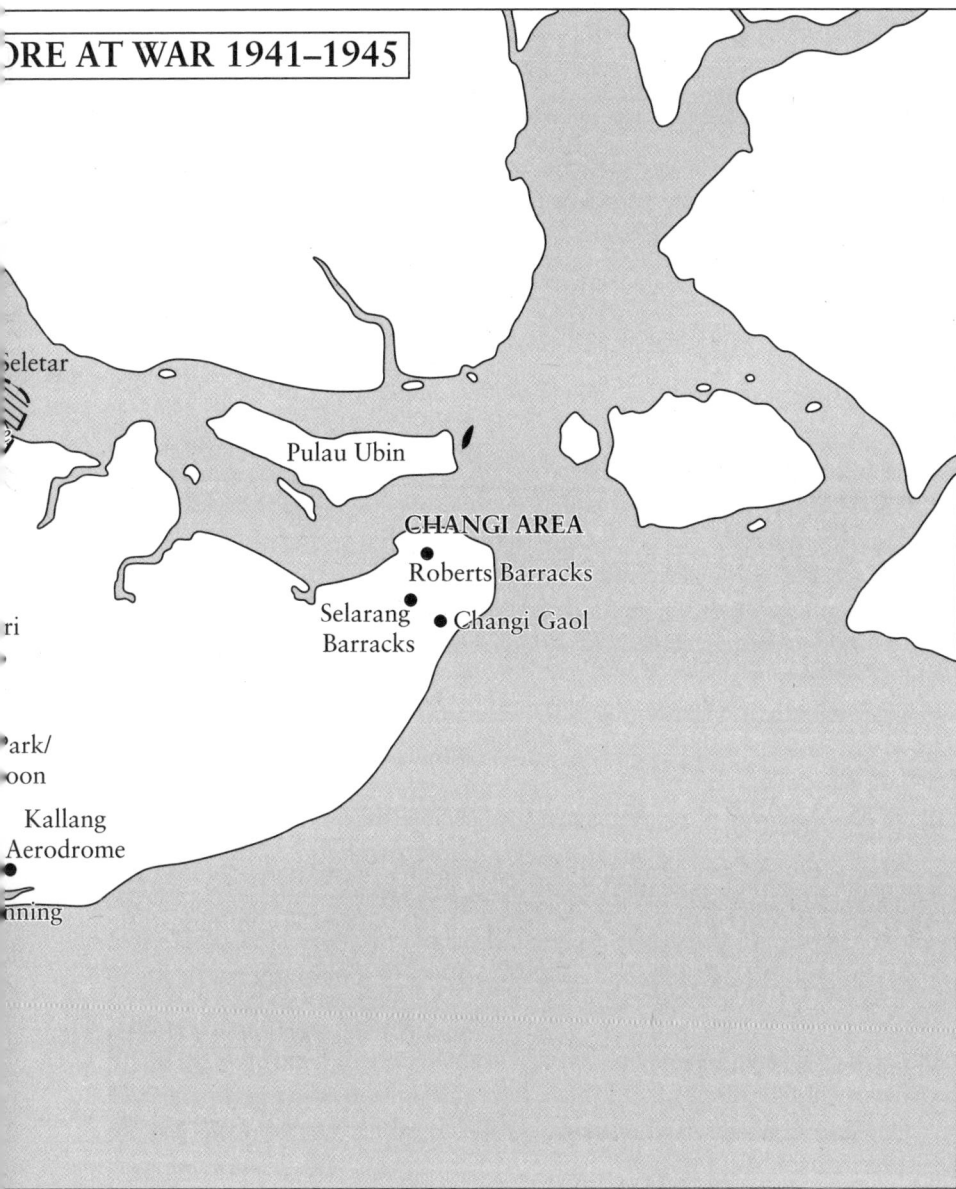

Seletar

Pulau Ubin

CHANGI AREA

Roberts Barracks

Selarang
Barracks

Changi Gaol

ri

ark/
oon

Kallang
Aerodrome

nning

INDEX